Teresa Martín & Luisa Menéndez

Teresa Martín & Luisa Menéndez

Indigenous Women from Appalachia in the Spanish Colonial Record

EDITED BY MELISSA D. BIRKHOFER AND PAUL M. WORLEY
FOREWORD BY ANNETTE SAUNOOKE CLAPSADDLE

Scholarly publisher for the Commonwealth,
serving Bellarmine University, Berea College, Centre
College of Kentucky, Eastern Kentucky University,
The Filson Historical Society, Georgetown College,
Kentucky Historical Society, Kentucky State University,
Morehead State University, Murray State University,
Northern Kentucky University, Spalding University,
Transylvania University, University of Kentucky,
University of Louisville, University of Pikeville, and
Western Kentucky University.

Editorial and Sales Offices: The University Press of Kentucky
663 South Limestone, Lexington, Kentucky 40508-4008
www.kentuckypress.com

Cataloging-in-Publication data is available from the Library of Congress.

ISBN 978-1-9859-0324-1 (hardcover)
ISBN 978-1-9859-0323-4 (pbk)
ISBN 978-1-9859-0326-5 (epub)
ISBN 978-1-9859-0325-8 (pdf)

This book will be made open access within three years of publication thanks to Path to Open, a program developed in partnership between JSTOR, the American Council of Learned Societies (ACLS), University of Michigan Press, and The University of North Carolina Press to bring about equitable access and impact for the entire scholarly community, including authors, researchers, libraries, and university presses around the world. Learn more at https://about.jstor.org/path-to-open/

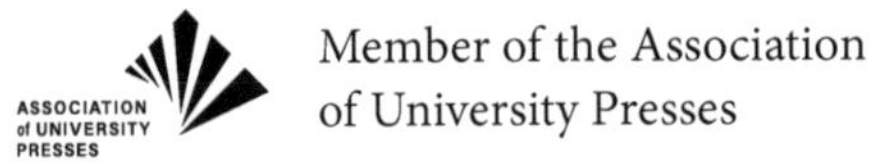

Member of the Association
of University Presses

Teresa, Luisa, Juliana, Mary, and Elena

Contents

Foreword

Never in human existence has the significant presence of women in any given civilization ever been questioned. Women have, of course, been a vital element of any society regardless of their assigned political standing within that society. However, the equal, measured hands of those who have been holding the pens and writing traditional Euro-American history have rarely recorded women's lives, voices, or political might.

Indigenous women of the Americas, in particular, enjoyed millennia of extraordinary influence within their own communities and through diplomacy outside of their communities before great erasures occurred in the documents that would supersede oral historiographies. The diplomatic balance of these precolonial nations—a balance centered on both men and women serving in leadership roles for tribes—was upended as European political structures invaded not only lands but also mindsets.

In *Teresa Martín & Luisa Menéndez*, two Indigenous women from what are termed today the Appalachian Mountains of Western North Carolina and extended lands stand before a colonial powerhouse as voices of economic sovereignty and political influence. Their declarations are largely unaltered by the retelling or reimaging that has so often occurred in colonial texts of the era. In a moment when their savvy, experience, and knowledge supersede any foreign notions of gender roles, these women represent their Indigenous cultures in a manner indicative of their cultural values and complexities.

Teresa and Luisa, as they would come to be called by their Spanish families, continued the multigenerational task of continuing to weave an invisible lifeline for all Indigenous women. Through their recorded presence and insistence on receiving their claims to power and influence, they have forever confirmed the reality that women's inherent rights on this continental soil are nonnegotiable.

Additionally, they make unwavering statements about citizenship and choice. Though uniquely empowered by cultural Indigenous feminine identity, they exercise their rights as Spanish citizens, dismissing European limiting factors of race or gender. These remarkable acts are almost unfathomable given the time and social structures. What stands as an even greater act is that they are making autonomous proclamations. They seek no representation. They are the wards of no one.

When Melissa Birkhofer and Paul Worley approached me with this project, I immediately felt simultaneously out of my depth of expertise and extraordinarily excited. On the one hand, I know little of Spanish colonial history and do not even speak conversational Spanish. However, the more Paul and Melissa described the project, the more I came to understand how this scholarship represents a complete paradigm shift.

As an Eastern Band Cherokee tribal citizen, a woman, a writer, and a student of our Cherokee history, I have often felt at odds with Western archival and archaeological scholarship that seeks to depict colonial interactions with Native peoples. This scholarship requires me to peer through a cloudy lens angled by someone else's hand and make broad claims about my ancestors based on the image before me. Colonial historical record has always been a translation of more than just words; it has been a translation of values, morals, ethics, and power dynamics. The translator has never had a lens that fit the cultural scope of an Indigenous eye.

What Melissa and Paul understood immediately was that the details that had been dismissed for centuries actually unlock new understanding regarding the diaspora of the Americas—an understanding critical to the future of Indigenous sovereignty. They had not contacted me to share more Spanish colonial history or the latest translation of a sixteenth-century Spanish document. They had contacted me to confirm that the Indigenous women of our region had something more to say, and an Indigenous lens might just want to take a look this time.

These accounts confirm that Teresa and Luisa never fully assimilated. They never chose to erase their Indigenous cultural values despite marrying Spanish men. As modern Indigenous women, we have carried echoes of such voices within our stories, and now we have the written accounts affirming our own modern calls for feminine sovereignty and influence.

For at least the three centuries following the account of Teresa and Luisa, attempts would be made by all manner of tactics to silence stories of Indigenous women. Misinterpretations, coercion, dismissal, suppression of Native languages, and religious doctrine would all aid in the general misunderstanding of who Indigenous women have been and who we are today. Romanticized iconography of "Indian maidens" found in both historical accounts and early colonial and American literatures relegates these women to the backdrop of historical landscapes. This has contemporary implications. The balanced leadership of men and women that many of these Indigenous cultures once thrived on has been dismantled over time and remade in the image of European and European-influenced systems of gendered power.

I like to believe that our Indigenous blood memory has not forgotten how to restore this balance—that we still hear the echoes of these women's stories, their tenacity, in the distance. The lifeline has not been broken, and we have the opportunity to pull these cultural influences closer.

Scholarship such as *Teresa Martín & Luisa Menéndez* does much to reset the fulcrum. It wipes the lens clean and brings it into focus from a new perspective. This time, the purpose is not to cement what *was* into the past but, perhaps, to better understand what *can be* in the future of both Indigenous scholarship and the diaspora of these lands. This time, women speak for themselves and lead the way forward.

Annette Saunooke Clapsaddle, author of *Even As We Breathe*, is an enrolled citizen of the Eastern Band of Cherokee Indians (EBCI). She holds degrees from Yale University and the College of William and Mary.

Introduction

Melissa D. Birkhofer and Paul M. Worley

It is hard to define the precise moment when any project, academic or not, begins, much less ends. This particular book has at least two beginnings that converge in a farmer's field known as the Berry Site in what, today, lies outside the town of Morganton in North Carolina (see Map of the US Southeast). It begins, on one level, when the residents of the ancestral Catawba town of Joara, which was situated on the land now called the Berry Site, greeted a contingent of Spanish troops led by Juan Pardo and allowed Pardo to build a small fort and to garrison his men there. From the perspective of the Spanish, in the year 1566, Juan Pardo left the town they called Santa Elena (now Parris Island, South Carolina) on a mission to feed his men (colonists in the capital were starving) and to begin the task of founding a chain of Spanish settlements all the way to the silver mines in Zacatecas in the colony of New Spain (present-day Mexico), among other reasons. Known as Cuenca, the Spanish settlement at Joara was the first inland European settlement in the colony known as La Florida.[1] It is during this time that the two Indigenous women who are the focus of this book, Teresa Martín and Luisa Menéndez, perhaps met and even married their husbands, Juan Martín de Badajoz and Juan de Ribas.[2] As noted by contributors Rachel V. Briggs, Christopher B. Rodning, Robin A. Beck, and David G. Moore in this volume, it is likely that they were among the "nonlocal" Indigenous women in Joara who were enslaved by the Spanish and made to serve them. It is also possible that, as Charles Hudson states, they appear later on the list of Indigenous women from the interior who were enslaved but then subsequently freed after becoming Christians. However, while a "Teresa" and a "Luisa" are listed, they are said to be married to other people, and Juan de Ribas himself is listed

---

This Introduction draws upon our article, "She Said That St. Augustine Is Worth Nothing Compared to Her Homeland: Teresa Martín and the Méndez Cancio Account of La Tama (1600)," *North Carolina Literary Review* 32 (2023): 122–42, which won the 2023 John Ehle Award.

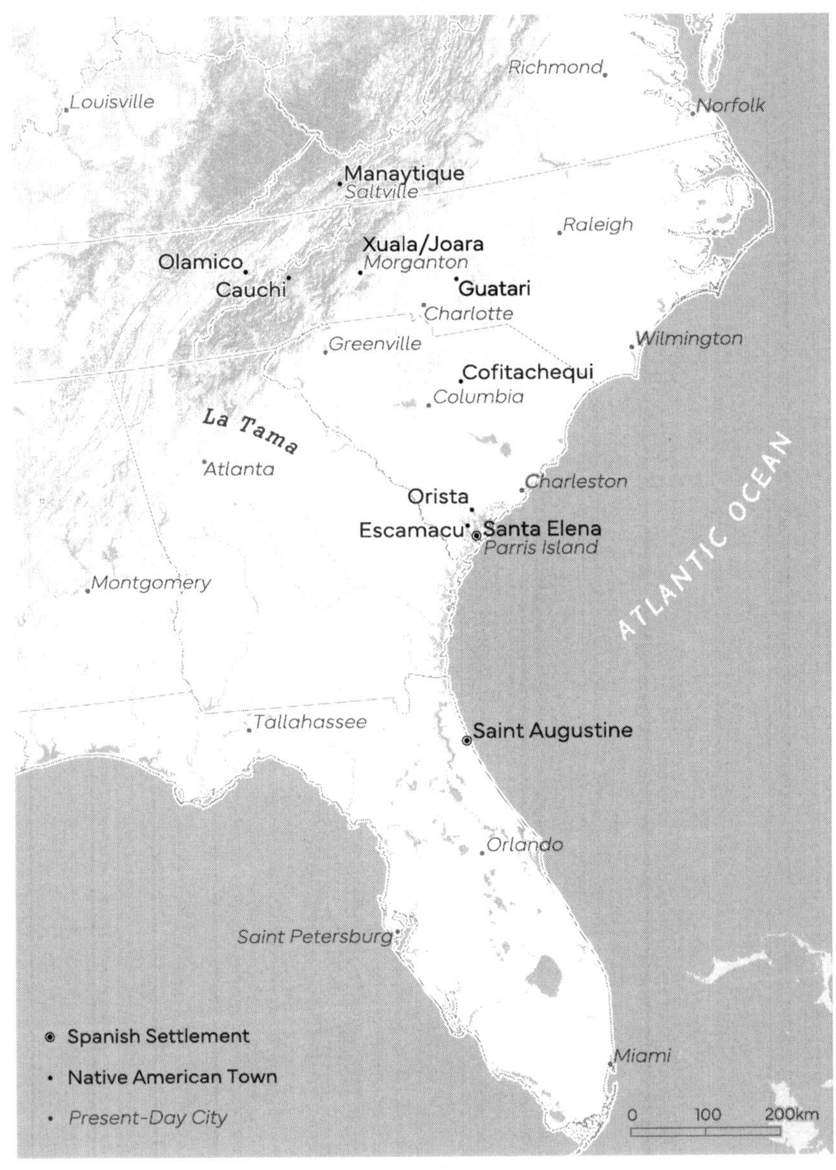

Map of the present-day US Southeast showing locations mentioned in the "Relación" (*Source:* Map data was sourced from the US Census Bureau and the USGS. [Courtesy of Josh Platt])

as married to a woman named Marina.[3] For his part, Juan Martín de Badajoz would seem to be one of the very few survivors, if not the only survivor, of the contingent stationed at the fort that Pardo built, Fort San Juan, and one can well imagine that the intervention of his wife, Teresa Martín, was crucial to his surviving the Catawbas' destruction of the fort in 1568, an act that ended European designs on settling the interior until the English began their push inland some years later. She would have been no less crucial in helping him navigate his long journey back to Santa Elena on the coast.[4] Whether or not these women had already met and married their husbands by the time the Spanish fort was destroyed, we do know that at some point Teresa Martín and Luisa Menéndez migrated from what was then their home in the foothills of the Appalachian Mountains to the colonial capital of Santa Elena on the coast before ultimately moving to St. Augustine, where they both gave testimonies about the colonial interior to the Spanish governor, Gonzalo Méndez de Canzo, in the year 1600.

This book also begins when we took students in Western Carolina University's inaugural Latinx Learning Community to visit the Berry Site as a way of underscoring the long histories of Indigenous Peoples and Spanish-speaking peoples in Western North Carolina, a region all too often coded as rural, isolated, English-speaking, and white. As we stood at the archaeological site, one of the contributors to this volume, David Moore, pointed toward the mountains in the west, which Pardo saw were capped with snow when he first arrived at Joara in 1566 and which, in turn, influenced his decision to stop for the winter and build a fort there. Moore also noted that one of the women (Teresa Martín) associated with the town in the colonial record had not only married a Spaniard (Juan Martín de Badajoz) at some point but also left an official testimony about her homeland some years later in the context of an official inquiry held by the Spanish governor of La Florida. As scholars of Latine/x and Indigenous literatures, we were aware of the foundational colonial texts about the region where we lived, such as Álvar Núñez Cabeza de Vaca's *Naufragios* and works associated with the expedition of Hernando de Soto, such as those by the Gentleman of Elvas or the stories El Inca Garcilaso said were told to him by his uncle. We were also well aware of the fact that scholars of US literatures typically only make passing reference to these, if they do so at all, given the field's tendency toward Anglophilic monolingualism. Despite our own training, it had never occurred to us there could be much more of interest in that part of the colonial record, much less a multipage testimony given by an Indigenous woman from what are now the mountains of North Carolina.

To our amazement, the document in which Martín's testimony appears—the "Relación de la Tama y su tierra, y de la población de ingleses" (1600), or "An Account of La Tama and Its Land, and the English Settlement"—also contains the testimony of Luisa Menéndez.[5] Both women are later mentioned in a letter by Méndez de Canzo dated June 28, 1600, in which the governor describes the contents of this previous inquiry, stating that it contains the "declarations of certain persons long resident in these provinces who have made excursions in the company of Captain John Pardo and Ensign Moyano, with whom there came two Indian girls from the farthest point inland to which the Captain and Ensign arrived. One of these girls is married to John de Ribas, a soldier of this garrison . . . and the other Teresa Martín, widow of another soldier of S . . . [missing]."[6,7] The mention of Martín's being a widow here is curious if only because it is not mentioned in the context of her earlier testimony. Further, this second letter would seem to confirm that the "Relación" is not even the first time that Martín intervenes directly in the colonial record, as she is undoubtedly the same "Teresa Martín" who, with her daughter Inés, collects her deceased Spanish husband's final pay as a soldier some twenty-three years prior in the former colonial capital of Santa Elena. The paylist from 1577 in which this action is recorded specifically refers to her as the widow of "Juan Martín de Badajoz." To the best of our knowledge, this book is the first time in which these documents, the "Relación" and the paylist, have been translated and published together.

In our view, the importance of these documents cannot be understated, and the present collection seeks to intervene in a number of scholarly disciplines and conversations, from Appalachian studies and US studies to Latine/x studies and Latin American studies. As an intervention into how we understand US history, the publication of Martín's and Menéndez's testimonies centers the voices and lives of Indigenous Peoples while reframing settler colonialism in the United States from a hemispheric perspective. In the twenty-first century, we are thus reminded that what is now the United States has always been intimately connected to what we now call Latin America and that this land belonged, belongs, and will belong to the Indigenous Peoples who have lived here for millennia. The typical reduction of colonial Florida to a footnote in most understandings of US history and culture sets aside the competition among would-be colonial powers in the region as well as erases the fact that Indigenous Peoples had a long history of engagement with and resistance to European intrusion that predates the arrival of the British. As literary scholars, we argue that the testimonies of Teresa Martín and Luisa Menéndez offer our disciplines the chance to rethink US literature in a way that echoes the dictum of the Muskogee Creek and Cherokee scholar Craig S. Womack, that "tribal literatures are not some branch waiting to be grafted onto the main trunk. Tribal literatures are the *tree*, the oldest literatures in the Americas, the most American of American literatures. We *are* the canon."[8] Further, as argued by Laguna Pueblo and Sioux scholar Paula Gunn Allen, "Native American literature should be important to Americans . . . as a major tradition that informs American writers." She goes on to note that Indigenous literatures are so significant that they are "fundamental to coherent understanding of non-Indian varieties of American literature."[9] Through their testimonies, Martín and Menéndez assert their agency as Indigenous women in a way that breaks the frame of the colonial document, pointing to how Indigenous histories, languages, cultures, literatures, oral traditions, and/or works in nonalphabetic writing systems exceed colonizing ways of understanding even as they are forced into them. In Womack's formulation, their testimonies underscore that yes, these "are the tree . . . the most American of American literatures." We would echo Allen and add that, as testimonies of multilingual Indigenous women from the sixteenth century, Martín's and Menéndez's voices are undoubtedly "fundamental" to any understanding of US literature, past, present, or future.

Indeed, Martín's and Menéndez's testimonies mark some of the earliest moments (1577 and 1600) that an Indigenous person from Appalachia and the US Southeast speaks directly into the colonial record. Chroniclers such as Cabeza de Vaca tend to write their accounts well after the incidents they describe occurred, and they use indirect speech when representing their interactions with Indigenous Peoples. For example, while fleeing enslavement under one Indigenous group, the four survivors of the disastrous Narváez expedition (1527) are taken in as healers by another Indigenous community, the Avavares. Given that the survivors have been in the land for a number of years at that point, they can apparently speak the language of the Avavares as "(al) though they are of a different nation and language, they understand the language of the ones we were with before." Cabeza de Vaca goes on to say that "the pueblo offered us a lot of tunas right away, because they had already heard news of us."[10] While here Cabeza de Vaca clearly breaks with the convention of communicating by "signs" found in most texts and does appear to communicate with the Avavares, he does not claim to quote any of the Avavares and glosses their conversation. Similarly, in his own account of French attempts to colonize La Florida, the would-be French governor René Laudionnière states that he understands his ally, Satouriona, well enough to pretend that he does not, in fact, understand him concerning the location of prisoners Satouriona had taken. He then says that "Satouriona then told his son Atore to find the prisoners and bring them to this place."[11] While telling us what Satouriona said, so to speak, as with Cabeza de Vaca, Laudionnière makes no effort to quote the leader's speech as though to give us his exact words. Like his Spanish counterpart, Laudionnière renders these for the reader on his own terms.

We can juxtapose these accounts with other testimonies as a way of showing how unique these documents really are. In the aftermath of the so-called Guale Uprising in 1597, the same governor, Méndez de Canzo, required a number of Guale men to go on record and explain how it came to pass that the Guale killed several Spanish friars who lived among them. Most of them speak through an interpreter, Gaspar de Salas, who coincidentally appears and gives his own testimony in the "Relación" from 1600, translated here. A notable exception is the cacique of San Pedro, known as don Juan, who gives his testimony in Spanish without the aid of an interpreter and even signs his own name.[12] To some extent these testimonies, even those that are given through an interpreter, move us toward a richer understanding of the complexity of these immediate interactions as well as of Indigenous-Spanish relations in general. The fact that don Juan both speaks Spanish and can sign his name speaks to sustained, long-term relations between his people and the Spanish, or at least between the Guale elite and the Spanish colonial system, in much the same way that the Spanish educated the children of Mexica nobles in central México. While these testimonies contain a variety of fascinating, conflicted perspectives on the 1597 uprising, they tend to be constrained insofar as these men are instructed to recount the details of a very specific series of events as opposed to answering more open-ended questions like the ones that Teresa Martín and Luisa Menéndez were apparently expected to answer in the "Relación de la Tama." We should also note that, as pointed out by Alejandra Dubcovsky, the inclusion of Indigenous women in such colonial records "often appears accidental or as nothing more than happenstance."[13] The inclusion of Menéndez and Martín in the "Relación" is crucial, however, as the Crown commands that the governor "become well informed about the disposition of that land through the caciques and Indians who are closer to the lands you intend to discover" p 63. In the absence of male caciques (it is of particular relevance here to note that Ribas claims his wife was a *cacica*, the feminine version of the word *cacique*), Martín's and Menéndez's testimonies are central to the governor's making his case for a return to La Tama.

Our introduction to these documents and the critical chapters that complete the volume seeks to serve several purposes. First, we hope to provide the reader with enough historical context about Menéndez and Martín and these documents such that readers, particularly if they are familiar with the Anglophilic literary canon and its histories, can better appreciate who these women were and why these two documents are important. Next, we describe our own approach to the Spanish-language transcription and English-language translation and annotation of these documents, highlighting the different archival resources we used. Finally, we provide a brief overview of the volume's critical pieces, each of which was solicited with the aim of thinking about these women and their testimonies from the perspectives of different academic disciplines. Rather than being an exercise in interdisciplinarity, we hope the intersections among these chapters demonstrate the inadequacy of monolingual or siloed approaches to human knowledge as well as the inherent limitations and consequences such approaches produce. In our view, only by attempting to holistically understand these women and their testimonies do we see how their voices do not simply mark an important moment in Appalachian, North Carolina, or US literatures but in hemispheric, if not global, Indigenous struggles for voice and representation under colonial conditions.

Sixteenth-Century La Florida

In order to understand these testimonies and their importance in Abiayala's literary history, we must begin by examining the contours of Indigenous-Spanish relations during the sixteenth century as well as the Spanish colonial genres.[14] The predominantly Anglophone trajectory of

US literature as a field has meant that Indigenous languages and other colonial languages such as Spanish have largely been set aside in the imagining of a US cultural and literary heritage with roots in English and the United Kingdom. This monolingualism of course means that a text like the "Relación," in which Martín's and Menéndez's respective testimonies appear, falls, almost by definition, outside of US, southern, or North Carolina literatures. As Sarah Dowling lays it out, we must recognize "the necessity of framing Spanish simultaneously as a colonized language within the US and as a colonial language in the hemisphere" while also understanding that "dominant multiculturalisms . . . uphold and enforce the settler monolingual paradigm and its white supremacist racial order."[15] Indeed, we find this intersection of language, monolingualism, and power, in Mixe linguist Yásnaya Elena Aguilar Gil's assertion that Indigenous languages are not so much dying out as they are murdered by their respective nation-states.[16] In short, engaging a document like this may require a number of potential monolingual, monocultural, white settler readers to reframe what they know or think they know about literary history, particularly as they are directly implicated in the ongoing murder (to use Aguilar Gil's terminology) of Indigenous languages in the twenty-first century.

Unlike Mexico, Guatemala, or Argentina, the Spanish colony known as La Florida did not become a modern nation-state. Rather, a mixture of conflicts with Indigenous Peoples in the region, competition with other colonies, a lack of gold and other resources, and pressures from other would-be imperial powers caused the Spanish to slowly abandon the region once thought of as, according to historian Paul Hoffman, "a new Andalucía (i.e., southern Spain) flowing with milk and honey, not to mention laden with pearls, gold, silver, wine grapes, and olives."[17] The 1819 Adams-Onis Treaty, in which the Spanish ceded what was left of the colony to the United States, closed the final chapter on a colonial holding that the Spanish Crown had struggled to fund, staff, and defend since its inception. Indeed, and particularly when compared to events in places like Anahúac (commonly referred to in English as the Aztec Empire) or Tahuantinsuyo (the Inca Empire), Spanish efforts to colonize La Florida were halting, sporadic, and all too often examples of abject European failure.

The first briefly successful attempt to settle this land by Europeans occurred in 1526 under the auspices of Lucas Vázquez de Ayllón. Setting out some thirteen years after the expedition of Juan

Ponce de León (1513), Ayllón was lured to the area precisely because he believed the land the Spanish referred to as *Chicora* was akin to the Spanish *Andalucía*. Importantly, his expedition also included a Catawba man, Francisco el Chicorano, who, having been abducted by the Spanish, had gone on to Spain where, according to Anna Brickhouse, "he entranced the Spanish court with a detailed account of his place of origin and its mineral wealth and agricultural abundance."[18] Despite or perhaps because of his extensive experience among Europeans, Francisco fled Ayllón's expedition soon after it touched land. The town Ayllón later established on September 28, 1526, San Miguel Gualdape, was gone by the end of that October due to harsh conditions, internal conflicts among would-be colonists, attacks from local Indigenous Peoples, and revolts by enslaved Africans.[19] Subsequent expeditions such as those of Pánfilo de Narváez (1527), which produced the famous account by one of its aforementioned survivors, Cabeza de Vaca, the aforementioned Hernando de Soto (1539), or Tristán de Luna y Arellano (1559–1561) proved no more successful. One of the entire colonial enterprise's foremost ironies is that, despite his improbable survival some years prior, Cabeza de Vaca apparently accepted an invitation to join Soto before eventually turning him down.[20]

There would be no permanent European settlement in the region until Pedro Menéndez de Avilés came on the scene in the 1560s. The first of these settlements, of course, is St. Augustine, which was founded in 1565. The second sustained Spanish settlement would be the town of Santa Elena in 1566. Somewhat ironically, Santa Elena was established, not at the site of an Indigenous town but at the site of a would-be French settlement and fort called Charlesfort on what today is Parris Island, South Carolina. That this competition among empires would eventually be won by the late-coming British underscores the contingency and uncertainty surrounding this area of US history as well as why this period is so often overlooked in the US popular imagination: This land was not a tabula rasa, even from the perspective of European imperialists and Indigenous resistance to European presence well predates the arrival of the British.[21] In the midst of this conflict among European powers—and particularly how it was playing out in the Caribbean—on December 1, 1566, Menéndez sent the Spaniard Juan Pardo out of Santa Elena with official instructions to, among other things, find an overland route to Spanish silver mines in

Zacatecas in the colony of New Spain, as such a route would enable Spanish ships to avoid the dangers of Caribbean piracy. Kimberly Borchard points out that this plan was not as offbeat as it might seem to us in the twenty-first century. After all, not only had the Spanish just conquered vast empires in México and Perú but, to Europeans at the time, it was "intuitive to assume that the riches discovered to the south would have a counterpart in the northern latitudes," such that Pardo might be expected to stumble on mineral wealth on the way to New Spain.[22] Pardo and his men thus set off with ambitions far beyond their official purpose. As suggested by the very title of Borchard's groundbreaking book, *Appalachia as Contested Borderland of the Early Modern Atlantic 1528–1715*, the region was thus not understood to be peripheral to the imperial designs of various European entities but integral to them. Less official but no less pressing was the fact that there was a food shortage in Santa Elena, with Menéndez's hope being that Pardo and his men would, like all sixteenth-century expeditions, be able "to obtain [food], by persuasion of force, from the people they encountered."[23] Of particular relevance to the present volume is the fact that Pardo and his men eventually came to Joara on December 27, 1566. While there, Pardo built a small fort, Fort San Juan, which was the first inland European settlement in North America. In keeping with common colonial practice, he named the would-be colony Cuenca, after the town in Spain where he was born.[24] Like virtually all other Spanish settlement attempts, Cuenca and Fort San Juan failed, as the Catawba killed all but perhaps a handful of the soldiers stationed there—with Juan Martín de Badajoz perhaps being the sole survivor—and burned the fort to the ground in May 1568.[25] The destruction of Fort San Juan was part of a larger series of events such as Sir Francis Drake's 1586 attack on St. Augustine that led the Spanish to abandon the original capital of Santa Elena in 1587 and retrench to St. Augustine and territories they could more capably maintain and defend. Although subsequent colonial governors entertained the possibility of expanding the colony back up the coast and into the interior, their proposals were never met with much support, and their plans were never realized. Further, the British establishing Jamestown in 1607 meant that the Spanish could not return to the interior without directly confronting another imperial power in a land that had always been unprofitable, ending any expansionist aspirations the Spanish may have had.

Reading the "Relación": Accounts and Testimonial Literature

The year 1600 was very much a hinge moment in the Spanish colonial undertaking known as La Florida. Santa Elena had only recently been abandoned and, as suggested by the second half of the title of the "Relación," the specter of English settlement loomed on the horizon. Further, the so-called Guale Uprising in 1597, which happened only a few short months after Gonzalo Méndez de Canzo had arrived in St. Augustine to assume the governorship, had likely shaken the colony to its core.[26] Having previously proposed an expedition to La Tama (in present-day Georgia), the newly minted expansionist governor was asked by the Crown to hold an official inquiry into the state of the interior, in which he recorded the testimonies of people with experience there and who could thus speak to the land, resources, and potential sources of wealth the Spanish could expect to find on their return. The document containing Martín's and Menéndez's testimonies bears a marginal note that reads "Relación de la Tama y su tierra, y de la población de ingleses" ("Account of La Tama and Its Land, and the English Settlement"). The appellation "relación" situates the document within a Spanish colonial genre that Walter Mignolo describes as being "account[s]/report[s] requested by the Crown."[27] Mignolo notes that one of the *relación*'s primary characteristics as a genre is that *relaciones* "do not 'freely' transcribe the observations of who is writing, what the person who is writing *sees*, but they *respond*, in a sense, to official requests."[28] Framing the actual testimonies, the voices of Méndez de Canzo and the notary, Juan Jiménez, even self-consciously refer to the fact that the Crown has "commanded" the governor to give an account of the land, with the present document representing the fulfillment of that command.

While the assertion that Menéndez's and Martín's testimonies are among the first pieces of Indigenous literature in the Southeast written in Latin script may seem strange to students and scholars of US literature schooled in the dominant, Anglophilic US canon, such a statement would be routine within the frameworks of Latin American literary study. Although similar genres are relegated to the literary margins here in the United States, texts as diverse as Columbus's diary and the letters of Hernán Cortés are understood to be foundational to the study of Latin American literature. Drawing on this tradition, scholars such as Luis Leal and Juan Bruce-Novoa have situated Cabeza de Vaca's *Naufragios* as a foundational work of Mexican American, Chicanx, and Latine/x literatures in order to give these a genealogical origin that precedes and exceeds British colonization.[29] As Mignolo argues, even if such texts may not have been written as literature per se, from the perspective of our own reception, we can nonetheless go back and understand these as possessing literary qualities.[30] Additionally, and in this particular case, we can use scholarship on the Latin American genre of the *testimonio* to inform our reading of Menéndez's and Martín's testimonies in the "Relación." To be clear, we do not claim that these testimonies are works of *testimonio* as such, given that *testimonio* has a very specific trajectory and history. Rather, we understand these testimonies as having certain *testimonio*-like qualities in the same way that Salvador Bueno notes how the Spanish friar Bernardino de Sahagún relied heavily on Mexica "informants" to narrate their experiences of the conquest and sing traditional songs to him in the production of his *Historia general de las cosas de Nueva España* (*General History of New Spain*; 1540–1585). Bueno thus asks whether these *tlacuilos* were "not, after all, giving testimony."[31] This dynamic of Indigenous people serving as informants for outsiders who then record their stories and disseminate them among a predominantly non-Indigenous audience has been a major preoccupation of Latin American cultural production from the colonial era to the present, encompassing to greater or lesser degrees such seemingly dissimilar works as Friar Diego de Landa's *Relación de las Cosas de Yucatán* (1566; trans. *Account of the Things of Yucatán*, 2023)[32] and the Venezuelan anthropologist Elisabeth Burgo-Debray and K'iche' Maya Rigoberta Menchú's controversial collaboration *Yo me llamo Rigoberta Menchú y así me nació la conciencia* (1983; *I, Rigoberta Menchú*, 1984).

Writing on the *testimonio*, John Beverley states that texts "like *I, Rigoberta Menchú* cannot be adequately contained within the category of 'literature' without putting the category itself into crisis; in its staging of voice, testimonio affirms the authority of oral culture against processes of cultural modernization and transculturation that privilege literacy and written language as norms of expression."[33] Put another way, the written recording of an oral voice, even one mandated by the Crown, perhaps, would ultimately seem to underscore the vibrancy and vitality of the oral culture the written words seek to domesticate. This assertion may seem paradoxical at first, particularly in a Latin American context in which, according to the Argentinian critic Ángel Rama, "the written word became the only binding one—in contradistinction to the spoken word, which belonged to the realm of things precarious and uncertain."[34] Further, this subjugation of the oral to the written was explicitly formulated as a weapon of empire beginning in the early colonial period. Writing on the Spanish humanist Antonio de Nebrija, whose 1492 *Gramática castellana* was the first grammar of a European vernacular language, Mignolo states that Nebrija "linguistically and philosophically was obsessed with the control of the voice by the mediation of the letter."[35] Nebrija's approach to language and writing, in turn, influenced men like Bernardo de Alderete, who published his own *Del orígen y principio de la lengua castellana* in 1606 and who, having "had the opportunity to read and listen to missionaries and men of letters who reported about Amerindian cultures and societies, [retained] their impression that lack of letters is equated with a lack of civilization."[36] As Mignolo points out later, in his *The Darker Side of the Renaissance*, "In Castile the theory of the latter led to a theory of writing that transcended the regionality of spoken languages and colonized the voice," whereas, in the Americas, "the application of the theory . . . led to the colonization of Amerindian languages (by writing their grammars) and the colonization of Amerindian memories (by writing their histories)."[37]

A key part of such projects, particularly during the early colonial period, were texts in which Indigenous subjects were interpolated to write or participate in the recording of their own stories. José Rabasa notes that the end of texts like those produced by the aforementioned Sahagún "was to lead [groups such as] the Nahua to objectify their own culture." Rabasa goes so far as to call these acts of ethnosuicide in which "Indians were asked to narrate and show how they had turned themselves into normalized Western subjects." Things are not, however, that simple, as Rabasa later claims that nonetheless "we witness the paradoxical turn of ethnosuicide into ethnogenesis."[38] We can productively relate Rabasa's claim to Beverley's notion above of the recorded orality of a given voice ultimately affirming the authority of that utterance, the person who speaks it, and orality itself despite the prevailing power dynamics in colonial, colonizing projects. In other words, at crucial moments when oppressed people may be invited or even required to participate in projects that would seemingly imply their subjugation, if not the disappearance of their peoples and their knowledges, they may, even as they participate, reaffirm these very things. As much as such texts may be invaluable for their truth value and sense of witness to particular historical events, these texts might be even more powerful when we notice and engage with their gaps, moments when the people forced to tell their stories decline to do just that, do so in a way that suggests their telling is intentionally incomplete, or even intentionally mislead their European interlocutors. As Doris Sommer famously remarks on *I, Rigoberta Menchú*, despite the apparent transparency many readers attribute to the narrative and its intentions, from "the beginning, the narrator tells us ever so clearly that she is not going to tell some things," with this "refusal to tell secrets remain[ing] on the page after the editing is done."[39]

Importantly, and as suggested by Rabasa's comments on Sahagún, such refusals have marked this textual production for over five hundred years. In the case of Landa, for example, it is widely known that one of his foremost informants on Maya culture was a young Maya-speaking man named Gaspar Antonio Chi, though Landa never mentions Chi in the text.[40] While the book was and remains something of a Rosetta Stone to writing in Maya glyphs, when someone (unattributed!) is asked to provide a sentence written in the glyphic system, he gives the example, "ma in ka ti" or "I do not want to."[41] From an example to which we will return to shortly, in Spanish friar Luis Cáncer's diary of his 1549 attempt to peaceably convert the Indigenous Peoples near Tampa Bay to Christianity, the Spaniard mentions that a woman named Madalena who is from the region will accompany him as an interpreter. As described in Scott Cave's brilliant article about Madalena and her life, she was abducted and enslaved during the De Soto expedition and subsequently spent over a decade in captivity in the Caribbean and Spain as a servant to the conquistador's widow, Isabel de Bobadilla.[42] From the Spanish perspective, these experiences would have made her the ideal interpreter. When Cáncer first meets a group of Indigenous men along the coast, he reports, "I said to them in their own language, 'He oça uluata,' which means, 'We are good men.'"[43] This bit of language, of course, presumably comes from Madalena in her role as interpreter. The fact that Cáncer's evangelization efforts ended in failure, with him being beaten to death in the surf a few days later, suggests that, like "ma in ka ti," the phrase "He oça uluata" may not be so straightforward, and may, in fact, be what Anna Brickhouse has referred to as a moment of "motivated mistranslation,"[44] in which we find the presence of a woman asserting her People's sovereignty and self-determination as opposed to being a willing agent of empire. We would argue such moments in which these voices can be read as undermining the written project and the written word itself are precisely those that, through their use of irony and other devices, make such texts literary in the fullest sense of the term.[45]

The Transcription and Translation of the "Relación" and the Paylist

First and foremost, we would like to recognize that the publication of texts like these is the result of efforts by hundreds of people whose work runs the gamut from preserving documents to ensuring the safety and accessibility of archives. Each of these people, whether or not we know their names, has played an important role in the current project. During our research we worked with people at three different archives: the Archivo General de Indias, or General Archive of the Indies (AGI), in Seville, Spain; the P. K. Yonge Library of Florida History, at the University of Florida in Gainesville; and the Georgia State Archives, near Atlanta.

The "Relación" is a fairly well-known document within scholarship on colonial Florida thanks to a transcription and translation done in the early twentieth century by the scholar Mary Letitia Ross. Her complete transcription and translation can be found among her papers in the Mary Letitia Ross Collection in the Georgia State Archives. The original copy of the "Relación" is housed at the AGI and is available through the AGI's digital portal PARES (https://pares.cultura.gob.es/inicio.html). During the early days of the COVID-19 pandemic, archivists in both locations were more than gracious in handling our queries, helping us access the complete original document via PARES (Seville) and Menéndez's and Martín's transcribed and translated testimonies from the "Relación" (Georgia). The AGI also houses Contaduria (CD) 944, one of the richly detailed bundles of St. Augustine's royal treasury records in which the paylist is located. Unfortunately, the AGI archivist reported that the entirety of that CD 944 (along with many others of early Florida's treasury records) suffered fire damage, and its pages are too deteriorated to be accessed. Fortunately, the University of Florida's P. K. Yonge Library houses extensive microfilm holdings of documents from the AGI, including a copy of CD 944. Having been denied funding for this project at our previous institution, in March 2023 we were able to use start-up funds from Worley's new position at Appalachian State to visit the Georgia Archive, obtain a complete copy of Ross's translation and transcription of the "Relación," and travel to the P. K. Yonge Library to search for the paylist. Thanks to, among other things, the efforts of the archivists who provided our daughter with craft supplies and books about cats while we looked through thousands of linear feet of microfiche, we were successful.

The transcription of the "Relación" presented here would have been impossible if not for the aforementioned efforts by Ross and Manuel Serrano y Sanz's *Documentos históricos de la Florida y la Luisiana, siglos XVI al XVIII* (1912), which is in turn a reedition of Iñigo Abad y Lassiera's *Relación del descubrimiento, conquista, y población de la provincias y costas de la Florida* (1785). Our first attempts at creating our own original transcription were halting and frustrating. Indeed, our preference would have been to simply publish Ross's work as much to recognize the fact that another scholar had already transcribed and translated the "Relación" in its entirety as to recognize her, specifically, as one of the most important scholars of the region. Indeed, her papers are an amazing, underutilized resource on the history of La Florida insofar as she has made a vast number of these documents available in English. It perhaps goes without saying that had she not given her papers to the Georgia Archives in the 1970s, current scholarship on the region would look very different. We were told that as Ross's bequest does not specifically allow for the future dissemination and publication of her papers, we could consult and cite from them but not publish them per se. Our research eventually led us to Serrano y Sanz's *Documentos históricos*, which contains a complete transcription of the "Relación" that faithfully follows the original colonial orthography. Given our limited skills as paleographers, or scholars who specialize in reading old manuscripts, we decided that the best course of action would be to update the Serrano y Sanz in conjunction with Ross's work so that the Spanish would be accessible to readers—and particularly undergraduate readers—in the early twenty-first century. We make no claim that this is the definitive transcription of the "Relación," and paleographers will no doubt find that we reproduce errors that may be found in earlier transcriptions by Ross and Abad. Scholars in the field who are capable of doing so will no doubt want to consult the original document. Further, inclusion of the transcription here is not mere window dressing, as it underscores the fact that Spanish has been spoken in what is now the US Southeast longer than English has been, even here in the mountains of present-day North Carolina. Given that there currently exists no transcription of the paylist, we asked our colleague Hannah Abrahamson if she would be up to the task. To our utter amazement, she returned a preliminary draft of the document to us within an hour of our having sent it to her. By comparison and as noted at the top of her transcription, this much shorter document hews more closely toward colonial conventions as reflected in the original itself.

Beyond our critical expertise, we have a good deal of experience as working translators. That said, we openly recognize that translating a notarial document written in La Florida in the year 1600 is a good bit different from translating a contemporary critical work of poetry. Rather than attempt to create a literal translation of the "Relación" and the paylist, at times we have opted to sacrifice some of the Spanish bureaucratic legalese in favor of contemporary readability. This choice does not so much reflect a particular aesthetic sensibility as it does the fact that we hope to make these documents accessible to as wide an audience as we can. When possible we have cross-checked our own translation with the three existing translations of which we are aware: the aforementioned complete translation by Ross, a partial translation by Katherine Reding that was published in the *Georgia Historical Quarterly* in 1924, and excerpts of adjacent documents that were published in David Beers Quinn's *The Roanoke Voyages 1584–1590* in 1967.[46] We are also indebted to the anonymous peer reviewers whose comments provided guidance on a number of difficult passages, and we readily claim any errors in our own translation. Differences between our own rendering and the aforementioned previous renderings are not, we would argue, corrections of errors but reflect our access to tools such as the internet that have greatly increased our access to linguistic and cultural information as well as sped up the overall translation process. These scholars were no less rigorous in their day than we endeavor to be in our own.

Along those lines, we would like to pay particular homage to Mary Ross and an apparent mistranslation in her work. Specifically, Ross translates *chagualas* as "cups." As evidence of Ross's importance to scholarship in this area, the notion that Luisa Menéndez and Teresa Martín mention ceremonies in which gold cups were brought out can be found throughout other scholars' work. Early drafts of our own translation followed this original translation until one of the contributors here, Kimberly Borchard, pointed out to us that the Real Academia Española translates *chagualas* as being "nose rings" or similar adornments. Again, we do not see this as an outright error so much as the work of a scholar doing the best she could within the limitations imposed on her by her own time. We do not seek to criticize Ross or her work but rather celebrate her and her enduring contributions to what we do know and can know about this particular time period. Further, we would argue that, given the magnitude and importance of Ross's work, her career offers a cautionary tale about how we, as professionals and academics, treat each other. According to at least one source, Ross seemed to have exited research and publication altogether after a fellow scholar scathingly corrected her misidentification of a group of ruins in present-day Georgia.[47] Had that conversation been handled differently, might Ross have continued to publish? And if she had, how might fields such as US literature and history have been fundamentally altered through the better dissemination of her research?

The Chapters in This Volume

In the spirit of collaboration and exchange, we are excited to present the reader with the following collection of chapters contributed by our friends and colleagues, old and new, from a variety of different disciplines. While the content is presented in a specific order, we should state at the outset that we requested that individual submissions engage different disciplinary lenses, such as Indigenous studies, Appalachian studies, and the study of colonial documents in Latin America, and that authors not shy away from writing for an undergraduate as opposed to an advanced academic audience. Indeed, we invited and encouraged personal reflection on these documents and what they mean as being integral to the overall project. On one level, our hope is that the current volume will have something of a popular readership and help people move beyond the dominant narratives of life in what we now call the United States, narratives that all too often ignore not only the fact that Spanish precedes English here by almost one hundred years but also that Indigenous languages and Peoples, from Cherokee, Yuchi, and Muscogee to Choctaw, Catawba, and Timucua, precede the presence of European languages and peoples by millennia. On another level, we hope that the diverse approaches taken in this volume highlight what different fields bring to the study of a text like this and how the production of knowledge is enriched when we stop to consider something from multiple perspectives instead of just one. While the chapters must reflect a particular order, given the linear nature of the book, we would encourage readers to begin with the chapter or approach that they may find most appealing and go from there.

As a prelude to the "Relación" itself, Kimberly Borchard's "Spanish Appalachia: The Méndez de Canzo Inquiry in the Context of La Florida" thinks about the inquiry by remapping the Spanish colony of La Florida and Appalachia in the contemporary imaginary. Analyzing the voices of each of the document's participants, Borchard underscores how the seldom-acknowledged history that the document represents can lead us to a different understanding of the past, present, and future of places such as Appalachia and North Carolina. "Indigenous Women and the Un/Making of Spanish Men in Northern La Florida, 1540–1568" by Rachel V. Briggs, Christopher B. Rodning, Robin A. Beck, and David G. Moore situates the "Relación" and Menéndez's and Martín's testimonies within the exciting archaeological work being done at the former site of Joara and Fort San Juan, using the archaeological record to demonstrate who these women may have been and what their relationships with the Spanish may have been like. Miriam Melton-Villanueva's "How Indigenous Women Created History in La Florida 1600" then connects the "Relación" to these larger hemispheric processes of European colonization, highlighting the role that notarial records can and do play in recovering the voices of everyday people who otherwise may be lost to history. "Making the 'Yaa' to the Governor in the Méndez de Canzo 'Account' and in Today's Florida" by Dolores Flores-Silva and Keith Cartwright meditates on the "Relación" in the context of contemporary politics and governors of (La) Florida past and present. In doing so, they understand contemporary events from a long view of negotiations between authorities and multiple actors and how, especially in the case of Luisa Menéndez, assent is not, perhaps, assent at all. In "Native American Women's Roles and Leadership in the 1500s–1800s," Elizabeth Coonrod Martínez considers the prominent role that Indigenous women have always played as leaders in their communities and beyond, as well as how colonization has sought to diminish and deny these facts. The final chapter in this volume, "Here, Now: Mapping Southeastern Indigenous Literature across Time" by Gina Caison situates Menéndez's and Martín's respective testimonies within a multiplicity of webs and worlds, showing how the two women "write home" in ways that defy domestication under European imperial designs. Powerfully connecting these women to contemporary writers and movements in Native American literature, Caison shows how Menéndez's and Martín's words resonate down to today. Her contribution thus provides a fitting close to the present work if one were to read it linearly, as well as a fitting beginning for future engagement with the "Relación."

With no further ado, we invite you to turn to the chapter you find most inviting, go back several hundred years, and meet Luisa Menéndez and Teresa Martín as they are called before the governor of La Florida to talk about La Tama.

Notes

1. In keeping with one of the Spanish conventions that can be found reflected in maps from throughout the hemisphere, Pardo named the colony itself Cuenca, after his hometown. See Robin A. Beck, Christopher B. Rodning, and David G. Moore, "Joara, Cuenca, and Fort San Juan," in *Fort San Juan and the Limits of Empire: Colonialism and Household Practice at the Berry Site*, ed. Robin A. Beck, Christopher B. Rodning, and David G. Moore (Gainesville: University Press of Florida, 2016), 1–3.

2. We refer to both Teresa Martín and Luisa Menéndez as "Indigenous" throughout this work given that there is no evidence that concretely gives a specific tribal affiliation to either. In the "Relación," Martín says she is from "Juacan," which was how the Spanish referred to the entirety of the so-called interior. Menéndez says that she is from Manaytique, present-day Saltville, Virginia.

3. Charles Hudson, *The Juan Pardo Expeditions: Explorations of the Carolinas and Tennessee, 1566–1568*, rev. ed. (Tuscaloosa: University of Alabama Press, 2005), 176, 197n.19.

4. See contributors to this volume Rachel V. Briggs et al., "Fear the Native Woman: Femininity, Food, and Power in the Sixteenth-Century North Carolina Piedmont," *American Anthropologist* 126, no. 1 (2024): 1–15. Drawing on Hudson and Worth, in this article they state that the three documented potential survivors were Martín's husband Juan Martín de Badajoz, Juan de Ribas, and "a Flemish fife." They note that all three had "married Native women" (5). To the best of our knowledge, Badajoz is only one of the three who was at the fort when it was burned.

5. In the "Relación," her name appears as "Menéndez" and "Meléndez," and she has been called "Luisa Méndez" in a number of scholarly works about this time period. Here we will follow the spelling as her name first appears: "Menéndez."

6. Katherine Reding, "Letter of Gonzalo Méndez de Canzo, Governor of Florida, to Phillip II of Spain, June 28, 1600," *Georgia Historical Quarterly* 8, no. 3 (1924): 216–17. A second translation of the same letter is included in Beers Quinn (826–38), cited below.

7. Note also that Martín and Menéndez are likely the two Indigenous women referred to in the León account, but given that they are not mentioned by name there, we do not include it here. John E. Worth, "Recollections of the Juan Pardo Expeditions: The 1584 Domingo de León Account," in *Fort San Juan and the Limits of Empire: Colonialism and Household Practice at the Berry Site*, ed. Robin A. Beck, Christopher B. Rodning, and David G. Moore (Gainesville: University Press of Florida, 2016), 58–80.

8. Craig S. Womack, *Red on Red: Native American Literary Separatism* (Minneapolis: University of Minnesota Press, 1999), 6–7.

9. Paula Gunn Allen, *The Sacred Hoop: Recovering the Feminine in American Indian Traditions* (Boston: Beacon Press, 1986), 4.

10. Álvar Núñez Cabeza de Vaca, *Chronicle of the Narváez Expedition*, trans. David Frye (New York: Norton, 2013), 46.

11. René Laudionnière, *Three Voyages*, trans. Charles E. Bennett (Tuscaloosa: University of Alabama Press, 1975), 86–87.

12. J. Michael Francis and Kathleen M. Kole, *Murder and Martyrdom in Spanish Florida: Don Juan and the Guale Uprising of 1597* (New York: American Museum of Natural History, 2011), 73–74.

13. Alejandra Dubcovsky, *Talking Back: Native Women and the Making of the Early South* (New Haven, CT: Yale University Press, 2023), 4.

14. By referring to the Hemisphere as Abiayala, we are not setting down geographic parameters along the lines of a national literature but understand the land as a living being capable of holding and possessing. In doing so, we are following the lead of two Indigenous scholars, the K'iche' scholar Emil Keme and the Dule scholar Sue Patricia Haglund. For his part, Keme proposes that we use this name as a "transhemispheric Indigenous bridge" (43). It is, as Keme points out, "the name the Guna use to refer to what for others is the American continent as a whole": Emil Keme, "For Abiayala to Live, the Americas Must Die: Towards a Transhemispheric Indigeneity," *NAIS* no. 5 (2018): 42. That said, Haglund argues the unintended, even colonizing consequences of this move insofar as the use of a Dule term by non-Dule risks the objectification of the land, as Abiayala is understood as a "what" as opposed to a "who." She powerfully states, "Abiayala is a relative, Abiayala is alive and present and is the evolution of Development with collective solidarity, not the chaos of destruction, because Abiayala is a live being. Abiayala is created in coexistence with our other realms. Not as a singular replacement but as a layering of previous worlds that came before it" (Sue Patricia Haglund, "Abundantly Abiayala/Abya Yala: Ethical Representation and Navigation in 'Othering' Dulegaya Terms in Non-Dule Spaces," Spanish and Portuguese Studies, University of Minnesota, November 16, 2022).

15. Sarah Dowling, *Translingual Poetics: Writing Personhood under Settler Colonialism* (Iowa City: University of Iowa Press, 2018), 26, 8.

16. Yásnaya Elena Aguilar Gil, "'Las lenguas no mueren, las matan': Lo que se esconde tras la extinción de las lenguas originarias en México," *Global Voices*, May 4, 2019, https://es.globalvoices.org/2019/04/05/nuestras-lenguas-no-mueren-las-matan.

17. Paul E. Hoffman, *A New Andalucia and a Way to the Orient: The American Southeast during the Sixteenth Century* (Baton Rouge: Louisiana State University Press, 1990), 4.

18. Anna Brickhouse, *The Unsettlement of America: Translation, Interpretation, and the Story of Don Luis de Velasco, 1560–1945* (Oxford: Oxford University Press, 2015), 27.

19. See the relevant passages from Gonzalo Fernández de Oviedo y Valdez's *Historia general y natural de las indias, islas, y tierra-firme del mar océano* (1535). These are available in English translation in J. Brent Morris's *Yes, Lord, I Know the Road: A Documentary History of African Americans in South Carolina, 1526–2008* (Columbia: University of South Carolina Press, 2017), 38–39. The exact location of this brief settlement is unknown. Possible places include Sapelo Sound, south of what is now Savannah, Georgia (Hoffman, *New Andalucia*, 72), or perhaps further north at the mouth of the Savannah River (Douglas T. Peck, "Lucas Vásquez de Ayllón's Doomed Colony of San Miguel de Gualdape," *Georgia Historical Quarterly* 85, no. 2 [2001]: 193).

20. Hoffman, *New Andalucia*, 89–90.

21. While some readers may chafe at this ("I certainly don't think that!"), we use this language intentionally and agree with the Guna Dule actor and artist-scholar Monique Mojica and her collaborator Brenda Farnell that ongoing violence against Indigenous bodies (what they refer to as *corpus nullis*) arises from European concepts that this land was indeed *terra nullis*. The notion that there was nothing here prior to Europeans' arrival is thus embedded in the world around us and is therefore something to be resisted and called out. See Monique Mojica and Brenda Farnell, *Chocolate Woman Dreams the Milkyway: Mapping Embodied Indigenous Performance* (Ann Arbor: University of Michigan Press, 2023), 19–20.

22. Kimberly C. Borchard, *Appalachia as Contested Borderland of the Early Modern Atlantic 1528–1715* (Tempe: Arizona State University Press for the Arizona Center for Medieval and Renaissance Studies, 2021), 95.

23. Hudson, *Juan Pardo Expeditions*, 24.

24. Beck et al., "Joara, Cuenca, and Fort San Juan."

25. See note 5.

26. Francis and Kole, *Murder and Martyrdom in Spanish Florida*.

27. "Relación de la Tama y su tierra y de la población de ingleses," in *Documentos históricos de la Florida y la Luisiana, Siglos XVI al XVIII*, ed. Iñigo Abad y Lasierra (Madrid: Librería general de Victoriano Suárez, 1912), 141–59; Walter Mignolo, "Cartas, crónicas, y relaciones del descubrimiento y la Conquista," in *Historia de la literatura hispanoamericana*, vol. 1, coord. Luis Íñigo Madrigal (Madrid: Cathedra, 1982), 70. Unless otherwise noted, translations from Spanish are our own.

28. Mignolo, "Cartas, crónicas, y relaciones del descubrimiento y la Conquista," 71.

29. See Luis Leal, "A Historical Perspective," in *A Luis Leal Reader*, ed. Ilan Stavans (Evanston: Northwestern University Press, 2007) 14–27; and Juan Bruce-Novoa, "Shipwrecked in the Seas of Signification: Cabeza de Vaca's *La*

Relación and Chicano Literature," in *Reconstructing a Chicano/a Literary Heritage: Hispanic Colonial Literature of the Southwest*, ed. María Herrera-Sobek (Tucson: University of Arizona Press, 2008), https://open.uapress.arizona.edu/projects/reconstructing-a-chicano-a-literary-heritage.

30. Mignolo, "Cartas, crónicas, y relaciones del descubrimiento y la Conquista," 59.

31. Margaret Randall, "¿Qué Es, y Cómo Se Hace un Testimonio?," *Revista de Crítica Literaria Latinoamericana*, 18, no. 36 (1992): 34.

32. The *Account* was recently republished in a critical edition: Matthew Restall et al., *The Friar and the Maya: Diego de Landa and the* Account of the Things of Yucatan (Denver: University Press of Colorado, 2023).

33. John Beverley, *Testimonio: On the Politics of Truth* (Minneapolis: University of Minnesota Press, 2004), 19.

34. Ángel Rama, *The Lettered City*, trans. and ed. John Charles Chasteen (Durham: Duke University Press, 1996), 6.

35. Walter Mignolo, *The Darker Side of the Renaissance: Literacy, Territoriality, and Colonization* (Ann Arbor: University of Michigan Press, 1995), 41.

36. Mignolo, *Darker Side of the Renaissance*, 43.

37. Ibid., 59.

38. José Rabasa, *Tell Me the Story of How I Conquered You: Elsewheres and Ethnosuicide in the Colonial Mesoamerican World* (Austin: University of Texas Press, 2021), 12–13.

39. Doris Sommer, "Rigoberta's Secrets," *Latin American Perspectives* 18, no. 3 (1991): 32.

40. Inga Clendinnen, *Maya Conquistador: Maya and Spaniard in Yucatan, 1517–1570* (Cambridge: Cambridge University Press, 1987), 119.

41. Diego de Landa, *Relación de las cosas de Yucatán* (Mexico: Conaculta, [1566] 1994), 186.

42. Scott Cave, "Madalena: The Entangled History of One Indigenous Floridian Woman in the Atlantic World," *Americas* 74, no. 2 (2017): 1.

43. John Worth, ed. and trans., *Discovering Florida: First-Contact Narratives from Spanish Expeditions along the Lower Gulf Coast* (Gainesville: University Press of Florida, 2014), 178. This comes from Luis Cáncer's diary, which was completed by his companion, the friar Gregorio de Beteta, upon Cáncer's death. A transcription and translation appear in Worth, which is the text we cite here.

44. Brickhouse, *Unsettlement of America*, 5.

45. A full exploration of the term "literature" and the scholarship on the "literariness" of different texts lies beyond the scope of the current project. Nonetheless, we will state that, following current trends in Indigenous literary studies, we understand the literary field as encompassing the traditional binary orality/literacy as well as a variety of media and expressive cultures. See, for example, Daniel Heath Justice, *Why Indigenous Literatures Matter* (Minneapolis: University of Minnesota Press, 2018) and Paul M. Worley and Rita M. Palacios, *Unwriting Maya Literature: Ts'íib as Recorded Knowledge* (Tucson: University of Arizona Press, 2019).

46. Katherine Reding, "Letter of Gonzalo Méndez de Canço, Governor of Florida, to Phillip II of Spain, June 28, 1600," *Georgia Historical Quarterly* 8, no. 3 (September 1924): 215–28; David Beers Quinn, *The Roanoke Voyages, 1584–1590: Documents to Illustrate the English Voyages to North America under the Patent Granted to Walter Raleigh in 1584*, vol. II (London: Halkyut Society, 1955), 826–38.

47. "Mary Ross—Teacher, Scholar, Historian," *Elegant Island Living*, April 27 2023, https://www.elegantislandliving.net/history/mary-ross-%E2%80%93-teacher-scholar-historian/

1

Spanish Appalachia

The Canzo Inquiry in the Context of La Florida

Kimberly C. Borchard

The Floridian Roots of Modern Appalachia

When you think "Florida," what do you think? For the average American, the word may conjure images of the Sunshine State: idyllic beaches, Disney World . . . perhaps memes about "Florida Man." An American schoolchild might recount something about a man by the name of Ponce de León who supposedly embarked on a journey to find the fountain of youth in 1513 and ended up giving the peninsula the name by which it is known today (the Spanish word meaning "flowery" or "full of flowers"). That same schoolchild may or may not know that de León died a few years later at the not-quite-youthful age of forty-seven, after the original inhabitants of the land reacted as those of any sovereign nation would to an unprovoked invasion of their territory: they greeted the foreign invaders with violence, and de León would soon die in Cuba from his injuries.[1]

This inglorious beginning of the attempted Spanish colonization of *La Florida* set a precedent for what would ultimately prove to be the protracted death of Spain's colonial empire north of Mexico. Because sixteenth-century Europeans had yet to make their way through the length and breadth of North America, "La Florida" constituted not only the Florida peninsula, as it is known today, but also everything beyond, over which Spain claimed sovereignty thanks to a papal bull of 1493.[2] Yet long before Spain's withdrawal from Florida in the eighteenth century, its colonial agents would set off centuries of violence across the American South in search of the purported gold mines of the Apalachee people.

In 1528, the Spanish shipwreck survivor Álvar Núñez Cabeza de Vaca washed up naked and shivering on a beach near contemporary Tampa and asked the Indigenous people whom he encountered there where he might find gold. When he heard the word he would later transcribe as *Apalache* in their response—uttered in a language that was unintelligible to him without the benefit of an interpreter—he became convinced that the people now known as the Apalachee possessed rich gold mines to rival the wealth wrested from the Mexica (better known as the Aztecs) by Hernán Cortés just seven years earlier. Even though those mines never existed, the promise alone was sufficient to fuel centuries of European attempts to find, seize, and exploit them.

Ultimately, the name of the Apalachee Indians[3] would be transposed to the mountain region today known as Appalachia by the French cartographer and illustrator Jacques Le Moyne de Morgues. Eager to emulate the highly profitable Spanish conquests of Mexico and Peru, French Huguenots[4] Jean Ribault and René Goulaine de Laudonnière set sail for "La Florida" in the latter half of the sixteenth century and founded two settlements on lands over which Spain claimed dominion: Charlesfort, on Parris Island, South Carolina (1562), and Fort Caroline, believed to be near contemporary Jacksonville, Florida (1565). Before fleeing a massacre at Fort Caroline led by Spanish admiral Pedro Menéndez de Avilés, Le Moyne would change the face of North American maps forever. He misappropriated the Apalachee name upon transposing a latinized version of *Apalache* onto a mountain range north of Florida, which he captioned with a tantalizing Latin legend, here rendered in English: "Appalachian Mountains, in which gold, silver, and copper are found." The rest, as they say, is history. Although the Apalachee people had no affiliation with the mountains to the north of their ancestral lands in Florida, Le Moyne's incorrect use of their name and the belief in the existence of concealed Appalachian mines would endure.

When he arrived in Florida in 1565 and put a violent end to Fort Caroline, Pedro Menéndez became convinced not only that the mountains to the north were rich in silver (which had recently surpassed gold in its importance to the Spanish imperial economy) but also that they constituted a vital military route to Spain's economic and administrative centers in Mexico. In fact, Menéndez believed that the Appalachian Mountains were a continuation of the mountains of Zacatecas (Mexico), in which Spain had already established highly profitable silver mines in the preceding two decades. While Menéndez did not refer to the eastern mountains as Appalachia or even as *Apalache* (Le Moyne's map would not be published for another quarter century), his conviction regarding the existence of mineral wealth throughout the range and his underestimation of the size of North America made his belief in the strategic importance of the Appalachian Mountains all the more urgent. In a letter of October 15, 1565, after describing the brutal slaughter of the French settlers at Fort Caroline (who had laid down their arms in exchange for the clemency that they learned too late they would never receive), Menéndez told King Philip II (r. 1556–1598) of Spain that the French settlers had "received news that a hundred leagues to the north-northwest of Santa Elena [Parris Island, South Carolina] lies the mountain range that comes from Zacatecas and which contains much silver; and Indians have come to them with many pieces [of this silver], and they were discovered to have possessed a quantity of five or six thousand ducats of these silver pieces, which the Indians of those lands brought to them."[5]

Menéndez was vehement not only that the Appalachian Mountains would yield rich mines but also that England and France were plotting to invade Havana, free the enslaved Africans and afro-descendants of the Caribbean, and sow chaos throughout Spain's "New" World colonies by provoking a pan-American slave revolt.[6] The resulting urgency to secure the Appalachian mines and fend off attacks by rival European empires thus provides the backdrop against which the Canzo inquiry, fully edited and published in a bilingual format for the first time in this volume, must be understood.

Pedro Menéndez de Avilés and the Fight for Spanish Appalachia

To fend off the threat of attack by rival European powers and ensure Spanish control of the Appalachian mines (as well as continued control of the mines of Zacatecas, which he believed to be much closer than they were), Menéndez believed it necessary to secure the Atlantic coast from Florida to Newfoundland. To do this, he proposed that Spain construct a fort in the Florida Keys to defend Spanish treasure fleets from the French and English pirates of the Caribbean, then permanently settle Santa Elena (Parris Island, South Carolina) and the Bahía de Santa María (Chesapeake Bay). To secure regions north, he contended that the settlement of Parris Island and the Chesapeake Bay would suffice, since he believed that "from there onward, toward Newfoundland, it's not necessary to settle [*poblar*], because to the north of this port eighty leagues inland, lie some mountain ranges, and at their foot, an arm of the sea that leads to Newfoundland . . . six hundred leagues."[7] In addition to his misguided belief that the mountains and silver mines of Zacatecas lay but a short journey to the south of the mountains of Virginia and the Carolinas, Menéndez hypothesized that a channel led directly from the Chesapeake Bay into the South Sea.[8] Having consolidated control over the eastern shores of North America from the Florida Keys to Newfoundland, Menéndez assured his sovereign that he would simultaneously protect the fleets carrying looted Mexican and Peruvian treasure through the Caribbean, dominate the northern fishing waters, link newly discovered Appalachian mines to those of Zacatecas, and ensure access to the South Pacific, China, and the Spice Islands.[9]

Menéndez's misguided optimism regarding the ease of conquering the whole of North America constituted not the exception but the rule in the European thinking of the era. Three-quarters of a century after Columbus cast anchor in the Bahamas and declared that he had successfully navigated a western route to Asia, Europeans remained overwhelmingly ignorant of the vastness of the "new" continent[10] to which the Genovese sailor had arrived. Foolhardy as his plan seems today, Menéndez was a shrewd strategist whose anticipation of threats from competing European empires reflected the challenges faced by Spain in its doomed attempt to maintain control over a sprawling colonial system that traversed the globe. While the wealth and sophistication of the Mexica and Inca empires that Spain had conquered in the first half of the sixteenth century now constitute common knowledge for anyone with a cursory knowledge of the New World, the European encounter with those empires had provided mind-boggling revelations regarding the fallibility of European geographers, classical philosophers, and even sacred Judeo-Christian texts in their day. Little did Menéndez suspect that prevailing European assumptions regarding geographical symmetry[11] to the north and south of the equator would soon prove equally fallacious.

Of interest to the current study is Menéndez's attempt to plot a land route across the Appalachian Mountains and southward to Zacatecas, which created the circumstances in which the Canzo inquiry would be produced. In an effort to find and protect against French and English rivals what he believed to be a direct path between present and future nerve centers of the Spanish Empire, Menéndez sent a soldier named Juan Pardo on two westward explorations from Santa Elena/Parris Island between December 1566 and March 1568. Menéndez charged Pardo with a general reconnaissance of the region, the discovery of a route to the silver mines of Zacatecas, and the establishment of peaceful relations with any Indigenous Peoples encountered along the way (whom Pardo would attempt to convert to Christianity). Of more immediate concern at the time, and unequivocally contributing to the ultimate failure of Pardo's mission to establish good relations with the Native inhabitants of the region, Menéndez also directed Pardo to feed half the men stationed at the inadequately provisioned settlement of Santa Elena by taking them along with him and feeding them with "tribute" to be collected from indeterminate Native people encountered along the way: Native people who undoubtedly were not anticipating the demand that they share their food with a literal army of uninvited guests.[12]

Florida archaeologist John Worth has noted that the first-person accounts of Pardo's expeditions offer a "final glimpse" of the Native societies of the mountain South: when the English finally penetrated the same region in the seventeenth century, the Indigenous societies they met there had already been transformed and decimated beyond recognition by the devastating effects of European contact.[13] The ongoing excavations of Fort San Juan, the only one of six forts built by Pardo discovered to date by contemporary archaeologists, continue to offer further glimpses of those societies on the cusp of irrevocable transformation.[14] Perhaps in anticipation, perhaps blissfully ignorant of the calamity to come, the Indigenous inhabitants of Joara (the Native town near which Fort San Juan was built) would burn the fort to the ground after only eighteen months, likely weary of material and sexual impositions by the Spanish soldiers housed there.[15]

The Canzo Inquiry: The Pinnacle of Myth and the Decline of Empire in the Language of Spanish Bureaucracy

It is in this context of imperial aspiration and struggle that the Canzo inquiry must be read. The year 1600, in which the inquiry was produced, would herald not merely a transition between centuries but a transition between Spanish monarchs and between European empires jockeying for control of the North American mainland.[16] News of the French settlements of Charlesfort (1562; Parris Island, South Carolina) and Fort Caroline (1565; near Jacksonville, Florida) had proven sufficiently alarming to Philip II to warrant dispatching Pedro Menéndez de Avilés with an armada to slaughter the "thieving pirates and perturbers of the public peace"[17] intruding in Spain's colonial domain just a few decades earlier. The Canzo inquiry, with its promises of incalculable wealth and warnings of English efforts to colonize the Virginia coast while ransacking Spanish ports throughout the Caribbean and Florida, prompted no such action by Spain's new king, Philip III (r. 1598–1621).

Rather than suggesting an imminent Spanish disengagement from North America, the letter that prompted the Canzo inquiry appears to express continuity with the expansionist politics of Philip II. Juan Jiménez, the scribe signing off on the inquiry, references a letter dated November 9, 1598, in which Philip III mentioned a previous allusion to the town of La Tama by Gonzalo Méndez de Canzo, governor and general captain of La Florida. Because the decision of whether or not to send more people to "populate" (read: attack and occupy) the (already populated) town hung in the balance, Phillip III charged Canzo "to become well informed about the disposition of that land through caciques and Indians . . . and the people with experience in the region who live in the garrison [of St. Augustine]" in order to provide the monarch with a "detailed account of everything," including "the layout and description of the land."[18] Such detailed accounts of the geography and natural resources of the New World constituted the cornerstone of the Spanish colonial archive, and—indeed—the whole of the Canzo inquiry is articulated in the legalese typical of Spanish imperial bureaucracy. The document privileges eyewitness testimony in the assessment of La Tama's potential for conquest, settlement, and profit, a rhetorical strategy used by agents of Spanish imperialism throughout the New World to bolster their epistemic authority and social rank since the time of Columbus.[19] This testimony is presented in the form of sworn statements by six declarants of varied extraction: one Spanish interpreter of the language of Guale (Gaspar de Salas), two Spanish soldiers (Juan de Ribas and Francisco Fernández de Ecija), two Native women (Teresa Martín and Luisa Menéndez), and an Irish soldier (David Glavid). Because these six witnesses made their statements individually in response to Canzo's inquiry,

"An Account of La Tama and Its Land, and the English Settlement" does not read as a neatly structured narrative but as a loosely connected set of accounts on a common subject. The most salient themes that reemerge throughout the accounts include the abundance of mineral resources, emphasized by all six witnesses; the suitability of the land for farming, hunting, and general subsistence, noted by five; pointed commentary on the relative civility of the Indigenous inhabitants of different regions of La Florida by the only two Indigenous witnesses; and generalized, multidirectional violence (Spanish-Spanish, Spanish-Native, Native-Spanish).

Gaspar de Salas

Given their diversity of backgrounds and complex relationships with La Florida, what is perhaps most striking about the inquiry is how much the declarants seem to have in common—at least as far as their perception of La Tama is concerned. Most notably, all six describe the area around La Tama as exceedingly rich in mineral resources. Gaspar de Salas, who served the Spanish Crown in both St. Augustine and Santa Elena/Parris Island "for more than twenty years," is the only one of the European witnesses featured in the inquiry to boast knowledge of a Native language, in this case "the language of the province of Guale and San Pedro."[20] Salas testifies that when he accompanied the Franciscan Friars Pedro Fernández de Chosas and Francisco de Veras on an inland exploration, they spent eight days in an unpopulated wilderness before reaching Tama, roughly fifty leagues (173 miles) from St. Augustine ("this presidio"). In the vicinity of La Tama, Salas declared that

> there are bare hills where he had seen different kinds of rocks containing metal and that elsewhere, he and the said friars, given that they had nothing to dig with, simply took rocks that were on top of the dirt that seemed to them to be metal. The declarant then gave some of these stones, and their dust to the governor, and others to a recently deceased silversmith who happened to be in the city. Having tested them while he was still alive, the silversmith told him that there was silver in the place *from which they had taken the rocks, as he had been able to draw silver from their dust . . . if you sought the vein there would be very rich mines.*[21]

(Italics added for emphasis.)

To these promises of rich mineral veins bursting from the mountains, Salas adds that if there were "someone who knew how to pan for gold could find it in those rivers."[22] This assurance of rich, easily exploitable mines and gold-bearing rivers echoes the hyperbolic accounts of Apalachee/Appalachian mines that proliferated in Spanish, Portuguese, and French following the initial encounter between Cabeza de Vaca and the inhabitants of western Florida. Salas's testimony of rich silver veins and fine "crystals" taken . . . "from those hills and from along the flowing rivers"[23] also echoes accounts of the Juan Pardo expeditions. Juan Pardo's scribe, Juan de la Bandera, reported finding a stone that "could be silver"; Domingo de León, who took part in both of Pardo's expeditions and was the first participant to learn the Native language spoken around Santa Elena, stated in terms similar to those used by Salas that Pardo's men had discovered a "bald hill" encrusted with unbreakable "crystals" as well as "many mines" of both gold and silver.[24]

Regarding the suitability of this idyllic mining region for conquest and settlement, Salas assures Canzo that although he and the Franciscan missionaries spent eight days in an unpopulated wilderness while traversing the region between Guale and Tama, once they reached Tama they observed an abundance of food crops, wild game, and fish,[25] suggesting land ideally suited for the establishment of a permanent settler colony. Beyond Tama, the people of Ocute dressed in a manner reminiscent of New Spain (Mexico) and greeted the Spaniards with the gift of ornate blankets (*mandiles*), hinting that Tama boasted as sophisticated a civilization as did Mexico, in addition to providing comparable mineral wealth. The people of Ocute, however, warned their guests that "if they continued ahead the Indians there would kill them" as they had done to De Soto some thirty years earlier.[26] In the testimony of Salas, La Tama thus appears as an oasis of mineral and natural abundance with wilderness on one side and hostile territory on the other, poised to become the outpost of the Spanish Empire on the North American frontier.

Juan de Ribas

Juan de Ribas served over thirty-four years in the presidio of St. Augustine, and while he never served in La Tama, Ribas accompanied Juan Pardo on his inland expeditions at the age of seventeen or eighteen.[27] Ribas mentions the abundance of pearls harvested from the Wateree

(Guatari) River (in today's South Carolina) and assures Canzo that a piper and his family who had stayed in that area "would be able to attest to the land's many riches" if found alive.[28] However, the pearls appear as a resource of secondary interest: the diamonds, gold, and silver in the mountains around Joara outshine all else. Ribas recounts that Hernando Moyano de Morales (whom Pardo had left in charge of Fort San Juan while exploring to the east)[29] had taken a small diamond from "a high hill which they called Diamonds" near Joara and sold it at a considerable profit in Spain, only to be told by the buyer that he "had not known what he had sold and that he [the buyer] would not return it to him for any price."[30] Further inland, traveling "more than twenty days" from Joara, Ribas claimed that Pardo's men found "mountains, where they marked many gold and silver mines, according to what he heard the alchemists and silversmiths," say as well as Native women wearing jewelry of gold, silver, and pearls.[31] Finally, Ribas attested to hearing that roughly a week's travel from the town where De Soto had died, through hostile territory, lay a city called the Great Copal, which was rich in silver and inhabited by people living in stone houses.[32]

Regarding the suitability of the region for conquest, Ribas assures Canzo that "[N]one of the towns at which they arrived had any defenses,"[33] a detail clearly intended to underscore the vulnerability of the rich mountain mining region to invasion. He adds that "the fertility of the land means that there is a diverse abundance of food of all kinds, and . . . if His Majesty knew about that land, he would not be able to stop himself from populating and conquering it and that, given the many mines that were found, the wealth of previously discovered lands cannot compare," noting that his wife (Luisa Menéndez, whom he does not name) and Teresa Martín, whose testimony is discussed below, "could speak about this and much more."[34] Despite his assurances regarding the defenseless mountain towns, however, this account of rich and fertile lands awaiting conquest is darkened by the specter of violence: Ribas notes that Moyano and all but one of the twenty-two men accompanying him were killed when they went to "pacify" an Indigenous revolt at Camacu and that this event aborted subsequent efforts to return to the mountain of Diamonds.[35]

Teresa Martín

Teresa Martín was a Native woman from the town of Joara who had been "taken back to Santa Elena on Pardo's second expedition"[36] when she was just a child.[37] Perhaps due to her youth at the time of Pardo's arrival and the fact that she was not a participant in his original expedition, Martín states that Pardo traveled 150 leagues (519 miles) to her home, three times farther than the distance mentioned by Salas. Married to the Spaniard Juan de Badajoz,[38] Martín assured Canzo that "when there were gatherings and dances among the Indians" of her homeland "they brought out . . . nose adornments of gold and silver" but that her young age at the time prevented her from having greater familiarity with this practice.[39] While she notes that pearls were harvested from a river a day's journey from her town and that many such pearls had been given to Pardo and Moyano as gifts, Martín's interviewer appears to dismiss the pearls and to privilege precious metals, as demonstrated when he follows up on her comments regarding the pearls with a question about gold: "Asked about the gold for the nose adornments that the Indians brought out in their dances particularly where the Indians found it and where they gathered it, she stated that three or four days' journey from her town there are some Indians who reside in a mountain range called Chisca, where they gather said gold . . . [F]rom these people they get the gold for the nose adornments they use in their dances, as well as the little solid gold tubes they wear dangling in their piercings."[40] Teresa Martín's attestation that Chisca[41] was the source of the gold used for ceremonial purposes in Joara echoed the account of a Portuguese participant in the Hernando de Soto expedition six decades earlier, who shared a report that in Chisca they smelted a metal of the same color as copper but "finer, and of a much more perfect color and much better appearance, that they did not make as much use of, for it was softer."[42] Martín also makes the curious observation that the people of Chisca "go around fully dressed, and they are very white, red haired, and blue-eyed, like the Flemish, because the hair they have is a little like gold."[43] Absent from her girlhood reminiscence is the fact that after Juan Pardo had left him in charge of Fort San Juan, Hernando Moyano ravaged a Chisca settlement in what Charles Hudson characterizes as the most violent act in either of the two Pardo expeditions. This massacre may be partially explained by further testimony from Juan de Ribas (not included in this volume) that Moyano had been paid in gold "for assisting [an unnamed] cacique against his [Chisca] rival."[44]

Regarding the ease of conquering and settling the region, Martín is as optimistic as Salas and Ribas, if not more so. She notes that St. Augustine, where she is being interviewed, "is worth nothing in comparison" to her homeland, "because in her land hunger is unknown."[45] She goes on to enumerate many of the food crops and game mentioned by the declarants discussed above, adding that the region also boasts valuable saltwater springs[46] and that decades earlier, Moyano needed only send a message ahead to towns on his route in order to be greeted with an abundance of foodstuffs upon arrival.[47] Indeed, at the beginning of her testimony, Martín notes that when Pardo and his infantry arrived in her land, her people shared generous amounts of food with them[48]—which was, of course, one of the intended outcomes of Pardo's decision to take with him half the hungry men at Santa Elena.

We should note, however, that Martín's anecdote about her people's generosity in feeding their unexpected guests may have as much to do with her relative assessment of her people as it does with her assessment of their land. When asked to compare her homeland to St. Augustine and its environs, she adds that in addition to the agricultural bounty that they enjoy, her people "are not fickle nor untruthful like those of this land [St. Augustine] . . . in this land they do nothing more than drink and take up the quiver and bow and go from one island to another and from one swamp to another, and fish and hunt, with no settlement."[49] This disparaging assessment of the people native to the area around St. Augustine contrasts sharply with that of her own town, which Martín describes as large, populous, and palisaded, with only four entry points, as much to ward off wild hogs that sometimes kill children as to defend the populace from human foes.[50] Without the terms "civilization" and "barbarism" so frequently invoked in discussions of the early Latin American literary canon, Martín thus effectively characterizes the Native inhabitants of St. Augustine as savages and her own people as civilized and politic. In the final assessment, Martín's testimony regarding the wealth, natural bounty, and polity of her native land creates the impression that not only is it ripe for Spanish settler colonists but that Martín may be actively encouraging those colonists to settle it.

Francisco Fernández de Ecija

Like Ribas and Martín, Francisco Fernández de Ecija professes no firsthand knowledge of La Tama, but the *alférez* boasts more than thirty-six years' experience in "these provinces," by which he presumably means the Florida peninsula and beyond.[51] He furthermore attests to having heard Juan Pardo and Hernando Moyano discuss La Tama at length while he accompanied them "into the interior together for more than two hundred leagues [692 miles]," implying that although he is not an eyewitness, he can offer secondhand testimony of the highest caliber.[52] While, as noted above, all witnesses interviewed for the inquiry attest to the mineral wealth of the inland mountains, most striking in Ecija's account is the consistency that it shows relative to the testimony of Gaspar de Salas as well as to the prior account of Domingo de León. After affirming the reliability of his sources, Ecija claims that

> about forty leagues, more or less from the coast, on said [Guatari or Wateree] river, *there was a crystalline hill, completely bare [pelado todo]*, without trees . . . *and that said hill was of diamonds and held great wealth*, because at the time when he returned from the entrada that he made with Juan Pardo and said alferez Moyano . . . he heard him say that . . . taking a very small point he carried it away and took it to Spain, not knowing the value it had, and selling it with another quantity of pearls that he took on said entrada, he heard him say that they gave him many ducats, and that he said they had tricked him for not knowing what he was selling.[53]

While those familiar with the Appalachian range may find such tales perplexing, there is striking consistency across these multiple accounts of "bald" hills littered with diamonds. Ecija goes on to explain that Moyano subsequently approached Pedro Menéndez in Spain to ask for men to accompany him and "discover" the diamond-studded hill again, but that since both Menéndez and Moyano then died, the plan had come to naught.[54] However, Ecija is happy to offer his own services "to go on this discovery. He would not do so out of his own interests, but those of His Majesty." He adds that he also has knowledge of the "very rich" mines discovered by Pardo's expedition and independently verified by alchemists, as well as the "very good pearls" that they obtained, assuring Canzo that should he support this mission "His Majesty would incur little expense and yet receive a great reward."[55]

Ecija dedicates little attention to the natural abundance of the land that the other declarants describe in such detail, other than to note that "it is a land that is well populated and well provisioned."[56] Though he stops short of Menéndez's assumption that the Appalachian Mountains provide a direct route to the mines of Zacatecas, Ecija nevertheless makes a similar underestimation of the breadth of the continent when he asserts that the region might be entered via New Mexico.[57] Ultimately, Ecija's voice can be counted among the chorus of the many before and after him who attested to bounteous, easily accessible mineral wealth in the Appalachian Mountains—despite repeated and lethal failures to secure more than anecdotal evidence of that wealth.[58]

David Glavid

David Glavid, an Irish soldier residing in St. Augustine at the time of the inquiry, constitutes something of an outlier among the witnesses called upon to testify to Canzo. Neither Spanish nor Native nor a longtime resident of La Florida (having lived in St. Augustine only five years), Glavid seems to have been selected because of his experience as an English hostage and his resulting knowledge of English designs on the continent. Indeed, Glavid claims to have been brought to Jacán (coastal Virginia) against his will by a man named Richard de Campoverde after his ship and its merchandise were hijacked by English pirates.[59] Like the other witnesses, Glavid testifies that "there were a lot of gold and pearls" in Jacán and that he saw Campoverde "recover more than one arroba of gold," though the metal was of low quality because "the Indians did not know how to refine it."[60] Like other declarants discussed above, Glavid states that the Natives wore golden nose adornments, though in his account it is the caciques and not the women who wear them.[61] Of greater potential concern to his Spanish interlocutor, however, is Glavid's assertion that "[T]he English also heard that forty leagues from there, upriver, at the foot of a mountain range at the headwaters of the river, there were gold mines." Although the English have thus far been unable to exploit the mines due to a lack of provisions on their aborted journey to discover them, Glavid warns Canzo that the "English are in said Jacán because it is a fertile land with so much gold and so many pearls," and that he does not believe they will readily give up their claims to it.[62]

Glavid's passing assurance that Jacán "is a fertile land," implicitly suitable for Spanish colonization, is easy to overlook. His testimony instead focuses on English piracy and threats to Spanish claims to the land soon to be known as Virginia, explaining that he originally arrived in North America only because "in the year of 1584 the English robbed a boat of his carrying merchandise and wine"[63] and Richard de Campoverde brought him forcibly across the Atlantic to Jacán along with 150 male colonists. Glavid notes that upon arrival in North America, the English began manufacturing bricks and roof tiles: an ominous indication of their intent to remain in this territory still claimed but yet to be conquered by Spain. Denied "passage," or means to leave, Glavid remained in Jacán until 1586, when Francis Drake famously sacked St. Augustine (as well as multiple other Spanish ports) and, in so doing, rounded up all the English colonists and returned them to England.[64]

Glavid notes the displeasure of Queen Elizabeth I at the removal of the colonists and reports that shortly thereafter, he witnessed in London the preparation of an even greater contingent of "two hundred men and a large number of colonists with their women"[65] to return to Jacán. Having accompanied the English fleet as far as Puerto Rico, Glavid alleges that he warned the governor of the English intent to attack the island, but to no avail.[66] Given that (he alleges) the English are already preparing a permanent settlement and have knowledge of the wealth hidden in the mountains, Glavid ends with the dire assessment that "as it is a fertile land with a lot of gold and many pearls, it did not seem to him that they [the English] would let go of it."[67]

Luisa Menéndez

The last of Canzo's witnesses, testifying two days after the rest of the declarants, was an Indigenous woman who was more than likely abducted as a girl by Juan Pardo from a town transcribed in the inquiry as "Manaytique,"[68] at or near the site of present-day Saltville, Virginia.[69] Likely due to her youth at the time she was taken from her land, some of Menéndez's testimony is confusing, even contradictory. Asked if there are precious metals or pearls in her homeland, Menéndez responds that "the Indians there wear golden nose adornments and that they obtain this gold from mountain ranges they call Chisca and that the Indians trade for it there."[70] She likewise affirms that her people harvested "many pearls" from a nearby river and gave them, along with gold nose rings, to Hernando Moyano. Yet, this seemingly straightforward affirmation notwithstanding, within the same utterance Menéndez declares that concerning silver "she does not know if there is any silver there, because although there are many mountains in her land, her people do not know how to mine for silver, or gold, of know anything about them. In her opinion, there is a lot of gold and silver in those mountains, but as she has stated, the Indians do not know about them."[71] It is perhaps due to these contradictions that Charles Hudson doubts Menéndez's claims regarding the presence of gold while affirming that "the Chiscas traded copper both to the people of Chiaha and the people of Joara."[72]

Like Teresa Martín, Luisa Menéndez affirms that the people of Chisca "are very white, and blue-eyed with red hair."[73] She similarly notes that "her land is very good and fertile with plenty of food," going on to enumerate abundant food crops and game and noting that "her town is established and very large. The houses there are made of wooden boards, covered with chestnut branches and juniper planks."[74] Finally, when asked if her land would provide sufficient sustenance "if many Spaniards were to go to that land," Menéndez replies that "regarding food, there would be no lack of it no matter how many people went, and that there was also a spring there with three or four heads of salt water from which the Indians make salt. The water there rises and falls, and in all of that land, there is no other salt water."[75]

In the end, with her assurances regarding the abundance of foodstuffs and the precious commodity of salt, Luisa Menéndez appears to encourage Canzo to make a new attempt to colonize her homeland. Yet her contradictions regarding mineral commodities raise many more questions than they answer. Why did she affirm that the Indians mined gold at Chisca, only to deny a moment later that her people had any knowledge of gold at all? Did she intend to make a distinction between those who she claimed did mine gold and her own people, who did not? Was she telling Canzo what she thought he wanted to hear? Menéndez apparently ended the line of questioning about precious metals by concluding that "as she was a young girl when she left her homeland, she cannot give as much information about the land as she would be able to say now that she is a grown woman. She says that her husband Juan de Ribas can better say what is in her land than she can, as he is Spanish and a man."[76] Was she deferring to her husband's testimony, either aware that he would be taken more seriously "as he is Spanish and a man" or because she was afraid of contradicting the testimony he had already provided? Or were her relatives possibly among those Chisca who were murdered by Moyano decades earlier and her recollections of her homeland and her youth distorted by trauma?

Whatever the reason for its contradictions, the testimony of Luisa Menéndez provides a fitting conclusion to the Canzo inquiry and an unintended shorthand for the previous seventy-two years of the European crusade to find the riches first of Apalachee, then of Appalachia: an unequivocal declaration of the existence of gold, followed by a straight-faced disavowal of any knowledge of how or where to mine that very gold. Like the decades of claims preceding it and the century of claims to come afterward until the Apalachee themselves were finally chased from their Florida home,[77] the Appalachian gold in Menéndez's testimony in the end appears as elusive as a mirage.

Conclusion: The Canzo Inquiry in the Twilight of Spanish Appalachia and Today

Transcribed nearly three-quarters of a century after Cabeza de Vaca's misapprehension that the Apalachee of western Florida were rich in gold, the Canzo inquiry offers a stunning snapshot of the moment when Spain's dream of conquering a northern El Dorado appeared to be on the brink of consummation. The testimony of six eyewitnesses representing a diverse cross section of colonial society and promising a motherlode of gold, silver, and diamonds ready for the taking must have provided a glimmer of hope that Spain could finally conquer its northern territorial claims and replenish the coffers of its overextended global empire. Yet while it shows hope for Spain's ultimate domination of a continent that had repelled attempts at conquest for nearly a century, the inquiry likewise betrays the anxiety of an empire on the cusp of decline. David Glavid's warning that "it doesn't seem . . . that [the English] would let go of such a fertile land . . . where there [is] so much gold and pearls" would be followed thirteen years later by that of Diego de Molina, a Spanish mariner gone to spy on the fledgling English settlement of Jamestown on the Virginia coast, who warned that if Spain did not send an armada to reassert its territorial claims, the English would soon be reaping the spoils of silver and gold mines in the mountains to the west.[78]

The questions at the heart of the Canzo inquiry regarding the availability of extractable resources and the suitability of the land for a lasting settler colony were clearly borne of a lingering imperialist intent. Yet despite the inquiry's promises of easy riches and warnings that Spain's new earthly paradise could soon be lost, the dawn of a new century and rise of a new monarch marked the end of Spain's vainglorious attempt to conquer an entire hemisphere. The result of Philip III's passivity in the face of the new colony founded at Jamestown just seven years later hardly need be remarked on here (much less in the language of the empire whose aspirations David Glavid accurately predicted).

Because the inquiry did not result in the northwestern expansion implicitly and explicitly elicited by Canzo's witnesses, today's reader may find the text idiosyncratic, anticlimactic, even anachronistic. Yet if we read the inquiry with one mindful eye turned toward the past and another toward the turbulent present, its implications are difficult to overstate. In a decade initiated by the most widespread movement for racial justice that this country has ever seen, while national leaders of all stripes polemicize the migrant crisis at the southern border of the United States for political gain, what does the Canzo inquiry mean for the never-ending debate about who does or does not have a right to be considered American? If we consider that some of the most compelling testimony about the wealth and abundance of Appalachia was provided by Indigenous women speaking Spanish, what does the inquiry say about what it means to be Appalachian? Southern? North Carolinian or Virginian? Even, perhaps, Latin American?

In the end, the Canzo inquiry raises more questions than it answers. Certainly, it raises more questions than Gonzalo Méndez de Canzo ever asked. In a young and striving nation reeling in the aftermath of a global pandemic and the greatest political crisis in nearly two centuries, the answers to those questions may prove more valuable than a mountain of silver, diamonds, and gold.

Notes

1. It is all but impossible that de León actually attempted to find the fountain of youth. For an overview of de León and the origins of this myth, see Matthew Shaer, "Ponce De Leon Never Searched for the Fountain of Youth," *Smithsonian Magazine*, June 2013, https://www.smithsonianmag.com/history/ponce-de-leon-never-searched-for-the-fountain-of-youth-72629888.

2. Mercedes Serna, *La Conquista del Nuevo Mundo: Textos y documentos de la aventura americana* (Barcelona: Castalia, 2012), 100.

3. Though "Indian" has fallen out of favor in much academic usage, I use it here because it is the term used today by descendants of the Apalachee who first encountered European explorers in Florida, the Talimali Band, the Apalachee Indians of Louisiana. See https://talimaliband.com.

4. French Protestants, the Huguenots, were a persecuted minority in the overwhelmingly Catholic France of the sixteenth and seventeenth centuries.

5. "[H]allaron por nuevas que al nornoroeste de Santa Elena cien leguas, tienen la serranía que viene de las Zacatecas y que es de mucha plata, y han venido indios a ellos con muchos pedazos, y hallóseles destos pedazos de plata, que los indios de aquellas partes les traían, cantidad de cinco o seis mil ducados." Pedro Menéndez de Avilés, *Cartas sobre la Florida (1555–1574)*, ed. Juan Carlos Mercado (Frankfurt: Iberoamericana-Vervuert, 2002), 145.

6. Ibid., 145–46.

7. "[A]llí adelante, hacia la Tierra Nova, no hay que poblar, a causa de que al norte deste puerto, a la tierra adentro, ochenta lenguas, hállanse unas sierras y al pie dellas un brazo de mar que va a salir a la Tierra Nova . . . seiscientas leguas." Ibid., 148–49.

8. That is, the south Pacific.

9. Menéndez de Avilés, *Cartas sobre la Florida*, 149.

10. In Spanish, North and South America are considered merely different regions of a single continent: *América*.

11. European thought of the era held that different regions of the earth at the same latitude featured both similar climates and similar natural resources. Karen Ordahl Kupperman, "The Puzzle of the American Climate in the Early Colonial Period," *American Historical Review* 87, no. 5 (December 1982): 1267.

12. Charles Hudson, *The Juan Pardo Expeditions: Exploration of the Carolinas and Tennessee, 1566–1568 [1990]* (Tuscaloosa: University of Alabama Press, 2005), 3, 23, and Robin A. Beck, Christopher B. Rodning, and David G. Moore, "Limiting Resistance: Juan Pardo and the Shrinking of Spanish La Florida, 1566–68," in *Enduring Conquests: Rethinking the Archaeology of Resistance to Spanish Colonialism in the Americas*, ed. Matthew Liebmann and Melissa S. Murphy (Santa Fe, NM: SAR Press, 2011), 19–39, here 21.

13. John Worth, "Recollections of the Juan Pardo Expeditions: The 1584 Domingo de León Account," in *Fort San Juan and the Limits of Empire: Colonialism and Household Practice at the Berry Site*, ed. Robin A. Beck, Christopher B. Rodning, and David G. Moore (Gainesville: University Press of Florida, 2016), 58.

14. The bibliography on Fort San Juan is abundant and rapidly growing, but key studies include Hudson, *Juan Pardo Expeditions*; Robin A. Beck Jr., David G. Moore, and Christopher B. Rodning, "Identifying Fort San Juan: A Sixteenth-Century Spanish Occupation at the Berry Site, North Carolina," *Southeastern Archaeology* 25, no. 1 (2006): 65–77; Robin A. Beck Jr., Christopher B. Rodning, and David G. Moore, "Limiting Resistance," in *Fort San Juan and the Limits of Empire: Colonialism and Household Practice at the Berry Site* (Gainesville: University Press of Florida, 2016); Robin A. Beck et al., "The Politics of Provisioning: Food and Gender at Fort San Juan de Joara, 1566–1568," *American Antiquity* 81, no. 1 (2016): 3–26; and Robin A. Beck et al., "A Road to Zacatecas: Fort San Juan and the Defenses of Spanish La Florida," *American Antiquity* 83, no. 4 (2018): 577–97.

15. See Beck, Rodning, and Moore, "Limiting Resistance," 19–20, 26; Robin Beck, *Chiefdoms, Collapse, and Coalescence in the Early American South* (Cambridge: Cambridge University Press, 2013), 90–92; and Robin A. Beck, David G.

Moore, and Christopher B. Rodning, "Introduction," in *Fort San Juan and the Limits of Empire*, 5–26, here 15–16.

16. We refer here to North America *north of Mexico*. While recognizing the bias inherent to this usage, the term "America" is equally problematic (see note 10) and attempts at greater specificity inevitably wordy.

17. Philip II in a letter to the French Queen Mother, Catherine de Medici, quoted in Stefan Lorant, *The New World: The First Pictures of America* (New York: Duell, Sloan, and Pearce, 1946), 18. For his part, Menéndez promised his sovereign he would "burn and hang whatever French Lutherans he found" (quemar y ahorcar a los franceses luteranos que hallase) upon arrival in Florida, a promise on which he most gruesomely made good. Menéndez de Avilés, *Cartas sobre la Florida*, 131.

18. "An Account of La Tama and Its Land, and the English Settlement (1600)," in *Teresa Martín & Luisa Menéndez: Indigenous Women from Appalachia in the Spanish Colonial Record*, eds. Melissa D. Birkhofer and Paul M. Worley (University Press of Kentucky, 2025), 63–64.

19. The invocation of eyewitness authority in accounts of New World exploration and conquest likewise bolstered the epistemic and social authority of colonial authors. As Ralph Bauer has explained, "whereas the authority of the historian in the Old World rested mainly on his noble social standing, few of the chroniclers of the New World, typically of humble social origins, could shore up their trustworthiness with names and titles. . . . The *relación* [account of deeds and services rendered by the first-person witness] . . . in its New World context . . . becomes defined by its positionality and directionality not only in social space but also in geographic space." Ralph Bauer, *The Cultural Geography of Colonial Latin American Literatures: Empire, Travel, Modernity* (Cambridge: Cambridge University Press, 2003), 36. For a now-canonical study on the privileged place of eyewitness testimony in early colonial historiography, see Rolena Adorno, "The Discursive Encounter of Spain and America: The Authority of Eyewitness Testimony in the Writing of History," *William and Mary Quarterly* 49, no. 2 (April 1992): 210–28.

20. Guale was located in the northeastern Florida peninsula, north of St. Augustine. See John Worth, "Places of Spanish Florida," accessed July 9, 2022, https://pages.uwf.edu/jworth/jw_spanfla_places.html; and "An Account of La Tama," 64.

21. "An Account of La Tama," 65.

22. Ibid., 66.

23. Ibid., 65.

24. Worth, "Recollections," 60. For an overview of claims regarding precious metals and jewels in the Appalachian Mountains during the Pardo expeditions, see Kimberly C. Borchard, *Appalachia as Contested Borderland of the Early Modern Atlantic, 1528–1715* (Tempe: Arizona State University Press for the Arizona Center for Medieval and Renaissance Studies, 2021), 99–102.

25. "An Account of La Tama," 65.

26. Ibid., 66.

27. Ibid.

28. Ibid., 67.

29. Borchard, *Appalachia as Contested Borderland*, 98.

30. "An Account of La Tama," 67; Hudson contends that the stone in question was likely quartz or corundum. Hudson, *Juan Pardo Expeditions*, 189.

31. "An Account of La Tama," 67–68; Ribas stated that the women wore *chagualas*. The *Diccionario de la Real Academia Española* defines *chaguala* as an "earring that Indians wore in the nose" (Pendiente que los indios llevaban en la nariz) (https://dle.rae.es/chaguala?m=form).

32. "An Account of La Tama," 68; La Gran Copal had been mentioned previously by Pedro Morales, a Spaniard captured by Francis Drake in 1586 when the latter raided St. Augustine and burned the city to the ground. For Morales's account in the context of colonial Appalachia, see Borchard, *Appalachia as Contested Borderland*, 60–61. For the Morales's account itself (in English), see Richard Hakluyt, ed. and trans., *The Principal Navigations, Voyages, Traffiques & Discoveries of the English Nation* [1587], 12 vols. (Glasgow: Printed at the University Press by Robert Maclehose for James Maclehose, Publishers to the University of Glasgow, 1904), 9: 112–13, https://tinyurl.com/cd8dm9km.

33. "An Account of La Tama," 68.

34. Ibid., 69.

35. Ibid., 67. John Worth notes that these killings, in 1576, were a response to the abuses of Lieutenant Governor Juan de Solís and his men. See Worth, "Recollections," 63. Ribas also makes the curious observation that many members of the De Soto expedition perished after the death of their leader "because [after] the General had died there had been among them a fight about who was to be in charge, and . . . they killed each other . . . and as people without a caudillo, the Indians killed some" ("An Account of La Tama," 68).

36. Beck, Moore, and Rodning, "Introduction," 16. While the scholarship is vague on this point, it is my assumption that Martín was abducted or that, at the very least, she had little say in her departure with the Spanish troops. See note 69.

37. "An Account of La Tama," 70.

38. Beck, Moore, and Rodning, "Introduction," 16.

39. "An Account of La Tama," 70.

40. Ibid.

41. Charles Hudson hypothesized that Chisca territory was "in and to the other side of the mountains north of Joara, including the area along the upper course of the Nolichucky River." Hudson, *Juan Pardo Expeditions*, 27. In more recent scholarship, Robbie Ethridge places the Chisca "somewhere in present southwestern Virginia and eastern Tennessee at the time of the Pardo and Soto expeditions" and notes that by 1624, the Chisca were conducting raids on "mission Indians" in Spanish Florida. Robbie Ethridge, "Introduction," in *Mapping the Mississippian Shatter Zone: The Colonial Indian Slave Trade and Regional Instability in the American South*, ed. Robbie Ethridge and Sheri M. Shuck-Hall (Lincoln: University of Nebraska Press, 2009), 1–62, here 33. John Worth notes that the Chiscas were one member of a broader English-Native coalition that attacked a Spanish-led group of "some eight hundred Apalachees, Chacatos, and Timucuans" in 1702, leading to a devastating loss for the Spanish-led group in a confrontation now known as the Battle of the Blankets. John Worth, "Razing Florida: The Indian Slave Trade

and the Devastation of Spanish Florida, 1659–1715," in *Mapping the Mississippian Shatter Zone*, ed. Ethridge and Shuck-Hall, 295–311, here 301.

42. An anonymous Portuguese expeditionary and author known only as the Fidalgo d'Elvas, or Gentleman from Elvas, recalled that a visiting cacique had told De Soto that "to the north there was a province called Chisca, and that there, there was melting of copper and another metal of that [same] color . . . [but] finer, and of a much more perfect color and much better appearance, that they did not make as much use of, for it was softer" (Pera ho norta auia huma prouincia que Chisca se chamaua e que alli auia fundiçam de cobre e outro metal de aquella cor . . . mais acendrado, e de muyto mais perfecto cor e muyto melhor ao parecer e que nao se aproueitauam tanto delle por ser mais brando). Fidalgo d'Elvas, quoted in Borchard, *Appalachia as Contested Borderland*, 47–48. For further bibliography and the framing of the account of Chisca gold during the De Soto expedition within the broader search for Apalachee/Appalachian mines, see Borchard, *Appalachia as Contested Borderland*, 47–48.

43. "An Account of La Tama," 70.

44. Hudson, *Juan Pardo Expeditions*, 29. For an overall framing of the rumor of Chisca gold within the broader search for Apalachee/Appalachian gold, see Hudson, *Juan Pardo Expeditions*, 27–29, and Beck, *Chiefdoms, Collapse, and Coalescence*, 75–76.

45. "An Account of La Tama," 72.

46. Ibid. While the origins of Teresa Martín are not specified in the inquiry, the other woman interviewed by Canzo, Luisa Menéndez, was from Manaytique/Maniatique, believed to be near the saltwater springs of Saltville, Virginia (see note 75). The scholarship has referred to this woman as both "Luisa Méndez" and "Luisa Menéndez." Noting the variant transcribed in the inquiry in the present volume, we privilege "Menéndez."

47. "An Account of La Tama," 72.

48. Ibid., 69.

49. Ibid., 72.

50. Ibid.

51. Ibid., 73.

52. Ibid.

53. Ibid.

54. Ibid., 73–74.

55. Ibid., 74.

56. Ibid.

57. Ibid., all citations.

58. Ecija's activities in North America would soon include espionage. On July 8, 1609, Ecija arrived on the Virginia coast to reconnoiter Jamestown and reported to his superiors in Madrid "that the English had 'built a fort [. . .] made of wood'" but that the fort walls were surrounded by piles of stone, implying plans for reinforcement. See William S. Goldman, "Spain and the Founding of Jamestown," *William and Mary Quarterly* 68, no. 3 (July 2011): 427–59, here 441. For a more detailed account of this spying expedition, see James Horn, "Imperfect

Understandings: Rumor, Knowledge, and Uncertainty in Early Virginia," in *The Atlantic World and Virginia, 1550–1624*, ed. Peter C. Mancall (Chapel Hill: Published for the Omohundro Institute of Early American History and Culture by the University of North Carolina Press, 2007), 534–37.

59. "An Account of La Tama," 75.

60. Ibid., 76.

61. Ibid.

62. Ibid., 76–77, all citations.

63. Ibid., 75.

64. Ibid.

65. Ibid.

66. Glavid refers to the governor of Puerto Rico as "Menéndez." The reader should note that the governor of Puerto Rico at the time was Diego Menéndez de Valdes, not Pedro Menéndez de Avilés, who died in 1574. "Diego Menéndez de Valdés," accessed June 30, 2022, https://dbe.rah.es/biografias/122739/diego-menendez-de-valdes; and 156.

67. "An Account of La Tama," 76–77; 59.

68. Ibid., 77.

69. Hudson describes Luisa Menéndez (whose name he renders "Méndez") as "an Indian woman from the interior who had been brought out as a girl by Pardo, probably as a hostage." Hudson, *Juan Pardo Expeditions*, 190. While Hudson does not elucidate on his reasons for assuming Menéndez had been a hostage, it seems safe to assume that no child would willingly leave her home, her family, and all she knew in the company of an invading army of adult men. See also Borchard, *Appalachia as Contested Borderland*, 98n.

70. "An Account of La Tama," 77.

71. Ibid.

72. Hudson, *Juan Pardo Expeditions*, 91.

73. "An Account of La Tama," 77.

74. Ibid.

75. Ibid., 79. The saltwater springs near Manaytique/Maniatique were "one of the most important brines in the American South and one of just three where rock salt is available." Beck, Rodning, and Moore, "Introduction," 10.

76. "An Account of La Tama," 79.

77. For an account of the events leading to the final expulsion of the much-diminished Apalachee polity from Florida in the context of the colonial trade in Native enslaved people, see Worth, "Razing Florida." For a contextualization of the Apalachee diaspora within the longer quest for Apalachee/Appalachian wealth, see Borchard, *Appalachia as Contested Borderland*, 153–63.

78. Borchard, *Appalachia as Contested Borderland*, 117.

Relación de la Tama y su tierra, y de la población de ingleses (1600), updated transcription by Melissa D. Birkhofer and Paul M. Worley

España. Ministerio de Cultura y Deporte. Archivo General de Indias, Santo Domingo, 224, R.5, N.36, F.258r-267v.

San Agustín, febrero del año 1600

En la ciudad de San Agustín de las provincias de la Florida, a cuatro de febrero de mil y seiscientos años, Gonzalo Méndez de Canzo, gobernador y capitán general de estas provincias de la Florida por el Rey nuestro señor, dijo que a los dieciocho de enero pasado de este presente año recibió una carta del rey nuestro señor, cerrada y sellada, firmada de su real nombre y rubricada de los señores de su real Consejo de las Indias, y refrendada de Juan de Ibarra, su secretario; su fecha en Madrid a nueve de noviembre del año pasado de noventa y ocho, en la cual dicha carta hay un capítulo que mandó a mí, escribano, saque un tanto de él, que es del tenor siguiente:

Capítulo de la carta de Su Majestad, de 9 de noviembre de 98, acerca de la Tama

Se ha entendido la advertencia que hacéis de la disposición de esa tierra, y lo que importaría que se os enviase gente para poblar un pueblo donde llaman la Tama, cuarenta leguas de ese presidio, y de allí hacer una entrada y descubrimiento hasta dar en el Nuevo México, que se entiende está doscientas leguas de la dicha Tama, y porque este es negocio de la consideración que ves, os encargo y mando que os informéis muy particularmente de la disposición de la dicha tierra, por medio de las caciques e indios más cercanos a lo que pretendéis descubrir, y habiéndolo comunicado con las personas de más experiencia que hubiere en este presidio, y con algunos caciques, me enviaréis relación particular de todo, y siendo posible, la planta y descripción de la dicha tierra en que queréis hacer la entrada.

Corregido y concertado fue el dicho traslado del dicho capítulo de carta del Rey nuestro señor, de donde fue sacado, que queda en el poder del dicho gobernador y capitán general, originalmente, y va cierto y verdadero; de que yo el escribano doy fe.

Y el dicho gobernador y capitán general dijo que para que se cumpla lo que Su Majestad manda por el dicho capítulo de carta, y se pueda enviar una relación con mayor claridad que ser pueda de la dicha tierra de la Tama, y descripción de ella, manda se tome declaración con juramento en forma, a las personas que han estado en la Tama, y asimismo de las que han entrado por el río de Guatari, treinta leguas hacia el norte de Santa Elena, donde estaba el presidio de Su Majestad, con el capitán Juan Pardo y el alférez Moyano, que han entrado a la tierra adentro cantidad de leguas, y asimismo David Glavid, irlandés, que ha estado en el Jacan con Richarte de Campoverde, que allí hizo población, y de las mujeres indias naturales que hay en este presidio, naturales de dicha tierra adentro donde llegó el dicho capitán Juan Pardo, y de otras personas que se entiende tendrán relación o noticia de ello, y para ello mando parecer ante su merced para que digan y declaren lo que cerca de lo susodicho saben y han oído, y lo firmo de su nombre.—*Gonzalo Méndez de Canzo.*—Ante mí, *Juan Jiménez*, escribano.

Testigo, Gaspar de Salas, soldado

Y luego incontinente el dicho gobernador y capitán general hizo parecer ante sí a Gaspar de Salas, soldado de este presidio, del cual fue tomado y recibido juramento en forma de Derecho, debajo del cargo del cual prometió de decir la verdad de lo que le fuese preguntado, y siéndole preguntado diga y declare al tenor de dicho capítulo de carta; y lo que sabe de la disposición y planta de la dicha Tama y pueblo de Ocute, por haber ido y estado en ella, dijo este declarante que a más de veinte años que sirve a Su Majestad en este presidio y en el de Santa Elena, y que por entender la lengua de la provincia de Guale y de San Pedro, el dicho señor general le ordenó el año pasado de noventa y siete fuese en compañía de los padres de la orden de San Francisco fray Pedro Fernández de Chozas y fray Francisco de Veráscula, en la que asimismo fueron con orden de su prelado y del dicho gobernador a descubrir tierra adentro, y llegó en compañía de los dichos padres al pueblo que llaman de la Tama, que a su parecer habrá cincuenta leguas, poco más o menos, de este presidio, y aunque salieron de Guale para la dicha Tama y tardaron ocho días y los siete de despoblado, no hallaron en todo el dicho camino buena tierra hasta llegar a la dicha Tama, donde había cantidad de comida de maíz y frijol y mucha caza de venados y gallinas de papada y otras muchas aves y volatería, y mucha cantidad de pescado y sollos que se llaman reales en España, y asimismo frutas, como son uvas muy gruesas y de grandes racimos y de tan buen gusto como las de España, y ciruelas blancas a manera de ciruela de monje, y cerezas y sandías y otras frutas; que a la redonda del dicho pueblo de la Tama y sus confines es muy buena tierra parada, y que en lloviendo se pega a los pies como greda, y tiene a partes muchos cerros pelados a donde ha visto géneros de piedras de metales, y que en algunas partes, él y los dichos religiosos, de las que parecía ser de metal tomaban de lo que estaba encima de la tierra, por no tener con qué cavar, y que tomó este declarante algunas de aquellas piedras, y trayendo los polvos de ellas los dio al gobernador parte de ellos, y otros a un platero que había a la sazón en esta ciudad y se murió los días pasados, y habiendo en su vida el dicho platero hecho la experiencia de ellas, le dijo que de donde se sacaban aquellos polvos había plata, porque la había sacado de ellos, y que sacando la dicha plata de los dichos polvos, por ser de la escoria y espuma de la dicha mina; que si se buscase la veta de ella serían minas muy ricas, y esto lo podrá saber mejor el dicho señor gobernador porque también él está informado e hizo la experiencia con el dicho platero; y asimismo, junto a estas dichas minas produce una yerba que los indios estiman mucho para medicinas con que se curan, y para heridas, que le llaman guitamo real, y asimismo han cogido este confesante y los dichos religiosos algunas piedras que en los dichos cerros y junto a los ríos caudales, a manera de cristal nacen, y otras cristal fino. De allí a la Tama hicieron, una jornada más adelante, a Ocute, donde fueron muy bien recibidos del cacique, regalándolos mucho, y las mujeres traían de allá sus cobijas, que llaman mandiles, a manera de carpetas pintadas, que dicen algunos que han estado en la Nueva España que imitan el traje de allá; y queriendo pasar adelante, el cacique del dicho pueblo de Ocute se lo estorbó con muchas veras y llorando con ellos, diciendo que si iban adelante los habían de matar los indios, porque muchos tiempos antes, que se entiende cuando pasó Soto, con llevar a mucha gente que iban a caballo, mataron de ellos, y que mejor matarían a ellos, pues que eran pocos, y que a esta causa no pasaron adelante y se volvieron desde allí; y asimismo oyeron decir a los indios de aquel pueblo, y a los Salchiches, que pasado una sierra cuatro jornadas de allí, muy alta, que había relumbraba cuando salía el sol como un fuego, y que de la otra parte de ella había gente que traía el cabello cortado, y que los pinos hallaban cortados con hachas, y que le parece que semejantes señas no pueden ser sino de gente española, y la dicha tierra le parece y es muy suficiente para producir cualquier género de grano y aunque sea trigo, y muchas vegas y sabanas para ganados, y ríos de agua dulce a trechos, y que le parece que si hubiera quien supiera lavar oro, se cogiera en aquellos ríos, y que se volvieron por otro camino diferente de él que habían ido, muy mejor y más poblado, porque no hay más de dos días de despoblado, y por el otro hay siete, y el caballo que los dichos frailes llevaron vino más al gusto hasta Yufera y Cascangue, pueblos de indios amigos, donde fueron muy regalados, hasta volver a San Pedro del cacique don Juan, y esto dijo que sabe por haberlo visto y oído como dicho es; y dijo ser de edad de treinta y ocho años, poco más o menos, y no firmó por no saber, y el dicho gobernador lo firmó—*Gonzalo Méndez de Canzo.*—Ante mí, *Juan Jiménez*, escribano.

Testigo, Juan de Ribas, soldado

Y luego incontinente, el dicho día cuatro de febrero susodicho, el dicho señor gobernador mandó parecer ante sí a Juan de Ribas, soldado de este presidio, al cual le fue recibido juramento en forma de derecho, bajo cargo del cual prometió decir la verdad, y siéndole preguntado por el tenor del dicho auto, dijo que él, aunque a más de treinta y cuatro años sirve a Su Majestad en estas provincias, no ha estado en el pueblo de la Tama, más de que siendo mozo de edad de diecisiete o dieciocho años, estando en el presidio de Santa Elena habiendo falta de comida, el capitán Juan Pardo se salió de dicho presidio con hasta ciento y cincuenta soldados para ir a la tierra adentro a descubrir, con orden del adelantado Pedro Menéndez, y entre otras personas que el dicho adelantado envió con el dicho Juan Pardo para que se quedasen con algunos caciques para aprender las lenguas, fue este declarante, para el dicho efecto, con el dicho capitán Juan Pardo, y se fueron desde Santa Elena a Topaz y a Uma y a la Buida, una legua de Canos, donde hay un río muy grande y caudaloso que llaman Guatari y va a la mar, y allí sacan cantidad de perlas, y quedó allí un pífano con su mujer y dos niños, y hasta hoy no ha salido de allí el dicho pífano, ni su mujer ni hijos; que hallarse vivo ahora alguno de ellos, le parece a este declarante sería de mucha consideración, porque declararían muchas riquezas de la tierra; porque de allí se fue todo el río arriba este declarante con el dicho capitán Juan Pardo, de Canos a Cayagua, y de allí a Cauichi, y de allí a Joaraz, y cerca de este dicho pueblo de Joaraz está un cerro alto donde llaman los Diamantes, y que volviendo de la tierra adentro el alférez Moyano, que lo había dejado el dicho Juan Pardo, tuvo nuevas de estos diamantes y se fue a él, y aunque hizo diligencias para romper en el con bandarrias y con cuñas de hierro, no hacía operación ni podía romper, y este declarante lo vio así, y sacando una puntilla pequeña de ello la llevó al dicho alférez Moyano, y yendo a España volvió otra vez el dicho alférez Moyano en compañía de don Diego de Velasco, yerno del dicho adelantado, con fin de que el dicho don Diego de Velasco le diera gente para volver a los dichos diamantes, y oyó al dicho alférez Moyano que por aquella puntilla que había sacado de los dichos diamantes, le habían dado en España mucha cantidad de dinero, y que le había dicho la persona que se lo había comprado, que no había sabido lo que se había vendido, que por ningún precio se lo volviera a dar; y el dicho don Diego de Velasco lo volviera a enviar y le diera gente, sino que enviándolo a el Escamacu con veintidós soldados a apaciguar a aquel cacique, que estaba rebelando, debajo de cautela le dijeron los indios que mandase a los soldados que apagaran las cuerdas, que tenían temor las mujeres y que no osarían llegar si no las apagaban, y mandando apagarlas dieron sobre el dicho alférez y soldados y los mataron a todos, excepto un soldado sólo que se escapó, que le llamaban Calderón, y así cesó de volver el dicho Moyano al descubrimiento de estas piedras; y de Joaraz, marchando el dicho capitán Juan Pardo con su gente pasaron adelante, y este testigo con él, más de veinte jornadas, y por el camino donde iban había muchas poblaciones, y a muchas partes sierras y montañas donde registraron muchas minas de oro y plata, según oyó decir a alquimistas y plateros que llevaba el dicho capitán, y en ningún pueblo que llegaron tuvieron defensa ninguna, sino buen acogimiento y tierra muy harta y abundosa de comidas de maíz, frijol, y calabaza, y mucha cantidad de castaña apilada; frutas de diversas maneras; la uva como la de España, y en algunas partes mejor, y entre las dichas indias había chagualas de oro y plata y muchas perlas, porque las veía dar al dicho capitán Juan Pardo y al alférez Moyano, y que en el pueblo de Arameco y Joaraz dejó cantidad de soldados repartidos hasta en cantidad de veinticinco hombres en cada uno, y se volvió dejando dicho a los caciques que dentro de tres o cuatro lunas volvería, y este declarante se quedó también para aprender la lengua, y pasó más adelante tres o cuatro jornadas y llegó a donde murió el adelantado de la Isla Hispañola, Soto, y allí halló relación de la gente que con él fue y vio allí cotas y armas y ropas de los españoles, y le dijeron los indios que como se había muerto el general había habido entre ellos pendencia sobre quién había de mandar y que se mataban unos a otros y que se habían dividido cada uno por su parte, y como gente sin caudillo, unos habían muerto los indios y otros siguiendo la tierra, y este declarante llevaba noticia de un piloto portugués que se llamaba Olmedo, con su mujer, que había quedado aprendiendo la lengua en Cauchi, y que de allí se fue solo con su mujer y aportó allí a donde murió el dicho Soto, a donde dijeron los indios que un cacique que está más adelante lo había muerto porque había dado con un palo a un hijo suyo, y que la mujer, de allí a algunas lunas habían venido unos hombres de a caballo y que la tomaron a las ancas de los caballos y que la llevaron, y que allí vio pintados en las paredes de las casas los caballos y las lanzas y el hábito de españoles, y que en aquel dicho pueblo donde murió el dicho general Soto le dieron relación los indios de una gran ciudad a quien ellos llaman la Gran Copala, y que para ir a ella se tardan siete u ocho días y van por agua en canoas, pegadas unas a otras, y con sus pavesadas, porque pasan por algunos pasos de indios de guerra, y que de la grandeza de esta ciudad no sabían acabar de decir de ella, y dejando algunos metales de platos de plata y peltre del dicho general Soto, decían los indios que en aquella ciudad las ollas eran de aquel metal, y que las casas decían que las tenían de piedra y de altos en aquella ciudad; a de allí se volvió a donde estaba el alférez Moyano en Joaraz, y se volvieron a Santa Elena, dejando en el dicho pueblo gente y cabeza de ellos, y por lo que ha visto, la fertilidad de la tierra y abundancia de comida que tiene de todos géneros, como tiene dicho, y vacas pequeñas a manera de las de Berbería, le parece que si se hubiera dado cuenta a Su Majestad, no pudiera dejar de hacerla poblar y conquistar, porque tiene para sí que no debe de haber tierra descubierta más rica que ella, por las muchas minas que como tiene dicho hallaron, y que esto y mucho más lo podía decir su mujer, que es natural de aquella tierra y la trajo el dicho capitán Juan Pardo, muchacha, y asimismo Teresa Martín que también es natural india de aquella tierra y la dicha su mujer, era la cacica de aquella tierra que llaman Guanaytique y que vuelve a declarar y advertir que la mina de los diamantes tiene para consigo que es la mayor riqueza que se sabe, y que el volver el dicho Moyano desde España a estas partes fue con intento de volver a donde los hay, como dicho es, por habérselo oído decir este declarante en su vida; y que esto es lo que sabe para el juramento que fecho tiene, y en ello se afirma y ratifica, y que es de edad de cincuenta y seis años, poco más o menos, y no firmó por no saber, y el dicho gobernador lo firmó de su nombre.—*Gonzalo Méndez de Canzo*.—Ante mí, *Juan Jiménez*, escribano.

Testigo Teresa Martín, india

Y después de lo susodicho, el dicho día atrás referido, cuatro de febrero de mil y seiscientos años, el dicho gobernador mandó parecer ante sí a Teresa Martín, india natural de la tierra adentro llamado Juacan, adonde entró el capitán Juan Pardo que partió de Santa Elena, de la cual fue tomado y recibido juramento sobre una señal de cruz [+] en que puso su mano derecha, la cual habiéndolo hecho con la solemnidad que se requiere y siéndole preguntado al tenor del auto proveído por el dicho señor gobernador, dijo que lo que puede decir y saber es que un capitán que se llamaba Juan Pardo llegó a su tierra con infantería, que sería a su parecer más de ciento y cincuenta leguas de la costa por la tierra adentro desde Santa Elena, que es costa de la mar, y en su tierra vio a los indios naturales de ella y sus parientes regalarle y estimarle a él y a la dicha su gente, dándoles mucha comida de la que ellos tenía para su sustento, como era maíz, frijol, calabaza, castaña apilada, carnes de vaca, venados y gallinas de papada, y otra mucha caza en gran cantidad, y pescados de ríos y lagunas en gran cantidad, y que si había de ir el dicho Juan Pardo de un pueblo a otro lo llevaban en andas gran cantidad de indios, limpiando los caminos por donde había de pasar, y sabe que el dicho Juan Pardo cuando se hubo que volver dejó algunos soldados repartidos en algunas partes a manera de fuertes, diciendo que de allí a tres o cuatro lunas volvería con mucha gente, y los indios naturales entendiéndolo así, lo estuvieron aguardando, y pasándose mucho tiempo no volvió, a cuya causa los soldados hicieron desórdenes con los indios y sus mujeres, y en aquel tiempo, esta que declara, siendo muchacha, se vino en compañía del alférez Moyano y no supo en lo que pararon los soldados; y tanto responde. Fuele preguntado si en su tierra hay oro u plata o perlas: dijo que cuando había juntas y baile de indios, sacaban algunas chagualas de oro y plata, pero que como era muchacha no lo conocía, y que hay perlas, las cuales sacaban en un río caudal que estará una jornada de su pueblo, y que al dicho capitán Juan Pardo y a el alférez Moyano les presentaron mucha cantidad en petacas, y que se acuerda ver al alférez Moyano en petacas tener muchas perlas grandes, blancas y redondas, y que vio partir para España al dicho alférez Moyano, y después le vio volver y le oyó decir que deseaba tener ocasión para volver a aquella tierra, y que le parece que pues tenía deseo, algún interés le debió de mover, y que en este tiempo le mataron los indios en Escamacu y así no tuvo efecto.

Preguntado que si el oro de las chagualas que los indios traen en sus bailes, que de a donde lo hallan o lo cogen, dijo que a tres o cuatro jornadas de su pueblo hay unos indios que residen en una sierra que llaman Chisca donde cogen el dicho oro, y los dichos indios andan vestidos y son muy blancos, rojos, y zarcos, a manera de flamencos, porque los cabellos que tienen son como un poco de oro, y de esta gente es la que da el oro para las chagualas de los bailes, y asimismo cañutos de oro macizos con sus agujeros, que los traen colgados.

Preguntado si hay grandes lugares y poblaciones en su tierra y en qué casas viven dijo que su pueblo es muy grande y de mucha vecindad de hombres y mujeres, y que no puede acordarse del número de la vecindad, que es muy mucha, y que tienen cercado todo el pueblo alrededor, y que no hay más de cuatro puertas principales y que las cierran de noche por causa de las guerras y puercos grandes que hay, que si no las cerrasen las puertas entrarían y suelen matar algunos niños, y que las casas son de madera y rajones, cubiertas con cortezas de palos.

Fuele preguntado que cual le parece mejor tierra y más fértil de comida, esta de San Agustín o su tierra: dijo que esta tierra de San Agustín no vale nada en comparación de la suya, porque en la suya no se sabe conocer hambre, que de dos y tres años tienen de maíz, frijoles, y calabazas y castañas, sin mucha cantidad de pescados que hay en los ríos y lagunas y que es en tanta cantidad la nuez que hay que sacan aceite de ella, y que al pie de una sierra que está cerca de su pueblo salen cuatro o cinco ojos de agua salada, que del agua que echan de ellos, con cierto artificio de fuego que tienen los indios hacen sal en gran abundancia; y el proceder de la gente de su tierra es diferente que él de esta, porque es gente de población y vecindad asentadas, con hijos y nietos y bisnietos, y no son mudables ni mentirosos como los de esta tierra, que en esta tierra no hacen más de tomar el carcax y el arco e irse de una isla a otra y de un pantano a otro, y mariscar y cazar, sin más asiento.

Fuele preguntado que si se fuese con cantidad de gente a su tierra, si tendrían comida por los caminos por donde hubiesen de ir, para sustentarse: dijo que por lo que ha visto cuando venían de su tierra le parece no puede faltar comida aunque el número de la gente sea mucha, porque el alférez Moyano no hacía más de enviar un correo delante al pueblo, y cuando llegaba había comida en abundancia.

Preguntado si por aquella tierra pueden caminar caballos, dijo que como era muchacha cuando vino sabe poco de eso, y que hay apartes muy grandes sierras, y que le parece que hay muy poca necesidad de caballos, porque cuando Juan Pardo y Moyano querían pasar por algún vado, los indios que llevaban los pasaban y que le parece que pueden caminar caballos; y esto dijo y declaró bajo el cargo del juramento que fecho tiene y en ello se afirmó y rectificó habiéndole sido tornado a leer, y que será de cuarenta años, poco más o menos, y no lo firmó por no saber, y el señor gobernador lo firmó de su nombre.—*Gonzalo Méndez de Canzo*.—Ante mí, *Juan Jiménez*, escribano.

Testigo el alférez Francisco Fernández de Ecija

E después de lo susodicho, el dicho día, mes, y año atrás referido, cuatro de este presente es de febrero de mil y seiscientos años, dicho señor gobernador hizo parecer ante si al alférez Francisco Fernández de Ecija, por ser hombre de mucha experiencia en estas provincias, y que a que sirve a Su Majestad en ellas más de treinta y seis años, del cual fue tomado y recibido juramento en forma debida de derecho, bajo el cargo del cual prometió de decir la verdad, y siendo leído el dicho auto y capítulo de carta de Su Majestad, dijo que él no ha ido al pueblo de la Tama que refiere el dicho capítulo de carta más de que tiene noticia de él, y lo que puede informar y decir en cumplimiento del dicho capítulo de carta y de lo que entiende y ha oído platicar al capitán Juan Pardo y al alférez Moyano que entraron con su compañía por la tierra adentro más de doscientas leguas, y que la perfecta entrada y descubrimiento en que estas provincias se puede hacer y es de más consideración es por el río de Guatari, que está en altura de treinta y cuatro grados, poco más o menos, por donde entró el dicho Juan Pardo y el dicho alférez Moyano, a quien oyó decir muchas veces, como camarada que ha sido del dicho alférez Moyano, que como cuarenta leguas poco más o menos de la costa por el dicho río, había un cerro cristalino, pelado todo, sin árboles, y que echaba muchas puyas, y que el dicho cerro era de diamantes y de gran riqueza, porque al tiempo que se retiró de la entrada que hizo con Juan Pardo dio en el dicho cerro el alférez

Moyano, y que le oyó decir que aunque procuró deshacerlo y sacar algunas piedras con mandarrias y cuñas aceradas, se las deshacía y no pudo romper en él, y que sacando una punta bien chica de él la llevó y fue a España, no sabiendo el valor que tenía, y vendiéndola con otra cantidad de perlas que llevó de la dicha entrada, le oyó decir que le dieron muy muchos ducados, y que decía que le habían engañado por no saber lo que se había vendido, y con la dicha codicia se fue el dicho Moyano al adelantado Pedro Menéndez, que estaba en aquella sazón en España, y que le había dicho: señor, yo soy el alférez Moyano, que entré con el capitán Juan Pardo en el descubrimiento de la Florida, y si vuestra señoría me da gente, yo entraré cuarenta leguas de la costa a descubrir un cerro de diamantes que tiene gran riqueza; y que el adelantado le había abrazado y le había dicho se holgaba mucho de lo que le decía, y que se fuese por el alférez de Don Diego de Velasco, su yerno, que le enviaba por gobernador de Santa Elena, y que llegado que fuese allí, él llegaría con mucha brevedad y le daría gente y lo necesario para la dicha entrada y descubrimiento del dicho cerro; y en este tiempo le ocupó Su Majestad al dicho adelantado en la armada de Santander, donde murió, y el dicho don Diego de Velasco, teniendo guerra con el cacique de Escamacu, envió al dicho alférez Moyano con veintidós soldados a quietar y pacificar el dicho cacique e indios, donde con cautela los dichos indios le dijeron que mandase a sus soldados apagar las cuerdas, porque las mujeres y los niños tenían mucho miedo que los querían matar, y mandándolo hacer así y visto los indios las cuerdas apagadas, cerraron con ellos, y como eran muchos los mataron sin escapar ninguno, sino fue uno que llamaban Calderón, que a cabo de tres días vino a Santa Elena a dar la nueva, con gran trabajo y riesgo, pasando bahías, por cuya causa cesó el descubrimiento del dicho cerro, sin haber hasta ahora quien tratase de ello; y este declarante es de parecer que Su Majestad debe de mandar acudir y saber de una empresa de tanto interés como es, y que aunque tiene treinta y seis años de servicio y trabajos en estas provincias, se holgaría de ir a este descubrimiento, y no por el interés que de ello le podría redundar, sino por el de Su Majestad, y deseos que siempre ha tenido de servirle y que sus tierras y patrimonios reales vayan en aumento; además, que ha sabido del dicho capitán y alférez de las minas muy ricas que habían descubierto y dejaron registradas por haber llevado alquimistas y plateros que lo entendían, y les vio traer cantidad de perlas muy buenas de la dicha entrada, y asimismo le parece y tiene para consigo que si por alguna parte se podría encontrar con los que bajan del Nuevo México es por aquella altura de los treinta y cuatro y treinta y cinco grados, y por ser tierra muy poblada y de muchos bastimentos y conocida y descubierta y que se sabe, y que Su Majestad podrá tener poco costo y grande aprovechamiento, y este es su parecer y lo que ha oído para el juramento que fecho tiene, y en ello se afirma y rectifica; y siéndole por mí, escribano, leído, lo firmó de su nombre, por ser así verdad lo que dicho y declarado tiene, y dijo ser de edad de cincuenta y seis años, poco más o poco menos tiempo.—*Francisco Fernández.*—Ante mí, *Juan Jiménez*, escribano.

Testigo David Glavid, irlandés, soldado

En este dicho día mes y año susodicho, el dicho gobernador y capitán general Gonzalo Méndez de Canzo mandó parecer ante sí a David Glavid, irlandés, soldado de este presidio, del cual fue tomado y recibido juramento en forma de debida de derecho, sobre una señal de cruz [+] que hizo con su mano derecha, y siéndole leído el auto de atrás proveído por el dicho señor gobernador, y capítulo de carta de Su Majestad que ya va incluso en él, sacado a la letra del tanto original, el cual habiéndolo entendido, dijo que él nunca ha estado en la Tama, ni sabe la tierra que es; que lo que sabe de estas provincias es que reside en ellas y en este presidio de San Agustín a más de cinco años, y que el año de ochenta y cuatro le robaron ingleses un navío suyo cargado de mercaderías y vinos, doblando el cabo de la Surlinga, saliendo de Nantes en la provincia de Bretaña, y le trajeron consigo la vuelta a las Indias, y venía por general de nueve velas pequeñas y grandes,[1] Richarte de Campoverde, y lo trajo hasta venir al Jacan, que es en esta costa, en altura de treinta y seis grados, y allí él tomó puerto y echó en tierra hasta en cantidad de ciento y cincuenta hombres pobladores y este declarante quedó con ellos, no le dando pasaje, y luego que saltaron en tierra empezaron a hacer ladrillos y teja para hacer un fuerte y casas, y estuvo allí con ellos año y medio hasta que vino por allí Francisco Draque con su armada, que saqueó algunos puertos de las Indias, y entre ellos este de San Agustín, y recogió en la dicha su armada los ingleses que allí había, y a este declarante, y los llevó a Inglaterra, y entendió en Londres este declarante como la reina se había desgraciado con el dicho Francisco Draque por el haber llevado la gente de Jacan, y luego vio que aprestaron en Londres dos navíos con doscientos hombre y mucha cantidad de pobladores con sus mujeres, para volver otra vez a la población del dicho Jacan, y a este que declara le volvieron a prender y embarcar para volver otra vez con ellos a Jacan, y así vino con ellos hasta la Isla de Puerto Rico, adonde en un puerto de la banda del sur tomaron aguada y refrescarse, y este declarante tuvo orden de huirse, como lo hizo, y dio aviso en Puerto Rico como en Inglaterra se aprestaban cinco naos con determinación de venir a tomar y saquear a Puerto Rico, y que habían de estar allí por Pascua de Espíritu Santo, para que estuviesen con cuidado, y mediante el aviso que dio a Diego Menéndez, que en aquel tiempo era gobernador, no hicieron efecto, por estar con aviso y cuidado, aunque vinieron los galeones por el dicho tiempo, y venían también con determinación de hecho aquel salto, traer más población al Jacan, e ir en seguimiento de los navíos en que este que declara vino, y así tiene por cosa cierta que los dichos ingleses están en el dicho Jacan; y para más confirmación dijo que hallándose el año pasado de noventa y nueve en la Habana, don Beltrán de la Cueva traía ciertos ingleses de Lima, de un navío inglés que allí tomó del hijo de Juan Acles, y entre ellos un mancebo le declaró y dijo que al tiempo que ellos partieron de Plemua [Plymouth] para el estrecho de Magallanes, habían partido en su compañía dos naos con socorro de gente, municiones, vestidos, herramientas, hachas y azadas, para los pobladores que estaban en el Jacan, por donde acaba de confirmar ser cierto estaren allí; y esto sabe.

Preguntado en el tiempo que estuvo en el dicho Jacan, que le ha parecido de la dicha tierra, y que si había oro o plata en ella, y qué frutas producía, dijo que en el tiempo que allí estuvo sembraron trigo y cebada y que lo que daba con gran abundancia, y que la tierra llevaba muchas frutas y muy buenas, como es uvas, ciruelas, manzanas, cerezas, castañas en mucha abundancia, y nuez, mucho maíz, frijol y calabaza, mucho pescado y de muchos géneros de manera en que cada luna entra su género de pescado, y asimismo había mucho oro y perlas, porque vio a Richarte de Campoverde rescatar más de una arroba de oro, y le parece a este declarante que no era oro muy subido, que oyó decir que sería de dieciséis a dieciocho quilates, y esto era porque estaba bruto, por no saber los indios acendrarlo, y entre los caciques vio que todos traían chagualas de oro, y asimismo había entre ellos mucha cantidad de perlas, y muy grandes, de que llevó el dicho Richarte de Campoverde gran cantidad, y este declarante rescató una perla grande de la hechura de una bellota, y mayor que bellota, muy transparente y muy buena, y viniéndolo a saber el dicho Richarte de Campoverde se la quitó, y así mismo tuvieron noticia los dichos ingleses como cuarenta leguas de allí, el río arriba, al pie de una sierra donde salía el río, había las minas de oro, y por faltarles la comida no llegaron y se volvieron de la mitad del camino, y que así como dicho tiene, los dichos ingleses están en el dicho Jacan, porque tierra tan fértil y donde había tanto oro y perlas, no le parece la dejarían de la mano, y que así por importar tanto al servicio de Su Majestad, ha dado esta cuenta al dicho general, para que él la de a Su Majestad; y esto es lo que sabe y ha visto para el juramento que fecho tiene, y en ello se afirma y rectifica, y siéndole leído su dicho y declaración lo firmó de su nombre, y dijo ser de edad de cuarenta años, poco más o menos tiempo.—*David Glavid*—. Ante mí, *Juan Jiménez*, escribano.

Testigo, Luisa Menéndez, india

En la ciudad de San Agustín a seis días del mes de febrero de mil y seiscientos, el dicho general Gonzalo Menéndez de Canzo hizo parecer ante sí a Luisa Menéndez, india natural de la tierra adentro de un pueblo que se llama Manaytique, donde entró el alférez Moyano, de la cual fue recibido juramento en forma debida de derecho, bajo el cargo del cual prometió decir verdad, y siéndole preguntado al tenor del dicho capítulo de carta y auto, y lo demás que sabe de su tierra, dijo que lo que sabe y se acuerda es que su tierra es muy buena tierra y fértil de mucha comida, como es maíz, castaña apilada, frijol y calabaza y nuez y mucha cantidad de venados y vacas y osos y gallinas de papada y patos y muchas aves de volatería, y que su pueblo es muy grande y de mucha vecindad, y que las casas son de tablones, cubiertas de cortezas de castaño y tablas de savina.

Preguntado si en su tierra hay oro u plata o perlas, dijo que oro hay entre los indios chagualas de oro, y que este oro lo traen de unas sierras que llaman de Chisca, y que los indios lo rescatan; y que los indios de aquella tierra son muy blancos y zarcos y de cabello rojo, y que la plata no sabe si la hay, porque aunque hay muchas sierras, los indios no saben sacar la plata, ni el oro, ni lo conocen que tiene para sí hay mucho oro y plata en aquellas sierras, más como dicho tiene, los indios no lo conocen.

Preguntado si hay perlas en aquella tierra, dijo que esta declarante con otras muchas mujeres y hombres fueron a un río donde sacaron muchas almejas grandes, y sacaron muchas perlas y las dieron al alférez Moyano, y asimismo le dieron los indios chagualas de oro, y que tiene por cierto, según hay muchas sierras y valles y grandes ríos, que si fuesen españoles sacarían muchas riquezas, y como era muchacha cuando salió de su tierra no puede dar tanta noticia de la tierra como diera ahora como es mujer de edad y que su marido Juan de Ribas dirá mejor lo que hay en su tierra, que ella, por ser hombre español.

Preguntado si fuesen muchos españoles por aquella tierra, si hallarían harta comida, dijo que lo que es comida que no les faltaría por muchos que vayan, y que asimismo sale un golpe de agua de tres o cuatro ojos de agua salada que los indios hacen sal de ella, y crece y mengua, y en toda aquella tierra no hay otra agua salada; y esto es lo que sabe y que se acuerda de su tierra, para el juramento que fecho tiene, y en ello se afirma y rectifica, y no firmó, que no supo; lo firmó el dicho señor general por ella.—*Gonzalo Méndez de Canzo*—. Ante mí, *Juan Jiménez*, escribano.

En la ciudad de San Agustín, provincias de la Florida, a seis días del mes de febrero de mil y seiscientos años, Gonzalo Méndez de Canzo, gobernador y capitán general de estas provincias por el Rey nuestro señor, dijo que atento que las personas pueden decir de la tierra que se ha visto y de que se tiene noticia en estas provincias y han andado españoles en ella, son las personas que en esta causa han declarado, atento a lo cual y por no haber al presente otras que en el caso puedan decir e informar según Su Majestad lo manda, manda a mí escribano, saque un testimonio o dos o más de todo, y se los dé autorizados en pública forma y manera que haga fe, y esto proveyo, mando y firmo de su nombre; en los cuales dichos traslado dijo que interponía e interpuso su autoridad y judicial decreto.—*Gonzalo Méndez de Canzo*. Ante mí, *Juan Jiménez*, escribano.

E yo, Juan Jiménez, escribano público mayor de gobernación de estas provincias, ciudad y fuerte de San Agustín de la Florida, de mandamiento del gobernador y capitán general Gonzalo Méndez de Canzo, hice sacar y saqué este traslado del tanto original que ante mi pasó y en mi poder queda, y va cierto y verdadero y concuerda con él, y en fe y testimonio de verdad lo signo y firmo de mi nombre

The first page of the "Relación" (España. Ministerio de Cultura y Deporte. Archivo General de Indias, SANTO DOMINGO, 224, R.5, N.36, F.258r.)

acostumbrado, que es a tal.—*Gonzalo Méndez de Canzo.—Juan Jiménez*, escribano.

Derechos, gratis.

Note

1. As noted by an anonymous peer reviewer, this is described in a marginal note as an "Armada de ingleses que entró en la Florida en el Jacán en altura de 36 grados."

An Account of La Tama and Its Land, and the English Settlement (1600), translation by Melissa D. Birkhofer and Paul M. Worley

España. Ministerio de Cultura y Deporte. Archivo General de Indias, Santo Domingo, 224, R.5, N.36, F.258r-267v.

Saint Augustine, February, 1600

On the fourth of February, 1600, in the city of St. Augustine in the provinces of La Florida, Gonzalo Méndez de Canzo,[1] who was made governor and general captain of these provinces of La Florida by our Lordship the King,[2] reported that on the eighteenth of January of the present year he received a letter[3] from our Lordship the King, sealed, stamped, and signed with his royal name, as well as with the names of the members of the royal Council of the Indies. The letter was also countersigned by the King's secretary, Juan de Ibarra, dated the ninth of November, 1598, in the city of Madrid. There is a section of that letter that I, the notary, was asked to excerpt, the tenor of which is as follows:

Section of the Letter from His Majesty concerning La Tama, dated 9th of November 98

The information that you have sent concerning the disposition of the land has been understood, as well as how important it would be to send you people to populate a town referred to as La Tama, forty leagues from the garrison at St. Augustine, and for you then to make a foray into the interior, discovering what you can until arriving in New Mexico,[4] which is understood to be two hundred leagues from said Tama. As you believe the matter to be of great importance, I charge you and command you to become well informed about the disposition of that land through the caciques and Indians who are closer to

For Paul Hoffman, La Tama was "the name given to the peoples of De Soto's Altamaha, Ocute, and Cofaqui chiefdoms." See *Florida's Frontiers* (Bloomington: Indiana University Press, 2002), 82. Based on the description of the Spanish soldier Juan de the lands you intend to discover, so that once you have spoken with the people with experience in the region who live in the garrison and these caciques, you can send me a detailed account of everything, and if possible, the layout and description of the land into which you want to make the foray.

The copy of said chapter from the letter of our Lord the King was thus corrected and compared with said section of the letter from our Lordship the King. I, the notary, verify that the original, certain, and truthful letter remains in the possession of the governor and captain general.

The governor and captain general[5] said that in order for His Majesty's orders in the above chapter of the letter to be carried out, and to be able to send His Majesty the clearest account and description possible about the land of La Tama, statements should be taken under oath from people who have been in La Tama, as well as from those who have been to the territory of the Guatari River,[6] thirty leagues to the north of Santa Elena, where there was once a garrison of His Majesty's, under the command of Captain Juan Pardo and his second lieutenant Moyano, who had penetrated a number of leagues inland[7]; as well as from David Glavid,[8] an Irishman, who had been in Jacan[9] with Richard Grenville,[10] who established a settlement there; from the Indigenous women who live here in the garrison, and who are from the land in the interior where Captain Juan Pardo went; and from other persons who are understood to have some account or news about that land. And so, he ordered them to appear before his grace so that they could say and swear

---

Lara, John Worth states that "Tama was the political center of a province of the same name." See "Late Spanish Military Expeditions in the Southeast," in *The Forgotten Centuries: Indians and Europeans in the American South, 1521–1704*, ed. Charles Hudson and Carmen Chaves Tesser (Athens: University of Georgia Press, 1994), 110. Worth also cites a letter from Méndez de Canzo in which the governor advocates going into Tama *and* Ocute, which suggests that the Spaniard understood these as somewhat distinct; see "Late Spanish," 109. Appropriately, Worth's map treats these as separate places, with Tama being more or less in what is today in central Georgia and Ocute lying a bit to the North ("Late Spanish," 107). However, writing on a 1602 inquiry, Charles Hudson notes that "the Spaniards often used 'Tama' to refer to the entire interior"; see *The Juan Pardo Expeditions: Exploration of the Carolinas and Tennessee, 1566*–1568 (Tuscaloosa: University of Alabama Press, 1990), 192–93. We provide the reader with these potentially conflicting, somewhat nebulous descriptions to give a notion of the region where the Spanish wished to go and to underscore the underlying uncertainties of their intentions.

what they know and have heard about the aforementioned, signed in his name—Gonzalo Méndez de Canzo—Before me, Juan Jiménez, notary.

Witness, Gaspar de Salas, Soldier

Immediately thereafter, the governor and captain general sent for Gaspar de Salas, a soldier in this garrison, to appear before him. In accordance with the law, Salas took an oath in which he promised to tell the truth concerning what he was asked and that, being asked, he would speak and declare regarding the contents of the section from the letter. As to what the declarant knows about the disposition and layout of said Tama and the town of Ocute,[11] as he has gone and been there, he stated that he has served His Majesty in this garrison and in Santa Elena[12] for more than twenty years, and because he understood the language of the province of Guale and San Pedro,[13] in 1597, the Lord General ordered him to accompany two priests from the Order of San Francisco,[14] Friar Pedro Fernández de Chozas and Friar Francisco de Veráscula,[15] who themselves had orders from their prelate and the governor to discover what they could in the interior. He arrived with the Fathers at the town they call Tama, which seems to him to be fifty leagues away, more or less, from this garrison. Although they traveled to Tama from Guale, with the journey taking eight days, seven of which were through uninhabited wilderness, they did not find good land at any point in the journey until they reached Tama, where there was a large quantity of food: corn and beans, deer for hunting, as well as turkeys and many other birds you can eat, a large number of fish and sturgeon that they call *reales* in Spain, as well as fruits such as large grapes that grow in large bunches and have a good flavor like those in Spain, and white plums like the *ciruela de monje*,[16] and cherries and watermelon and other fruits. He said that all around the town of La Tama and its confines there is very good, dark earth and that when it rains the soil sticks to one's feet like clay. He also said that in some areas there are bare hills where he had seen different kinds of rocks containing metal and that elsewhere, he and the said friars, given that they had nothing to dig with, simply took rocks that were on top of the dirt that seemed to them to be metal.[17] The declarant then gave some of these stones and their dust to the governor, and others to a recently deceased silversmith who happened to be in the city. Having tested them while he was still alive, the silversmith told him that there was silver in the place from which they had taken the rocks, as he had been able to draw silver from their dust, which would be from the dross and scum from a mine, saying that if you sought the vein there would be very rich mines there. Salas then said that the said Lord Governor also knew this because he has likewise been informed of it by the silversmith. Moreover, the land next to the mines produces a plant that the Indians greatly esteem for its use in medicines to heal, and for wounds, that they call *dictamo real*.[18] The witness and the friars also took stones from those hills and from along the flowing rivers where they grow like crystals, some of them fine. From La Tama they went farther on to Ocute, where they were well received by the cacique, who gave them many things. The women there brought them blankets, which they call *mandiles*, and which are like painted carpets. Those who have been to New Spain[19] say that these are similar to textiles people wear there. They wanted to continue their journey, but the cacique of Ocute told them they could not, weeping and saying that if they continued ahead the Indians there would kill them. According to the cacique, a long time before then, meaning when Soto passed through,[20] the Indians there killed a large group who were on horseback and that these same Indians would probably kill them as well, since they were so few. This is why they did not continue on and came back. They also heard both the Indians from that town and the Salchiches[21] say that past a tall mountain range four days from there, there was a fiery brilliance when the sun rose. That on the other side of the range there were people who wore their hair short, and that the trees there were cut with hatchets, and that other, similar signs could only mean the presence of Spaniards. It seemed to him that the land could produce any kind of grain, even wheat, that it had many meadows and fields for cattle, and long rivers with fresh water, and it seemed to him that someone who knew how to pan for gold could find it in those rivers. They returned by a better and more populated route than the one they had taken, that only had two days of uninhabited territory, as compared to seven the other way. The friars' horse had an easier time traveling back via Yufera and Cascangue,[22] towns of friendly Indians where they were well received, until they returned to San Pedro and its cacique don Juan.[23] He said that he knows all of this because he saw it and heard it as it is recorded here. He stated he was thirty-eight years old, more or less, and he did not sign because he does not know how. The governor signed it—Gonzalo Méndez de Canzo—Before me, Juan Jiménez, notary.

Witness, Juan de Ribas, Soldier

Immediately thereafter, on the said day of February 4, the Lord Governor ordered to appear before him Juan de Ribas, a soldier in this garrison. In accordance with the law, Ribas took an oath in which he promised to tell the truth. Being asked about the contents of the letter, he stated that while he has been in the service of His Majesty in these provinces for more than thirty-four years, he has not been in the town of La Tama. However, as a young man of the age of seventeen or eighteen years, he served in the garrison at Santa Elena. As there was a lack of food there,[24] Captain Juan Pardo left Santa Elena with up to 150 soldiers, going into the interior to discover what he might under the orders of the *Adelantado* Pedro Menéndez.[25] The declarant was one of the people the *adelantado* sent with Pardo to stay with the caciques there and learn their languages. They traveled from Santa Elena to Topaz and to Uma and to La Buida,[26] one league from Canos,[27] where there is a large, wide, fast-flowing river named Guatari[28] that flows to the ocean and where they harvest a great number of pearls. A piper stayed to live there with his wife and two children, and to this day the piper has not returned from there, nor has his wife or children. The declarant thinks that it would be of great importance to find any of them alive, as they would be able to attest to the land's many riches. From there, the declarant traveled upriver with Captain Juan Pardo, from Canos[29] to Cayagua,[30] and from there to Cauichi,[31] and from there to Joara. Near the town of Joara,[32] there was a high hill which they called The Diamonds.[33] Returning from the interior, Lieutenant Moyano, who had been left there by said Captain Juan Pardo, received news of these diamonds, and he went there. Although he tried to break them then with iron mauls and wedges, these did not work and the diamonds could not be broken. Seeing this, the declarant saw Lieutenant Moyano take a small point of one. He then went to Spain, returning in the company of Don Diego Velasco, son-in-law of said *adelantado*,[34] with his goal being that Don Diego de Velasco would give him people to return to gather those diamonds. The declarant heard Lieutenant Moyano say that in Spain they had given him a large sum of money in exchange for the tiny point that he had taken from among those diamonds and that the person who had bought it had told him that Moyano had not known what he had sold and that he would not return it to him for any price. Don Diego de Velasco would have sent him again and given him people, but instead sent him to Escamacu[35] with twenty-two soldiers to pacify that cacique who had rebelled. The Indians treacherously told Moyano to order his soldiers to extinguish the match cords on their arquebuses, as the women were afraid and would not come back unless the match cords were put out. But once Moyano told his men to extinguish their match cords, the Indians fell on the lieutenant and his men, killing them all with the exception of a single soldier who escaped, whom they called Calderón.[36] This is why Moyano never returned to where those stones were discovered. Captain Pardo and his people went on ahead, marching from Joara, this witness among them. They traveled more than twenty days, and on the road on which they traveled, there were many settled towns and, in many parts, hills and mountains, where they marked many gold and silver mines, according to what he heard the alchemists and silversmiths that the captain brought say. None of the towns at which they arrived had any defenses. All were very welcoming, the land very full and abundant in foods, corn, beans, squash, and large stores of chestnuts; diverse kinds of fruits; grapes like the ones in Spain, and elsewhere better ones. Among the Indians there were nose adornments of gold, as well as silver and many pearls, because he saw them give them to Captain Pardo and Lieutenant Moyano. He divided up his men, leaving a number of soldiers in the towns of Arameco and Joara,[37] up to twenty-five in each, and he left for Santa Elena after telling the caciques that he would return in three or four moons. This declarant stayed behind as well to learn the language, and later went on a journey of three or four days and arrived at where Soto, the *adelantado* of the island of Hispaniola, died.[38] There he learned stories about the people who had been with Soto, and he saw coats of mail and weapons, as well as Spanish clothing. The Indians told him how when the general had died, there had been among them a fight about who was to be in charge. They said that the Spanish then killed each other, dividing up with each going to his own fate. As a people without a leader, the Indians killed some of them, while others lived off the land. This declarant carried news of a Portuguese pilot named Olmedo,[39] who, together with his wife, had remained in Cauchi to learn the language.[40] He said that he and his wife had gone alone from there and reached the place where Soto had died. The Indians there said that a cacique further on had killed the pilot because he had hit one of the cacique's sons with a stick[41] and that months later some men had come on horseback and taken the wife, tying her to the back of a horse and carrying her away.

There he saw horses, spears, and Spanish clothing painted on the walls of the houses. And in that town where General Soto died, the Indians told him about a grand city they called the Great Copla.[42] They said it took seven or eight days to get there, by water in canoes, one right next to the other, with their banners raised because they would pass through territories with warlike Indians. The greatness of the place was such that they could not stop talking about it. Pointing to metal plates of silver and pewter that belonged to General Soto, the Indians said that in that city there were bowls of that same material and that there were tall houses of stone. From there, Ribas returned to where Lieutenant Moyano was in Joara, and they all returned to Santa Elena, leaving others there in charge. As has been said, from what he saw, the fertility of the land means that there is a diverse abundance of food of all kinds, and small cows like those found in Barbary.[43] It seemed to him that if His Majesty knew about that land, he would not be able to stop himself from populating and conquering it and that, given the many mines that were found, the wealth of previously discovered lands cannot compare.

Ribas said his wife could speak about this and much more, since she is a Native of that land.[44] Captain Juan Pardo brought her from there when she was a young girl, as well as Teresa Martín, who is also an Indigenous Native woman from that land. And his said wife was the *cacica* of that land, which they call Guanaytique.[45] Ribas once again declares and notes that he believes that the diamond mine there holds the greatest wealth ever known, and Moyano's return from Spain to these parts was with the intention of going back to those mines, as stated, as this declarant himself heard him say while he was alive.

This is everything he knows by the oath he has taken, and which he affirms and ratifies. He is fifty-six years of age, more or less, and does not sign because he does not know how. The said governor signed it in his name—Gonzalo Méndez de Canzo—Before me, Juan Jiménez, notary.

Witness Theresa Martín, Indian

Following the aforementioned, on the same day referenced above, the fourth of February 1600, the Lord Governor called to appear before him Teresa[46] Martín, an Indian woman from the inland area called

Juacan,[47] to which Captain Pardo, who had departed from Santa Elena, had made a foray. She took the oath on a sign of the cross [+] on which she placed her right hand. Having done so with the requisite solemnity, she was asked about the content of the proceedings undertaken by Lord Governor. She stated that she was only able to declare what she knows, which is that a captain named Juan Pardo came to her land with infantry, and which seemed to her to be 150 leagues from the coast over the land from Santa Elena, which is on the coast by the sea. She saw the Indians from her land and her relatives give gifts to Pardo and esteem him and his people, giving them a lot of food from what they had for their own sustenance, such as corn, beans, squash, chestnuts, beef,[48] deer, and turkeys, and many other things to hunt in great quantities, as well as fish from rivers and lakes in great number. She said that if the aforementioned Juan Pardo had to go from one town to another, a great number of Indians carried him on a platform, clearing the roads where he would have to pass. She knows that when said Juan Pardo had to return, he left his soldiers divided up in different areas in a manner of forts, saying that he would be back with many more people in three or four moons. Understanding this, the Indians waited for him. A great deal of time passed and he did not return, because of which the soldiers caused disorders among the Indians and their women.[49] She declares that, being a young girl at that time, this declarant came in Lieutenant Moyano's company, and she does not know how the soldiers ended; so she responds.[50]

She was then asked if there is gold or silver or pearls in her land. She responded that when there were gatherings and dances among the Indians, they brought out some nose adornments of gold and silver, but since she was a young girl she never saw them. She then said that there are pearls, which they harvest from a large river about a day's journey from her town and that a great quantity of pearls in leather pouches were presented to both said Captain Juan Pardo and Lieutenant Moyano. She remembers seeing Lieutenant Moyano with pouches filled with many large, white, round pearls. She then saw said Lieutenant Moyano depart for Spain, and when he returned, she heard him say that he hoped to have a chance to return to that land. It seemed to her that some reason motivated him to return, but then Indians killed him in Escamacu,[51] and so he was unable to carry out his plan.

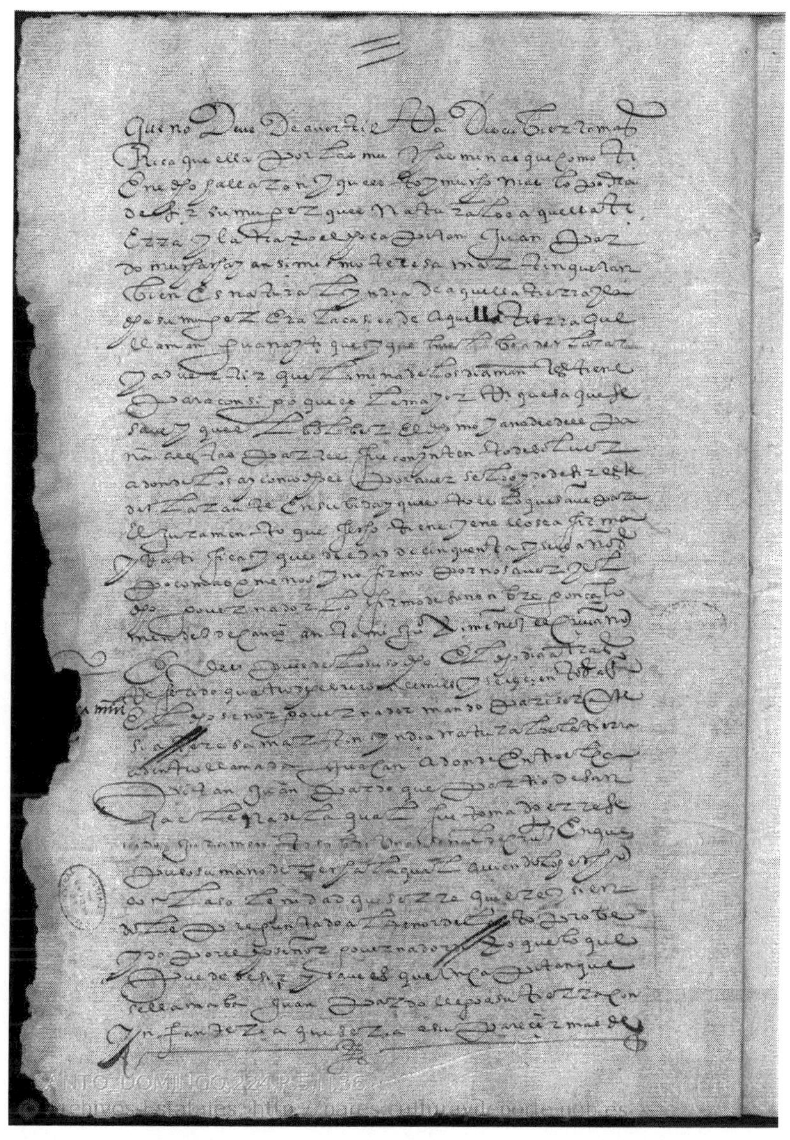

The beginning of Teresa Martín's testimony (España. Ministerio de Cultura y Deporte. Archivo General de Indias, SANTO DOMINGO, 224, R.5, N.36, F.261v.)

Asked about the gold for the nose adornments that the Indians brought out in their dances, and particularly where the Indians found it and where they gathered it, she stated that three or four days' journey from her town there are some Indians who reside in a mountain range called Chisca,[52] where they gather said gold. She then said that those Indians go around fully dressed, and they are very white, red haired, and blue-eyed, like the Flemish,[53] because the hair they have is a little like gold. From these people they get the gold for the nose adornments they use in their dances, as well as the little solid gold tubes they wear dangling in their piercings.

Asked if there are great places and large populations in her land, and in what kinds of houses they reside, she stated that her town is very large with many men and women. She cannot remember the number of people there, but the town is large, with a fence around the whole of it. There are no more than four main doors, and these are closed at night because of wars and the large pigs that there are. If they did not close the doors, the pigs would enter, and they tend to kill some of the children. The houses there are of wood and branches covered with tree bark.

She was then asked which seemed to her a better land and with more food, St. Augustine or her land. She replied that this land of St. Augustine is worth nothing in comparison to hers, because in her land hunger is unknown; they have enough corn, beans, squash, and chestnuts to last two or three years, as well as a large quantity of fish that are in the rivers and lakes. The nuts there are in such quantities that they extract oil from them and that at the foot of the mountain range near her town, there are four or five salt water springs. The Indians even have a way of using fire to make salt in great abundance with water from those springs.[54] The way of life of the people in her land is different from that of the people in this one, because they are settled and they live in permanent towns,[55] with children and grandchildren and great- grandchildren. They are not fickle nor untruthful like those of this land, as here the Indians do nothing more than take quivers and bows and go from one island to another and from one swamp to another, fishing and hunting, with no fixed settlement.

She was asked if she were to go with a number of people to her land, whether or not there would be enough food to sustain them along the way. She said that from what she had seen when the Spanish came to her land, it seemed to her that there would be no lack of food, even if the number of people were great, because Lieutenant Moyano did nothing more than send a message on ahead of him to a town, and when he arrived there was food in abundance.

Asked if horses would be able to walk in that land, she responded that as she was just a young girl when she left, she knows little about this. In places there are very large mountain ranges, and it seemed to her that horses would be of little necessity, because when Juan Pardo and Moyano wanted to go somewhere, the Indians they brought with them took them, so it seemed to her horses could pass through there as well. This she said and declared under the oath she made, which she affirmed and corrected after it was read to her. She appears to be forty years old, more or less, and she did not sign for not knowing how, and the Lord Governor signed in his name—Gonzalo Méndez de Canzo—Before me, Juan Jiménez, notary.

Witness Lieutenant Francisco Fernández de Ecija

After the aforementioned, and on the day, month, and year referred to above, the fourth of the present month of February 1600, said Lord Governor made appear before him the Lieutenant Francisco Fernández de Ecija, as he was a man with a lot of experience in these provinces who had served His Majesty in them more than thirty-six years. In accordance with the law, Ecija took an oath in which he promised to tell the truth. Having been read the acts and the section of the letter from His Majesty, he stated that he has not been to the town of La Tama to which the letter refers but that that he does have knowledge about it. The information he can give in fulfillment of the chapter from the letter, and what he understands from having heard Captain Juan Pardo and Lieutenant Moyano speak, is that they traveled into the interior together for more than two hundred leagues. He says that the best plan for a foray into and discovery of these provinces could be done along the Guatari River, which is thirty-four degrees latitude, more or less, and to where the aforementioned Juan Pardo and his lieutenant Moyano had made a foray previously. As he had been a comrade of said Lieutenant Moyano, he heard him state many times that somewhere along this river about forty leagues from the coast, more or less, there was a completely bare, crystalline hill, without trees, with many diamonds sticking out. The hill itself was made of diamonds and held great wealth. When Lieutenant Moyano returned from the foray that he made with Juan Pardo to said hill, the declarant heard him say that he tried to break loose and remove a few stones, even by using hammers and steel wedges, but these fell apart and the stones could not be broken. He then collected a very small point that he carried away and took to Spain. He did not know what kind of value it had and sold it along with a number of pearls that he took on the foray. Fernández heard him say that they gave him many ducats and that they had tricked him because he did not know what he was selling. Desiring to claim this wealth for himself, Moyano went to the *adelantado* Pedro Menéndez, who was at that time in Spain, and said to him, "Sir, I am Lieutenant Moyano, who traveled to the interior with Captain Juan Pardo in the discovery of La Florida. If your lordship were to give me people, I would enter forty leagues from the coast to find a hill of diamonds that holds incredible wealth." With that the *adelantado* embraced him and said that what he told him made him very happy. He then went to find Lieutenant don Diego de Velasco,[56] his son-in-law and the governor of Santa Elena, so that once he arrived he could immediately go there, and the governor would give him people and what was necessary for the foray to find the hill. At this time, His Majesty had placed the *adelantado* in charge of the Armada in Santander, where he died, and don Diego de Velasco, having made war against the cacique of Escamacu, sent said Lieutenant Moyano with twenty-two soldiers to calm and pacify the cacique. There some Indians treacherously told him to have his soldiers extinguish the match cords of their arquebuses because the women and children were very afraid that they wanted to kill them. Having them do this and the Indians seeing their match cords were extinguished, surrounded them. There were so many Indians they killed all the Spaniards without anyone escaping, save for one named Calderón[57] who, after three days and having crossed the bay at great effort and risk, came to Santa Elena to report the news. This is why attempts to find the mountain ceased, and why no one has attempted to find it until now. It appears to this declarant that it would be worthwhile for His Majesty to send someone to find out more about an enterprise of such great interest as this. Although he has spent thirty-six years of his service laboring in these provinces, he would be excited to go on this discovery. He would not do so out of his own interests, but those of His Majesty, as he has always wished to be of service to His Majesty and for his lands and royal patrimony to continue to increase. Further, he knows that the mines discovered by the captain and lieutenant are very rich as they were examined by alchemists and silversmiths who had been brought along and who understood such things. He saw them obtain a quantity of very good pearls during the foray. Additionally, it seems to him and he holds it to be true that if one could leave New México and enter those lands at any point, it would from that latitude of thirty-four or thirty-five degrees latitude. As it is a land that is well populated and well provisioned, known, and discovered, that His Majesty would incur little costs and yet receive a great reward. This is his opinion and what he has heard, given under an oath taken on this day, and which he affirmed and corrected; and having been read by me, the scribe, he signed it in his name, as what is said and declared within is true. He says that he is fifty-six years old, more or less—Francisco Fernández-—Before me, Juan Ximénez, notary.

Witness David Glavid, Irishman, Soldier

On this same day of the month and aforesaid year, Governor and Captain General Gonzalo Méndez de Canzo had appear before him David Glavid, Irishman, soldier of this garrison.[58] In accordance with the law, he took an oath on a sign of the cross [+] which he made with his right hand. The acts previously provided by the Lord Governor and the chapter of the letter from His Majesty that was included with it, taken to the letter from the original, were then read to him. Having understood these, he said that he has never been to La Tama, nor does he know that land. What he does know of these provinces is that he has resided in them and in the garrison of St. Augustine for more than five years and that in the year of 1584 the English robbed a boat of his carrying merchandise and wine as he rounded the Cape of Surlinga,[59] having left Nantes in the province of Brittany. They brought him with them back to the Indies, in a fleet of nine sails, large and small,[60] under the General Richard Grenville,[61] and they took him all the way to Jacan,[62] which is on the coast, at a latitude of thirty-six degrees. There he made port and landed up to 150 male settlers. This declarant stayed with them, as they did not give him passage. After they came onto the land they began to make bricks and tiles to make a fort and houses, and he was there a year and a half until Francis Drake[63] came there with his armada, which sacked several ports in the Indies, among them St. Augustine. Drake added the English people who were there to his armada, this declarant among them, and took them all to England. In London, this declarant came to understand that the Queen had become annoyed with Francis Drake for having removed these people from Jacan. He then saw how in London they had prepared ships with two hundred men and a large number of colonists with their wives, in order to return to the Jacan settlement. This declarant was again taken and put on a ship to return with them to Jacan again, and so he went with them to the island of Puerto Rico, where in port on the southern coast, they got water and refreshed themselves. This declarant was able to flee, as he then did, and he warned people in Puerto Rico that in England they were preparing five ships with the aim of taking and sacking Puerto Rico and that they meant to be there by Easter, so would need to be careful. And because of the warning he gave to Diego Menéndez, who was governor at that time, the attack had no effect, as he was prepared when the galleons appeared at the moment when the declarant said they would. The English had determined that after the assault they would bring more people to settle Jacan, and then follow the ships in which this declarant came, so he holds it to be true that the English are in Jacan.[64] As further confirmation of this, he said that, as he found himself in Havana last year, 1599, the declarant saw don Beltrán de la Cueva[65] bring several Englishmen to Havana from Lima, who had been onboard an English ship that he took there from the son of John Hawkins.[66] Among them was a young boy, who swore to him that when they left Plymouth[67] for the Strait of Magellan, they had in their company two ships with aid in the form of munitions, clothing, tools, axes, and hoes, for the colonists who were in Jacan, which he took to confirm that the English were there. And this is what he knows.

Asked about the time he spent in Jacan, and how land appeared to him, and if there were gold or silver there, and what fruits the land produced, he stated that while he was there, they planted wheat and barley, which the land produced in great abundance and that the land produced many great fruits, such as grapes, plums, apples, cherries, chestnuts in abundance, and nuts, a lot of corn, beans, and squash, and fish of many kinds, such that in every month there comes a different variety of fish. Likewise, there were a lot of gold and pearls, because he saw Richard Grenville recover more than one *arroba*[68] of gold. It seemed to this declarant that the gold was not of high grade; he heard it said that it was between sixteen and eighteen carats. This was due to the fact that it was raw, and the Indians did not know how to refine it. He saw that all of the caciques wore gold nose adornments and that they had a large quantity of very large pearls among them. Richard Grenville himself took a large quantity of pearls, and this declarant bartered for a large pearl in the shape of an acorn, but larger than an acorn, which was very clear and very good. Richard Grenville found out about it and took it from him. The English also heard that forty leagues from there, upriver, at the foot of a mountain range at the headwaters of the river, there were gold mines. They could not go there, however, because they lacked food and they turned back midway. As he has said, the English are in Jacan. As it is a fertile land with a lot of gold and many pearls, it did not seem to him that they would let go of it. Given the matter's importance to His Majesty's service, he has given this account to the governor so that he can give it to His Majesty. This is what he knows and has seen, as stated under oath on this date. He affirms and corrects it. Having read the declaration of what he said, he signed it in his name, and stated that he is forty years of age, more or less—David Glavid—Before me, Juan Jiménez, notary.

Witness, Luisa Menéndez, Indian

In the city of St. Augustine, on the sixth day of the month of February, 1600, the General Gonzalo Méndez de Canzo made appear before him Luisa Menéndez, [69] an Indigenous woman from the interior, from a town called Manaytique,[70] to which Lieutenant Moyano had made a foray. In accordance with the law, she took an oath in which she promised to tell the truth. Being asked about the content of the above section of the letter and the acts, and anything else she might know about her land, she said what she knows and remembers is that her land is very good and fertile with plenty of food, like corn, chestnuts, beans and squash, and nuts, and a large quantity of deer and cows[71] and wild turkeys and ducks, and many other birds you can eat. Her town is established and very large. The houses there are made of wooden boards, covered with chestnut branches and juniper planks. When asked if there is gold or silver or pearls in her land, she said that in

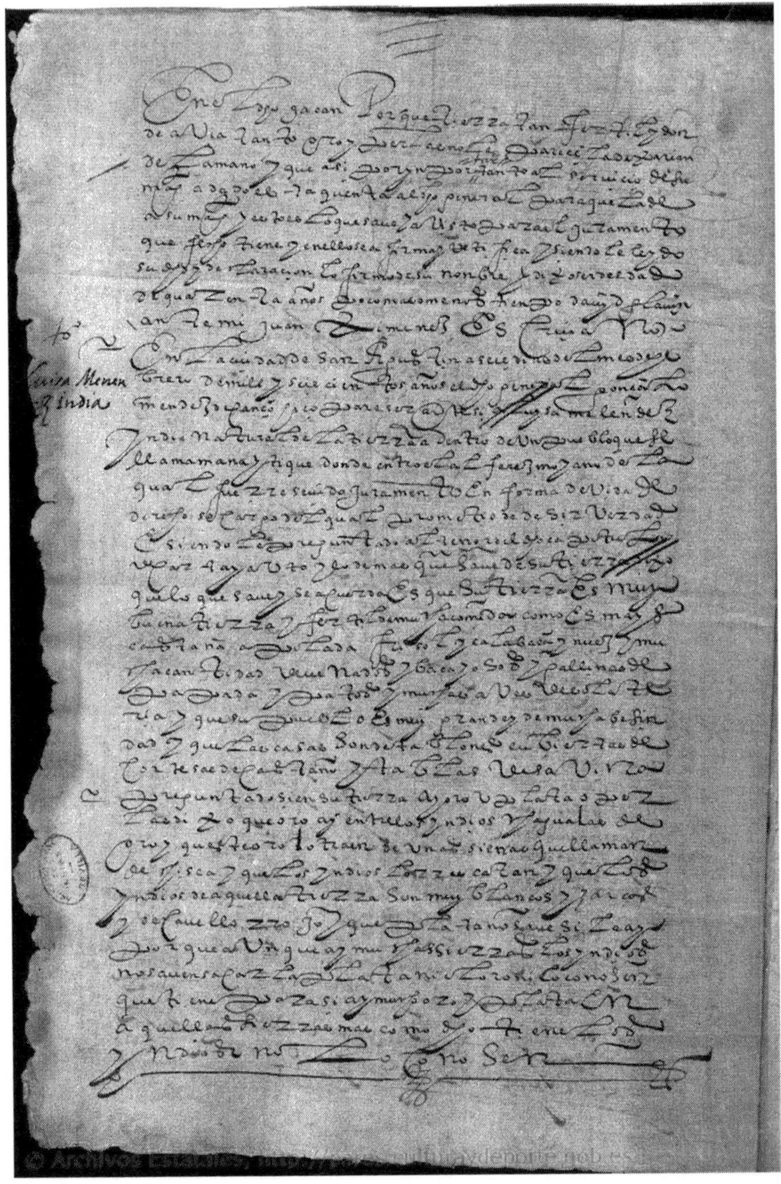

The beginning of Luisa Menéndez's testimony (España. Ministerio de Cultura y Deporte. Archivo General de Indias, SANTO DOMINGO, 224, R.5, N.36, F.266v.)

terms of gold the Indians there wear golden nose adornments and that they obtain this gold from mountain ranges they call Chisca and that the Indians trade for it there. She said that the Indians of that land are very white, and blue-eyed with red hair. She does not know if there is any silver there, because although there are many mountains in her land, her people do not know how to mine for silver, or gold, or know anything about them. In her opinion, there is a lot of gold and silver in those mountains, but as she has stated, the Indians do not know about them.

Asked if there are pearls in that land, this declarant said that with many other women and men, she went to a river where they took out many large clams, and they harvested many pearls and gave them to Lieutenant Moyano, and likewise the Indians gave him gold nose adornments. She knows for certain that, as there are many mountain ranges and valleys and large rivers, if the Spanish went there, they would obtain a lot of wealth, but as she was a young girl when she left her homeland, she cannot give as much information about the land as she would be able to say now that she is a grown woman. She says that her husband Juan de Ribas can better say what is in her land than she can, as he is Spanish and a man.

Asked if many Spaniards were to go to that land, whether or not they would find plentiful food, she stated that regarding food, there would be no lack of it no matter how many people went and that there was also a spring there with three or four heads of salt water from which the Indians make salt. The water there rises and falls, and in all of that land, there is no other salt water. This is what she knows and remembers about her land, taken under oath on this this date, and which she affirms and corrects. She did not sign it, as she did not know how, and the Lord General signed it for her.—Gonzalo Méndez de Canzo—Before me, Juan Jiménez, notary.

On the sixth day of the month of February of the year 1600, in the city of St. Augustine, province of La Florida, Gonzalo Méndez de Canzo, governor and captain general of these provinces by our Lord the King, said that people who can describe what they have seen in that land, and Spaniards who have been there and have knowledge of it, have made their declarations here. In view of this and the fact that there are at present no others who can speak and or provide information about this matter according to His Majesty's command, the governor orders me, the notary, to make one or two or more copies of all of these testimonies and have them certified in the necessary, public form and way. This he did, ordered, and signed in his name, with said copies being made under his authority and certified by judicial decree—Gonzalo Méndez de Canzo—Before me Juan Jiménez, notary.

And I, Juan Jiménez, the principal public scribe of the government in these provinces, the city and fort of St. Augustine of La Florida, on the orders of Governor and Captain General Gonzalo Méndez de Canzo, undertook to copy and made this copy of the original that was given to me and remains with me. This copy is accurate and true and follows it faithfully. As a show of faith and to testify that this is the truth, I put my mark and sign it in my accustomed name which is as such—Gonzalo Méndez de Canzo—Juan Jiménez, notary. Dues free.

Notes

1. According to Charles Arnade, Méndez de Canzo was born in Casariego de Tapia in Asturias, Spain, around 1554; see *Florida on Trial: An Eyewitness Account of Life in Florida Datelined at St. Augustine in 1602* (Coral Gables: University of Miami Press, 1959), 5. As admiral responsible for escorting Spanish ships laden with gold and silver, in 1595 he attacked two ships belonging to the English pirate Sir Francis Drake and captured the aptly named *Francis*. He then participated in the defense of San Juan, Puerto Rico, against Drake in November of that year, with his actions earning him the governorship of La Florida on May 22, 1596 (Arnade, 6–7).

2. Spanish monarch King Philip III (1578–1621; reign from 1598–1621).

3. This passage marks the document according to the generic conventions of the *relación*, literally "relation" or "account," which is a response to a direct request by the Spanish Crown; see Walter Mignolo, "Cartas, crónicas, y relaciones del descubrimiento y la Conquista," in *Historia de la literatura hispanoamericana*, vol. 1, coord. Luis Íñigo Madrigal (Madrid: Cathedra, 1982), 70.

4. The reader will immediately notice that any territory one would describe as "New Mexico" is a good bit farther away from central Georgia than two hundred leagues, and it recalls Juan Pardo's arriving at Joara, looking at the snow-capped mountains to the west, and thinking Zacatecas lay just beyond. These mistakes underscore how much Europeans thought they knew about this land versus what they actually knew.

5. That is, Méndez de Canzo.

6. Hudson mentions that the Guatari River is known as the "Santee-Wateree-Catawba River" today, see *The Juan Pardo Expeditions*), 192. This is not to be confused with the town of Guatari, which he describes as being "present-day Salisbury, North Carolina" (Hudson, *Juan Pardo Expeditions*, 26).

7. This is a reference to the expeditions of Juan Pardo, which Hudson describes as "failures" (Hudson, *Juan Pardo*, 3). The first of these left Santa Elena (present-day

Parris Island in Beaufort, South Carolina) in December 1566, while the second left in September 1567. It was on the first of these that Pardo, arriving in the town of Joara, established Fort San Juan, the first inland European settlement in this part of the hemisphere. For his part, Hernando Moyano de Morales was the man Pardo left in charge of the soldiers at the Fort San Juan garrison when he returned to Santa Elena. Moyano then set off on his own adventures, looking for gold, silver, and other resources, upon Pardo's departure. Hudson notes that Joara itself "was a border town in every sense of the word," linguistically and culturally (88) but ultimately claims that its residents spoke Cherokee (87). More recent scholarship seems to suggest that the town was more likely Catawba; see Robin A. Beck, Christopher B. Rodning, and David G. Moore, "Joara in Time and Space," in *Fort San Juan and the Limits of Empire: Colonialism and Household Practice at the Berry Site*, ed. Robin A. Beck, Christopher B. Rodning, and David G. Moore (Gainesville: University of Florida Press, 2016), 57.

8. Darby Glavid.

9. Jacan is the name of what is now known as Chesapeake Bay.

10. Sir Richard Grenville (1542–1591) who, along with Ralph Lane and under the sponsorship of Sir Walter Raleigh, made the first attempt to establish a Roanoke colony in 1585. See Kimberly C. Borchard, *Appalachia as Contested Borderland of the Early Modern Atlantic, 1528–1715* (Tempe: Arizona State University Press for the Arizona Center for Medieval and Renaissance Studies, 2021), 121–22; and Anna Brickhouse, *The Unsettlement of America: Translation, Interpretation, and the Story of Don Luis de Velasco, 1560–1945* (Oxford: Oxford University Press, 2015), 253.

11. Perhaps the town/chiefdom of Ocute, which was near Tama (see unnumbered note).

12. The second sustained European settlement in this part of the hemisphere, at the site of what is today the Parris Island Marine Base outside of Beaufort, South Carolina. The Spanish settled the area in 1566 at the site of a previous French settlement (1562–1564) and eventually abandoned it in favor of focusing on St. Augustine in 1587.

13. Guale is an area encompassing coastal Georgia and northern Florida; see John H. Hann, "Political Leadership among the Natives of Spanish Florida," *Florida Historical Quarterly* 71, no. 2 (1992): 199. San Pedro was perhaps a Guale village, or a village of a neighboring people (see Brickhouse, *Unsettlement of America*, 181–84, in which she describes how "Andrés de San Miguel" visits the Guale village of Asao before going to "San Pedro"). Hoffman lists a "San Pedro de Mocamo" in Guale as being Cumberland Island, Georgia (Hoffman, *Florida's*, 77).

14. The Franciscans, a religious order established by Saint Francis of Assisi in the early thirteenth century. It is notable that religious orders like the Franciscans frequently came into conflict with colonial officials like the governor, particularly over issues such as Indigenous rights, even as they were outright agents of empire through their evangelization efforts.

15. As evidenced by the very title of J. Michael Francis and Kathleen M. Kole's *Murder and Martyrdom in Spanish Florida: Don Juan and the Guale Uprising of*

1597 (New York: American Museum of Natural History, 2011), the friars had a rather harrowing experience.

16. Elsewhere, Katherine Reding translates this as "long green plum," which may be the green gage plum; see "Letter of Gonzalo Méndez de Canço, Governor of Florida, to Phillip II of Spain, June 28, 1600," *Georgia Historical Quarterly* 8, no. 3 (1924): 224. This translation would make sense, as—if the "white plum" description is of this fruit's meat—Salas could be referring to the paw paw.

17. Note that the anonymous peer reviewer states that this reads as though Salas and the friars are taking these stones from their footprints, or *huellas*. As *huellas* does not appear in either of the transcriptions done by Abad or Ross, we have opted to omit this from our translation.

18. *Euphorbia tithymaloides* or Devil's Backbone. According to Francis and Kole, it was, "highly valued for its medicinal properties" (*Murder and Martyrdom in Spanish Florida*, 38, n84).

19. Name originally given to the colony established by the Spanish after the fall of the Mexica (Aztec) Empire in 1521. It came to include much of what today is Central America, the US West and parts of Canada, as well as Louisiana.

20. See Charles Hudson, Marvin T. Smith, and Chester B. DePratter's "The Hernando de Soto Expedition: From Apalachee to Chiaha," *Southeastern Archeology* 3, no. 1 (1984): 65–77, for a fuller description of the Spaniard's wanderings through this area. For our purposes here, it is notable that the memory of Soto's disastrous expedition (1539–1543) is reported as continuing to live in the consciousness of the region's Indigenous Peoples almost sixty years after it took place.

21. Another Indigenous People who lived along the Georgia Coast. Francis and Kole place one of the principal Salchiche towns, Tulufina, as being "northwest of modern Ossabaw Island, Georgia" (*Murder and Martyrdom in Spanish Florida*, 35).

22. Perhaps towns in/near Guale. If so, it is notable that they might not be as "friendly" as reported here, as a young man from "Cascangue" was captured by the Spanish during the so-called Guale Uprising of 1597 (Francis and Kole, *Murder and Martyrdom in Spanish Florida*, 66).

23. This don Juan is not the same person as don Juan (or don Juanillo) from Tolomato, the alleged leader of the so-called Guale Uprising. According to Francis and Kole (*Murder and Martyrdom in Spanish Florida*, 42), this Don Juan's loyalty and professed Christianity earned him a salary from the Spanish Crown ("equivalent to that of a Spanish soldier") and perhaps was one of the reasons that made San Pedro a target of the Guale.

24. This would appear to be the first Pardo expedition in December 1566.

25. Pedro Menéndez de Avilés (1519–1574). Menéndez had a successful career in the service of the Spanish Crown as *capitán general* at different moments of both the Fleet of Flanders and the Fleet of the Indies, including being given a knighthood in the Order of Saint James (Santiago). In 1565 he was appointed *adelantado* of La Florida, with one of his first tasks being to oust the French from the region, who were led by Jean Ribault. Hoffman describes the victorious Menéndez as "sparing only a few Catholics and musicians"; see *A New Andalucia and a Way to the Orient: The American Southeast during the Sixteenth Century* (Baton Rouge: Louisiana State

University Press, 1990), 230. Menéndez de Avilés was also the founder of both St. Augustine and Santa Elena.

26. These names do not appear in the Bandera Account of the Pardo expedition or, as far as we can tell, elsewhere. One would infer that they are smaller towns on the road between Santa Elena and Cofitachequi. Perhaps they are simply given different names in the Bandera Account.

27. Hudson notes that when Pardo arrived, Canos was the name being used for the former Cofitachequi, which is currently understood to be near present-day Camden, South Carolina (*Juan Pardo Expeditions*, 25). The town was made famous by the Soto expedition for, among other things, having a female ruler.

28. See note 6.

29. See note 27.

30. This name does not appear in the Bandera Account of the Pardo expedition or, as far as we can tell, elsewhere.

31. Perhaps Cauchi? See note 40.

32. "Joaraz" or "Juaraz" in the text.

33. According to Hudson, "the location of this deposit, probably corundum, may have been near Carpenter's Knob in northern Cleveland County, North Carolina"(*Juan Pardo Expeditions*, 190). Nonetheless, the possibility that this could actually be a mountain made of diamond fired imperial imaginations. Andrade writes that when the pirate Sir Francis Drake attacked St. Augustine in 1586, his "avowed purpose was to capture the Moyano diamond" (*Juan Pardo Expeditions*, 41).

34. Son-in-law of the *adelantado* Pedro Méndez de Avilés who, upon the *adelantado*'s death, governed from Santa Elena from 1571 to 1576. See Hoffman, *Florida's Frontiers*, 64–65, particularly regarding Méndez de Avilés's apparently successful attempts to embed missionaries in Indigenous towns.

35. Escamacu or Uscama, a village north of Santa Elena involved in the Guale Uprising of 1576. Francis and Kole say that Moyano was sent "to retrieve some Indian laborers who had fled from Santa Elena after stealing some Spanish clothing. According to later Spanish testimonies, when Moyano and his men reached Escamacu, the Indians refused to feed them, as they had done in the past. In response, Moyano seized several pots filled with gacha (a type of gruel made from maize and/or acorn flour), and the Spaniards satiated their hunger. Early the next morning, Escamacu's warriors attacked the Spanish forces while they slept, killing Moyano and 24 of his men. Only one Spaniard, Andrés Calderón, survived the slaughter. Calderón returned to Santa Elena to convey the news" (*Murder and Martyrdom in Spanish Florida*, 24). Hoffman attributes Calderón's unlikely survival to the fact that he "had been attending to nature's call outside of the village" when the attack occurred (*Florida's Frontiers*, 66).

36. Andrés Calderón, see note 35.

37. This may be the moment when Pardo leaves some men garrisoned at Joara (Juaraz), but the reference to Arameco is unclear. This makes it sound as though Ribas was garrisoned at Fort San Juan, and ventured into what is now Tennessee.

38. Soto died of a fever along the banks of the Mississippi. In Hudson's rather poetic summation, Soto "lost his fortune, his life, and about half of his army [on his expedition]. His only discovery was that there was no populous native state in North America like the one Cortés has conquered in Mexico and the one Pizarro has conquered in Peru" (*Juan Pardo Expeditions*, 10).

39. Hudson records this as "Almeydo." He also notes that "his woman" in Ribas's words, was "presumably an Indian woman" (*Juan Pardo Expeditions*, 191), which would make this bond the third between a Spanish man and an Indigenous woman that appears in the Account.

40. The town referred to as Guasili by chroniclers of the Soto expedition (Hudson, Smith, and DePratter, "The Hernando de Soto Expedition," 26). Robin Beck notes that this is likely the Plum Grove Site near what is today Embreeville, Tennessee; see "From Joara to Chiaha: Spanish Exploration of the Appalachian Summit Area, 1540–1568," in *Southeastern Archeology* 16, no. 2 (1997): 164.

41. Hudson records this as a daughter as opposed to a son, and has the daughter as the woman carried off (*Juan Pardo Expeditions*, 174). In the original manuscript, however, the passage appears to read "hijo suyo," as it states in the transcription. This would suggest that these are separate, though related incidents, as we have rendered here.

42. La Gran Copla was a mythical city, much like El Dorado, Cibola, or the Seven Cities of Gold, and was said to be northwest of Santa Elena. See Hudson, *The Juan Pardo Expeditions*, 190–94 for a thorough explanation of Ribas's story of La Gran Copla, as well as the influence it had on the English.

43. The comparison here is presumably between a buffalo and *Alcelaphus buselaphus buselaphus*, the bubal hartebeest, a now extinct African antelope native to northern Africa.

44. "Natural de aquella tierra."

45. See the later note regarding Manaytique. Here, this scribe may be misspelling the name of Méndez's town, or Ribas may be mispronouncing it.

46. her name appears with an "h" in the original.

47. In their introduction to *Fort San Juan and the Limits of Empire*, Beck, Moore and Rodning write, "Martín was identified as a native of 'Juacan' (Joara) and was married to one of the thirty soldiers left at Fort San Juan after Pardo's first expedition, Juan Martín de Badajóz"; see *Fort San Juan and the Limits of Empire: Colonialism and Household Practice at the Berry Site* (Gainesville: University Press of Florida, 2016), 25. Although there may be others, to date this is the only source we have been able to locate that states that Juacan is Joara. Again, given the fact that Juan Martín is one of the very few survivors from among the Spaniards who were at the fort, as suggested by Hudson (*Juan Pardo Expeditions*, 176), the possibility that he and Teresa were married and lived together in Joara/Fort San Juan, would certainly support Teresa's being from the town. Hudson, Smith, and DePratter ("Hernando de Soto Expedition," 18) note that the town's name, "Joara," appears as "Xuala" in chronicles about the Soto expedition. However, in recent conversations with Rachel Briggs, a contributor to this volume and a member of the archaeological team at the Berry Site, Briggs suggested that Martín was from elsewhere, given that she says she was from a walled town and Joara was not walled. Perhaps Martín was

even from Manaytique or Guapere given that she, like Menéndez, talks about the prevalence of salt water springs near her hometown. See note 54.

48. This is "carnes de vaca" in the original. One can assume this is a reference to bison.

49. This would obviously have been the second Pardo expedition, which departed Santa Elena on September 1, 1567, arriving in Joara on September 24. Note that, contrary to what Ribas would seem to suggest, namely, that Martín and Menéndez left with Pardo, this would not have been the case if she were there when these events occurred. Pardo received word that Moyano, whom he left in charge of Fort San Juan and who had gone about the countryside looking for wealth, had got into trouble at Chiaha, and left around September 29 to rescue him. They found Moyano and his men at Olamico, in the kingdom of Chiaha, near what is now Dandridge, Tennessee, on October 7. He then continued on his travels, returning to Joara on November 6. He then left his ensign, Albert Escudero de Villamar, in charge of a garrison of thirty men at Fort San Juan, before leaving on November 24 to make his way back to Santa Elena (see Hudson, *Juan Pardo Expeditions*, 29–41). This is a fascinating moment in the text in which Martín likely describes sexual violence, which the scribe then renders as "disorders" in the account. Importantly, Juan Martín de Badajoz, Teresa's husband, seems to have been the primary informant for the friar Jaime Martínez, who describes Martín de Badajoz as saying, "These soldiers after they had waited long for the Spaniards to bring provisions, attempted to obtain them from the Indians. They left the fort deceived by the treacherous Indians who came together in great numbers and killed them all, inflicting on them the tortures related by Juan Martín. Martín escaped, traveling more than two hundred leagues over rough and mountainous country to St. Helen, guided by the intercession of our Lady of Guadalupe"; see Ruben Vargas Ugarte, "The First Jesuit Mission in Florida," *US Catholic-Historical Society: Historical Records and Studies* 25 (1935): 142.

50. See the previous note. Moyano left with Pardo for Santa Elena.

51. See note 35.

52. People who were recorded as having gold, dating back to Soto being told this in Chiaha (Hudson, *Juan Pardo Expeditions*, 10). Hudson says, "The territory of the Chiscas appears to have been in and to the other side of the mountains north of Joara, including the area along the upper course of the Nolichucky River," elsewhere noting that Chisca "was the name that Muskogean-speakers (and perhaps speakers of other languages) used to refer in general to the people who lived in the mountains and hills of the upper Tennessee Valley" (27, 90). According to Hudson, they traded copper in both Chiaha and Joara (91).

53. A fascinating moment in the text as both Martín and Menéndez report this obviously incorrect anecdote about the Chisca. Here, they are compared to the Flemish. Has Martín seen enough Flemish people in La Florida to draw the comparison herself, or is the scribe once again inserting himself in her testimony?

54. Also see note 47 for an additional discussion of Martín's potential hometown. From this information we could then begin making a case that Martín is, like Menéndez, from Manaytique or the surrounding area. This would explain how

she claims that she "joined the company of Lieutenant Moyano," as well as how she could provide some details about how Moyano was received on his so-called foray.

55. "Porque es gente de población y besinidad asentadas."

56. See note 34.

57. Andrés Calderón, see note 35.

58. According to David Beers Quinn, Glavid appears in one of Ralph Lane's (c. 1530–1603) lists of would-be Roanoke colonists under the name "Darby Glande"; see *The Roanoke Voyages, 1584–1590: Documents to Illustrate the English Voyages to North America under the Patent Granted to Walter Raleigh in 1584*, vol. II (London: Halkyut Society, 1955), 828, n. 1, 195. As noted by Beers Quinn, he later appears in John White's account of his voyage as the deserter "Darbie Glauen" (195, n. 4, 519). Beers Quinn also states that a "Elizabeth Glane" appears later in White's account in a list of women who "safely arriued in Virginia and remained to inhabite there" (539) in 1587 (541, n. 12). Regarding Glavid's account here, Beers Quinn suggests that "there is no reason to believe him when he says that on this occasion he was impressed as a colonist" (519).

59. The Isles of Scilly off of Cornwall, England. Referring to these as "Surlinga" appears to be a holdover from the Middle Ages; see J. Rendel Harris and D. Theol, "Scylla and Charybdis," *Bulletin of the John Rylands Library* 9 (1925): 88–89.

60. As noted by an anonymous peer reviewer, in a marginal note this is described as an "English armada that arrived in La Florida at Jacan at a latitude of 36 degrees."

61. See note 10.

62. See note 10.

63. The English pirate Sir Francis Drake, who attacked St. Augustine in 1586.

64. This would, of course, be a reference to the Roanoke settlement, which at this point had already disappeared. See note 10.

65. Admiral Beltrán Castro y Cueva (1550–1618).

66. In a note to his translation of Glavid's testimony, David Beers Quinn notes that Juan Acles was John Hawkins, with the reference here being to his son, Richard Hawkins (*The Roanoke Voyages*, 836 n5). Beers Quinn then cites J. A. Williamson's *Age of Drake* (New York: Macmillan, 1938), 350, for the story of how Beltrán captured Hawkins at the Bay of Atacames on June 18, 1594.

67. Plymouth, a port city in England.

68. Unit of measure equating to 11.5 kg, or twenty-five pounds (Real Academia Española, https://dle.rae.es/arroba).

69. In the original, her name appears as "Menéndez" here, and as "Meléndez" in her testimony.

70. According to Beck, "it is likely that Maniatique was located on the South Fork of the Holston River near present Saltville" which is located in southwest Virginia ("From Joara to Chiaha," 165). As recorded in the account of Domingo de León, one of the soldiers was at Joara at some point, Mayantique was, along with Guapere, one of the two towns destroyed by Moyano; see John Worth, "Recollections of the Juan Pardo Expeditions: The 1584 Domingo de León Account," in *Fort San Juan and the Limits of Empire*, ed. Robin A. Beck, Christopher B. Rodning, and David G. Moore (Gainesville: University Press of Florida, 2016).

Beck also notes that Manaytique "was probably the town referred to as Chisca by (Francisco) Martínez," whereas he states Guapere was likely somewhere along the upper Nolichucky or Watauga Rivers ("From Joara to Chiaha," 166). See also "The Martínez Relation," in Hudson's *Juan Pardo Expeditions*.

71. Again, the reference to "cows" here is mostly likely to bison.

Transcription of the Paylist (1577)

Hannah R. Abrahamson

AGI Contaduria 944, (17 de agosto, 1577) s/f.

Note: This transcription reflects the orthography of the original document as closely as possible. This allows students of Spanish to have a sense of how the "Relación" itself was written while also minimizing changes to the document's original structure and meaning.

Otra librança de quantia de çiento
y veynte y ocho rreales que mon-
tan quatro myll y trezientos
y cinquenta y dos maravedis

NEXT PAGE
que pareçe que pago a Juan de
Ribas por rrazon de ocho baras
de cañamaço a çinco rreales y
una caldera de cobre en ocho ducados
que esta firmada del dicho general y ofiçiales por ante el
dicho Pedro Guerra fecha a diez y
siete de agosto de setenta y siete
y pareçe estar tomada la rrazon y carta de pago ante el dicho
Pedro Guerra

[Next entry]
Otra librança de quantia de diez
y seis myll y quatroçientos y hon-
ze maravedis que pareçe que pago
a Teresa Martin como a tutora
e curadora de Ynes Martin su
hija y a ella como a hija eredera
de Juan Martin de Badajoz su padre
soldado que fue destas pro-

vinçias ya defunto que los uvo
de aver de rrazion y sueldo de
ocho meses y siete dias de cabo descuadra en Santa Elena
desde quinze de nobienbre de setenta y çinco hasta veynte
y dos de jullio de setenta y seis
que le mataron yndios que esta
firmada del dicho general y ofiçiales
por ante el dicho Pedro Guerra fecha
a diez y siete de agosto de setenta y
siete y pareçe estar tomada la
rrazon y carta de pago y un tes-
timonyo de ciertos autos escritos en tres
ojas firmados del dicho Pedro Guerra de la Vega, escrivano.

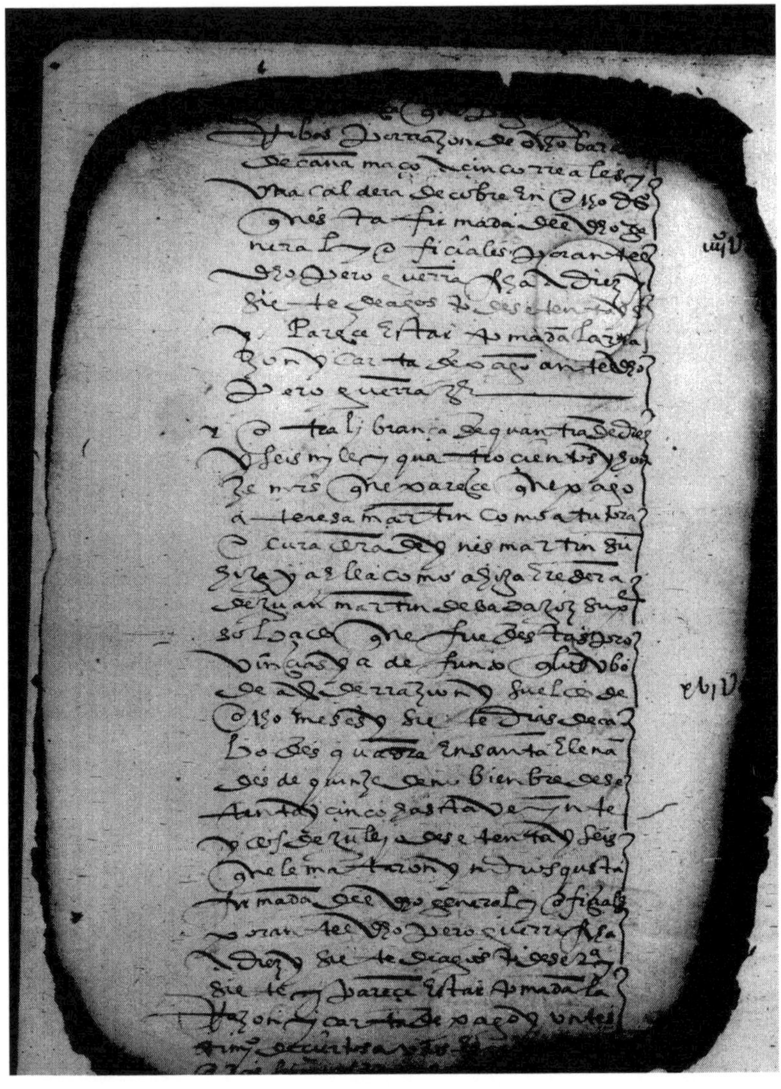

The paylist in which Teresa Martín claims Juan Martín de Badajoz's pay on the behalf of their daughter, Inés (España. Ministerio de Cultura y Deporte. Archivo General de Indias, CONTADURIA, 944. Accessible on Reel 2, Legajo 944 at the P. K. Yonge Library of Florida History, Special and Area Studies Collections, George A. Smathers Libraries, University of Florida.)

Translation of the Paylist (1577)

Melissa D. Birkhofer and Paul M. Worley

Another issue in the amount of one hundred
and twenty-eight reales that come to
[damage] four thousand and three hundred
[damage] fifty-two maravedis

NEXT PAGE
recorded here as paid to Juan de
Ribas a ration of eight
bundles of cloth worth five reales and
a copper pot worth eight ducats
which is signed by the aforementioned
general and the officials before
the aforementioned Pedro Guerra on the date of August
seventeen seventy-seven
and appearing here the reason and acknowledgment
of payment before the aforementioned
Pedro Guerra

[Next entry]
another issue in the sum of sixteen
thousand four hundred and eleven
maravedis recorded here as paid
to Teresa Martín as the guardian
and executor of Inés Martín her
daughter and to her as the daughter and heir
of Juan Martín de Badajoz her father
a deceased soldier from these
provinces to whom are owed
rations and pay for
a total of eight months and
seven days in Santa Elena
from the fifteenth of November of
Seventy-five until the twenty-
second of July of seventy-six

when he was killed by Indians. This is signed by the said general and officials
before said Pedro Guerra, dated
the seventeenth of August seventy-seven
and appearing here the reason and acknowledgment
of payment, and a testimony
of certain written records
on three pages signed by said Pedro Guerra de la Vega, notary.

2

Indigenous Women and the Un/Making of Spanish Men in Northern La Florida, 1540–1568

Rachel V. Briggs, Christopher B. Rodning, Robin A. Beck, and David G. Moore

Contributions to this volume draw on documents derived from the Méndez de Canzo Inquiry (1600) and other sources to emphasize the voices and viewpoints of Indigenous people in the colonial history of La Florida. Material evidence from sixteenth-century archaeological sites in the US Southeast offers other perspectives on the experiences of Indigenous Peoples during this period, including archaeological finds from the Berry Site, located in Western North Carolina, and a site connected to the lives of Teresa Martín, Luisa Menéndez, and other Native people who shaped the landscape and lifeways of the residents of La Tama and of the "new world" formed through Indigenous engagements with Spanish colonialism in La Florida. Written accounts of testimony by Martín and Menéndez, and other documentary sources associated with Spanish entradas *led by Hernando de Soto (1539–1543) and Juan Pardo (1566–1568) reflect retrospective accounts of life and lives in La Florida. Archaeological evidence reflects in part the material outcomes of everyday life and major events captured in those written accounts, and the archaeology complements the documentary sources (and vice versa) in shedding light on aspects of the lived experiences of this history by the diverse peoples entangled within it.*

This chapter is a revised version of our previously published article, "Fear the Native Woman: Femininity, Food, and Power in the Sixteenth-Century North Carolina Piedmont," published in 2024 in the journal *American Anthropologist* 126 (1): 32–46. This chapter has been adapted with an eye toward the new translations of the La Tama documents featured in this volume. We are grateful to the editorial staff of *American Anthropologist* for allowing us the opportunity to include our work here, and for the opportunity to revise it to fit the themes of this volume.

***

In 1566, when the governor of La Florida Pedro Menéndez de Avilés ordered Captain Juan Pardo and a company of 125 soldiers on the first of two expeditions into the interior of the Carolinas, Pardo knew that he and his men would be depending on the voluntary and conscripted labor and resources of Native women.[1] Colonists in the Spanish town of Santa Elena were starving,[2] and though Spanish men were capable agriculturalists, little progress had been made to make La Florida a food-secure colony. Instead, both raw food resources (like maize, beans, and chestnuts) as well as the tools, labor, and knowledge to transform those materials into "edible dishes" (like hominy and hickory nut soups) were taken from Native towns, and those agents within Native towns who had this knowledge and controlled these resources were Native women.[3] Throughout the southeastern United States (hereafter, the Southeast), Native women were the farmers of their communities, tending to fields and harvesting crops, and they were also the cooks, responsible for preparing the meals and dishes that resulted from their labor. And though local and regional chiefs had the power to demand food resources from their communities and to distribute those resources as they saw fit, a considerable amount of power remained in the care of the domestic unit, and thus in the hands of Native women, who had the social power to choose to share or not to share their stores. Spanish soldiers, explorers, and colonists witnessed this authority firsthand—they saw Native women in fields tending to plants, in their homes preparing pots of food, and women sharing their voices in council houses. They saw powerful Native women *micos* (regional chiefs) carried on litters and *oratas* (local chiefs), both of whom drew authority from their powerful, elite matrilineages.[4] This feminine presence is threaded throughout the Pardo chronicles, but researchers have had a hard time "reading women" into them. Indeed, because Native women, specifically, and their labor, more broadly, are rarely explicitly highlighted in the writing of the chronicles, researchers have implicitly written them out of history.[5]

However, the lack of explicit documentation of Native women does not mean that their presence and power was not felt nor that they were inert forces shaping Spanish colonial outcomes. Too often, we have interpreted colonial entanglements from a modern Western perspective, applying Western concepts of power and gender to the interpretation of early Spanish colonial enterprises.[6] Native women are often misconceptualized through this lens, portrayed not as *Native* women but instead in much the same way as that of sixteenth-century *European* women. Though a weak social force in sixteenth-century Spain, femininity was a powerful force in Native societies throughout La Florida, providing Native women with control and power that were palpable not only within their own communities but within Spanish colonial enterprises as well.[7] Women's control over fields, food stores, cooking tools, and cooked foods was a source of feminine social power, providing them with opportunities for sharing their opinions, for achieving social recognition, and for achieving elevated status within their communities.[8] And this power, though infrequently mentioned, directly contributed to the "unsettling" of the sixteenth-century Spanish colonies in the Southeast.[9]

Here, our goal is to demonstrate how Native women like Teresa Martín and Luisa Menéndez possessed a recognized and real power through their relationship with food and cooking that was a source of anxiety for sixteenth-century Spaniards stationed in the interior at the colonial site of Fort San Juan. Fort San Juan was a short-lived Spanish colonial outpost established in the winter of 1566 by Captain Juan Pardo at the Native town of Joara, located in Western North Carolina at the Berry Site (31BK22), near present-day Morganton, North Carolina. Joara may have been the ancestral home of Teresa Martín,[10] and Fort San Juan potentially the short-lived home to Luisa Menéndez (if she became attached to Juan de Ribas while he was stationed at the fort). Within a year and a half, that fort, along with the other forts that Pardo established in the region, was razed by Native groups, and most of the Spaniards garrisoned in the interior were killed.[11] Here, we consider two realms of power available to Native women throughout La Florida through their control of food, which we believe significantly shaped the interactions and outcomes between Native groups of the upper Catawba River Valley and surrounding areas with the mid-sixteenth-century Spanish *entradas* led by Captain Juan Pardo (1566–1568; map of Indigenous towns visited by Pardo).[12] First, we critically explore the chiefly, or political, power that elite Indigenous women like Luisa Menéndez could, and did, hold, as recorded in the Spanish documentary evidence and informed with a critical understanding of Native gender roles. We suggest that though the chiefly office was gender neutral,[13] one of the reasons Native women likely attained chiefly

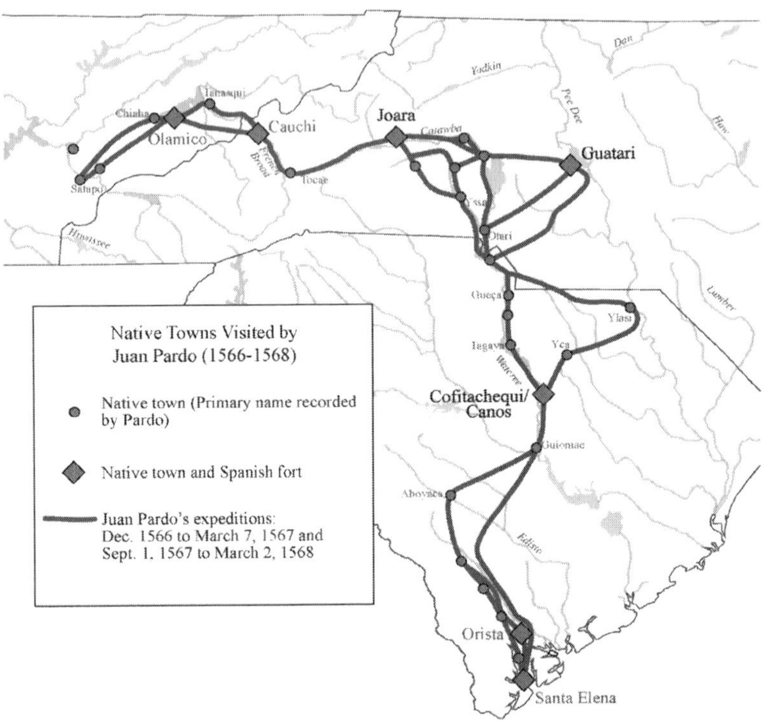

Potential locations of Indigenous towns visited by Pardo and the forts he established (Map by chapter authors)

status less often than Native men was because of other important social opportunities afforded Native women through their control over food.

Second, we explore the symbolic power held by Native women through the control and preparation of food both within their own communities and with respect to the men garrisoned at Spanish colonial outposts through both the ethnohistoric and archaeological records from the Spanish Fort San Juan and the Indigenous town of Joara.[14] Symbolic power is defined by Pierre Bourdieu as an agent-dependent form of power that is drawn when a person, or group, exerts domination over symbolic, tacit, and even unconscious cultural domains manifested in the everyday social habits of societies.[15] Symbolic power is often countered to the absolute power of imperialism, militarism, and warfare; whereas the force of a weapon might be unquestionable, symbols and ideologies hold sway because people believe in them. While the control over food can mean the difference between life and death, following the prevailing Galenic humoral system of medicine for sixteenth-century Europe, the incorporation of food into the body was believed to fundamentally impact not only health but also the presentation of various physical traits such as skin color, height, and even body hair.[16]

Through these considerations, we present two forms of power derived from the control and transformation of food into culinary products that Native women in the sixteenth century could and did enact during the sixteenth-century Spanish colonial *entradas* into the Carolina Piedmont, as well as throughout various parts of La Florida. With these new considerations, we present a revised model for conceptualizing the demise of Fort San Juan and its sister forts in 1568 that attributes the outcome to a social cleave between the Spanish soldiers and Native women, which stemmed from growing anxieties and fears that the Spaniards developed over the power that Native women wielded in their daily lives. Native women were not static resources to be controlled within the Spanish colonial system but, instead, dynamic and powerful actors whose actions were strongly informed by their own social constructions of gender and, in many cases, food. While our story ends with the destruction of Fort San Juan, we believe there needs to be greater consideration of Native women's power throughout the colonial Southeast and that we can only begin to understand the words and actions of Native women like Luisa Menéndez and Teresa Martín once we stop portraying them as sixteenth-century European women and start conceptualizing them through a Native feminine lens.

Feminine Chiefly Power

In 1566, Pedro Menéndez de Avilés ordered Captain Juan Pardo and a company of soldiers on the first of two expeditions intended to establish a series of outposts that would serve as waystations along a secure terrestrial route stretching from the Carolina coast to the increasingly important Spanish silver mines in Zacatecas, Mexico.[17] This route was to extend from Santa Elena, located near present-day Parris Island, South Carolina, through the Carolina Piedmont and across the southern Appalachians (see map of Indigenous towns visited by Pardo). In the Catawba River Valley, Pardo visited the Indigenous town of Joara, where he stayed for two weeks and established Fort San Juan.[18] Over the next year and a half and during two separate expeditions, Pardo and his men established several other forts: Fort Santiago at the town of Guatari, Fort San Pablo at Cauchi, Fort San Pedro at the town of Olamico, and Fort

Santo Tomás at Canos (or Cofitachequi) (see map of Indigenous towns visited by Pardo).[19] None of these forts lasted long. In 1568, a coordinated Native attack was leveled on all five forts, reportedly killing nearly all the Spaniards garrisoned at them. While others may have escaped, the only documented Spanish survivors were Juan Martín de Badajoz (husband to Teresa Martín), Juan de Ribas (husband to Luisa Menéndez), and a "Flemish fife" located at Canos, all of whom married Native women either during or after the uprising.[20] According to Jaime Martínez, who drew on the account of Juan Martín de Badajoz, the attacks were prompted by food demands; further, as we learn in her testimony, Teresa Martín reported that she believed that anxieties at Joara grew as the soldiers stationed at the fort "caused disorders with the Indians and the women."[21] In both cases, the implication is that Native women, in particular, were central to the reason behind the destruction of the forts.

Throughout La Florida, Spaniards had limited access to their familiar Spanish foods: Hernando de Soto in 1539, for example, infamously traveled with a herd of European pigs, while Pardo was only able to bring limited supplies of wine, hard tack, cheese, oil, and grain on his journeys. Instead, they expected to be provisioned by the towns they visited, where they demanded supplies like maize, chestnuts, bear grease, deer meat, and hickory nuts, as well as the individuals and labor necessary for the transformation of these materials into edible dishes.[22] Yet these Indigenous individuals (almost exclusively women) are rarely mentioned. Instead, the credit for provisioning is entirely placed on the shoulders of chiefs, who were assumed to have the power to demand and then mobilize food resources.[23] For this reason, some of the only Indigenous women who appear in the mid-sixteenth-century Spanish chronicles of the Carolina Piedmont are women of chiefly status.

Feminine Power and the Chiefly Office

After a close reading of the documents produced from both expeditions, Ruth Trocolli reported that in the mid-sixteenth century, the *entradas* of both Hernando de Soto and Juan Pardo encountered approximately five Native women of chiefly status in the Carolina Piedmont, two of whom were *micos*, or leaders with regional authority: Tali Mico, known to the Spanish as the Lady of Cofitachequi, whom Soto encountered in 1540; Guatari Mico and a feminine local head chief, or *orata*, of Guatari, both of whom Pardo encountered in 1568; an "old *cacica*" (old feminine chief) at Joara whom Pardo encountered in 1568; and

Luisa Menéndez, a potential chief of unknown status, who eventually married Juan de Ribas.[24] As Trocolli demonstrated, the institution of feminine chiefs and leaders was neither rare nor a "last resort" when no suitable masculine leader was available; feminine leadership was widespread and persistent throughout the Southeast, and only among certain groups, like the Caddo, was feminine leadership exceptional.[25] Instead, while leadership and political office were firmly aligned with masculinity in sixteenth-century Western societies, these qualities were neither inherently masculine nor feminine among Native groups in the Southeast, making the chiefly office gender neutral. Further, while Native groups in the Southeast were socially stratified, they were not singularly hierarchical but, instead, heterarchical, meaning there were at least two complementary paths to leadership and social prestige based on different, merit-based paths.[26] This means that both men and women (and potentially third-gendered individuals as well) could attain chiefly rank so long as they met the singular universal qualification for holding office: they must be descendants of a socially high-ranking family.[27]

Based on Trocolli's arguments, then, the expectation would be that Native men and women held the office of chief in close to equal proportions, and yet in no part of the Southeast during the 1500s through 1700s that Spanish, English, or French colonists interacted with were women chiefs as abundant, let alone equal to, the number of masculine chiefs.[28] Could this discrepancy result from observer bias, and could feminine chiefs have been more common but generally overlooked by European observers? While feminine chiefs do appear to have been noteworthy from the perspective of at least some chroniclers, it is likely that other Europeans were not so struck, and thus some feminine chiefs went without notice or comment. However, in the Pardo accounts alone, Bandera only notes four feminine chiefs, while he potentially records upward of 120 masculine chiefs.[29] If this sample of chiefs, and the implied gendered ratio, experienced by Bandera and Pardo is representative of other areas and times in the Southeast as well (though we should be wary of this), then Western bias alone seems unable to account for the gendered discrepancy between masculine and feminine chiefs.

Could Native women have possessed less chiefly ambition than their masculine counterparts? In this case, the implication is not that males and females possess inherent behavioral differences resulting from endocrine differences but, instead, that as a social institution, the

Native chiefly office may have been less appealing to women because of social and cultural institutions that made "being chief" less desirable. We would like to suggest that masculine chiefs did outnumber feminine chiefs, despite the gender neutrality of the Native chiefly rank in the Southeast, and that the discrepancy between masculine and feminine actors attaining these offices may be attributed to the expectations and responsibilities inherent in Native gender roles, social constructs that ultimately shaped the behavior of all persons within Native societies.

Gender

Gender is a social, cultural, and historical construct and not a biologically essential category.[30] Gender is a form of social categorization that defines specific roles and responsibilities for social actors. While gender identity indicates how a person self-identifies, gender roles are structural phenomena that create categorized, patterned sets of practices and behaviors that each gendered category is expected to enact. Beginning in the fifteenth century, Western gender roles began permeating other parts of the world through the economic, colonial, and militaristic actions of Western powers. Historically, this resulted in naturalized ideas of gender rooted in Western ideologies. While Western ideas about gender certainly structured colonial entanglements in the sixteenth-century Southeast, and while Western bias allowed colonists to overlook and misunderstand many Indigenous behaviors, practices, and concepts related to gender, we believe there were numerous constructs of gender among southeastern Indigenous groups, and further, that elements of those gendered systems are discernible from the Western ethnohistoric record. In what many consider the most comprehensive ethnohistoric synthesis produced for the Native Southeast, Charles Hudson stated that Native women were primarily responsible for transforming raw food products into meals, a process that began with gathering wild resources and growing domesticated and semidomesticated plants, crafting ceramic tools such as cooking pots and serving ware, and then following a series of steps and practices to ultimately prepare dishes central to their cuisine.[31] While these gendered responsibilities are similar to those attributed to Western women, we do not believe they are the product of Western bias or expectations but instead reflect historical Indigenous gendered responsibilities.[32]

Another consideration impacting chiefly ambition stemming from gender-based differences between Native societies in the Southeast and European societies of the sixteenth century is kinship: Native societies were principally matrilineal and practiced matrilocality, while European societies were principally patrilineal and patriarchal. In the sixteenth-century Carolina Piedmont, matrilineality meant that not only kinship was traced through the mother's lineage but so, too, was corporate control of land and resources.[33] Men married into families, relocating to their wife's town; this meant that the only universal qualification for chiefship, hailing from an elite family, was also primarily traced through the mother's, perhaps even the wife's, lineage.

Based on the prescribed behaviors and practices for Indigenous women as noted, why, then, may they have developed less chiefly ambition compared to masculine counterparts? We propose that the social responsibilities expected from women generally inhibited them from attaining chiefly status as readily as men, stemming from the expectations placed on women to perform domestic duties, including agricultural duties, cooking, food procurement, and child-rearing. Consequently, Indigenous elite women may only have sought chiefly office when they had a sufficient number of close feminine relatives who could help care for their corporate holdings and responsibilities. In other words, domestic and corporate duties came first, then chiefly aspirations.

While this sentiment closely echoes systemic gendered inequalities still in play in the Western world today, there are important distinctions between these conceptions regarding power. Presently, gendered responsibilities, like childcare, eldercare, and domestic care, inhibit many women from attaining the same degree of career success as their masculine colleagues in the Western workforce; however, in sixteenth-century Indigenous southeastern societies, chiefship was just one avenue of power available to Native women in their heterarchical societies and perhaps not the most appealing avenue at that. What if, as a source of power, chiefship at virtually any level was "less powerful" than other avenues available to Native women, such as serving as matriarch or "Beloved Woman," and many of the responsibilities given to women were perceived, both individually and socially, as more important than those performed within the office of chief?[34] This sentiment is echoed by several Indigenous feminist scholars, who justly highlight that within many Native societies throughout North America, feminine actors and activities were valued equally to other gendered individuals and activities, including masculine actors and activities.[35]

In her essential collection of essays on the lived experience of contemporary Native women in North America, Wilma Mankiller highlights how Western feminist movements alienated Native women by calling for the abandonment of cherished gendered activities that were and still are exalted within many Native communities even though they oppress white women in Western circles.[36] While gender was mobilized historically as a systemic category of repression in Western societies to marginalize women and non–gender conformists, gendered categories within many Native societies may have only structured certain labor roles, without commodifying, objectifying, or disenfranchising individuals based on their gender identity or role.[37] In other words, within many Indigenous societies in the Southeast, women's domestic, agricultural, and culinary duties were not performed to socially elevate their husband's or partner's position but, instead, were performed in tandem with their partners and their families to elevate the unit and perhaps even themselves. This point is well illustrated in the creation of Timucua Eve, or the Timucuan version of the Judeo-Christian first woman, Eve. As Alejandra Dubcovsky tells us about why Eve ate the apple, "Timucua Eve 'loved her spouse,' but she did not want 'to serve him' for the rest of her days. She wanted more. She wanted to be a *nia parucusi* (a woman war-chief) and *hachibueno inemi nahiabancheta* (knower of all things)."[38]

Native women occupied complex and important social positions, but these positions were not limited to their societies alone. Within European colonial societies, Native women had unique and all-too-often misrepresented avenues for realizing their own ambitions and manifesting their own emboldened ideas of power.

Native Women and Symbolic Power

As noted, Native women were central to the survival of Spanish outposts and Spaniards themselves throughout their colonial enterprises in the sixteenth-century Southeast. Spanish colonists depended not simply on appropriated maize, chestnuts, bear fat, and other foodstuffs generated by the labor of Native women but even more so on the transformation of that raw material into culinary, or "edible," products like hominy, acorn porridge, and kunuchee.[39] We have very little evidence to suggest that Spanish men cooked, or even knew how to cook, many of the foodstuffs found in the Southeast.[40] For example, the culinary preparation of maize involved tools, skills, and knowledge unfamiliar to Spaniards; unlike European grains, maize must either be nixtamalized, or alkaline treated, to make it a complete dietary staple and to transform it into a dish of hominy or paired one-to-one with a complementary protein source like beans or venison.[41] In other words, it is not enough to simply find eatable plants and animals in a new place; the culinary system in which they are enmeshed many times determines the nutritional value of the dish relative to the corpus of dishes and meals within that system.

This intimate relationship between Native women and the life-sustaining power of food provided them with at least two domains of symbolic power: one vested in them from their own communities based on the roles and responsibilities attached to Native femininity, and the other vested in them by Spaniards based on their dependence on them for food. Bourdieu defined symbolic power as power derived from the domination of artificial, or ideological, structures within and between societies.[42] The source of symbolic power is the conscious acceptance and the deft navigation of a widespread social worldview. Unlike absolute power, symbolic power is conditional based on who is involved, with the basis of social power drawn from the consequences of being compliant with or rejecting that worldview. This can include social acceptance (people like you), popularity (a lot of people like you), dismissal (people ignore you and your opinion), refusal (people reject the right for you to exist), exile (a community forces you to leave), or even death (you are killed for the way you navigated a social system).

The responsibility vested in sixteenth-century Native women to grow, process, and cook most foodstuffs consumed not only within their own societies but also by Spanish garrisons was no small task; not only was the preparation of staple dishes like hominy labor-intensive, but provisioning people outside of their homes on a weekly, if not daily, basis certainly taxed both materials and labor. Did Native women have a choice in this matter? Were Native women throughout the Southeast complicit in the food provisioning of Spanish soldiers? Perhaps these women understood provisioning foreigners simply as a mandatory social duty—women in Mississippian societies were often expected to welcome and feed visitors, and as such, these women may not have even questioned this service.[43] Perhaps this was a matter of pride. In their testimonies, both Teresa Martín and Luisa Menéndez, when asked, noted how plentiful their homelands were, with Martín going as far as to say that hunger is unknown in her land.[44] Indeed, both women also indicate that any visitors to their homelands would receive more than enough to eat. While these comments could be read as a testament to the high agricultural yield of the region, perhaps they are instead boasts regarding the power of Native feminine work. As stated, Native women controlled all aspects of food production, from seed to field to pot, with considerable sovereignty over how their resources were used. If food shortages were expected and hunger known, it would perhaps reflect poorly on them, on their feminine relatives, and on their matrilineages by indicating that they were "not good at being women."[45]

Regardless of their complicity, by preparing food for Spanish soldiers, Native women throughout the Carolina Piedmont gained access, both socially and spatially, to Spaniards and their residences, a proximity that was both opportunistic and dangerous. The uncertain potential of this proximity is perhaps best showcased at Fort San Juan, where Native women, through cooking for Spaniards, gained greater access to coveted trade goods, information, and even potential social relationships, all of which could translate into greater symbolic power within their communities, but where simultaneously there is documentary evidence of potential sexual assault.[46] Archaeological evidence from the Berry Site, home to Fort San Juan and the Native town of Joara, suggests that cooking for Spanish colonists meant cooking *near* them (see the map of identified features and structures of the Spanish compound).[47] Over twenty years of fieldwork and analysis have been conducted at the Berry Site, first in 1986 and in each year since 2001 (except the summer of 2020). The first extended research chapter at the site was dedicated to the exposure and excavation of the Spanish compound associated with Fort San Juan,[48] the presence of which has been confirmed through, among other artifact finds, the recovery of olive jar fragments, fragments of Caparra Blue majolica, wrought iron nails, lead shot and molten lead sprue, and iron rings that might represent mail armor. Several cooking features and refuse pits are located within the identified Fort San Juan domestic compound, which is a set of five structures that housed, fed, and sheltered the Spaniards garrisoned at the fort. Feature 76 is a circular hearth associated with an open-air kitchen space used in the first half of the Spanish occupation.[49] It is important to note that this feature is not located near the compound but *inside it*, near Structures 1 and 3, closely positioning Native women using this cooking area to the Spaniards garrisoned in nearby houses. Later, Structure 5 was dedicated to cooking activities, serving as the compound's kitchen, and like its predecessor Feature 76,

Structure 5 was located inside the Spanish compound, closing the geographic gap between those women working in this kitchen and those men living in the compound.

And yet, despite the close proximity of Structure 5, spatial and architectural features suggest a more private space than the open-air kitchen of Feature 76 (see the map showing the kitchen and trash-disposal area in Berry Site). First, unlike Feature 76, which is in the center of the compound, Structure 5 is on the western edge and off the axis initially established for the first three buildings. Next, while the doorway has yet to be conclusively identified, we believe it was on the southwest corner, facing away from the compound and toward Joara. Finally, it appears two screens were erected around the structure on the northwest and northeast sides, creating partitions that obfuscated the viewshed of the structure from the compound.[50] Previously, we suggested that these partitions may have been erected to block smells wafting from disposal and cooking activities or to direct traffic of the Spaniards at mealtime.[51] However, is it possible these screens were designed to create greater social space between women working in the structure and the Spaniards living in the compound? And if so, why was space needed? Perhaps it was not simply Native women who understood the opportunities available through provisioning Spanish men; perhaps the Spaniards also felt, and were uncomfortable with, the desired closeness between them and Native women, and perhaps some of those garrisoned at Fort San Juan were even threatened by this proximity.

You Are What You Eat. . . .

If the sixteenth-century Spanish men traveling or stationed in the Southeast were fearful of Native women, they had good reason to be. Native women, after all, controlled their food in an otherwise foreign and hostile land. That dependency alone would be enough to cause anxiety. Destroy that relationship, and you can no longer eat. However, it is likely that the anxiety over the control held by Native women ran far deeper than a fear of death from starvation or social isolation; food, from the Spanish perspective, was central to preserving and maintaining the Spanish body and character.[52]

As Rebecca Earle writes, in sixteenth-century Europe, the prevailing theory for understanding the human body was Galenic humoralism, which held that the body was composed of both a complexion a person was born with and humors that were in constant flux creating

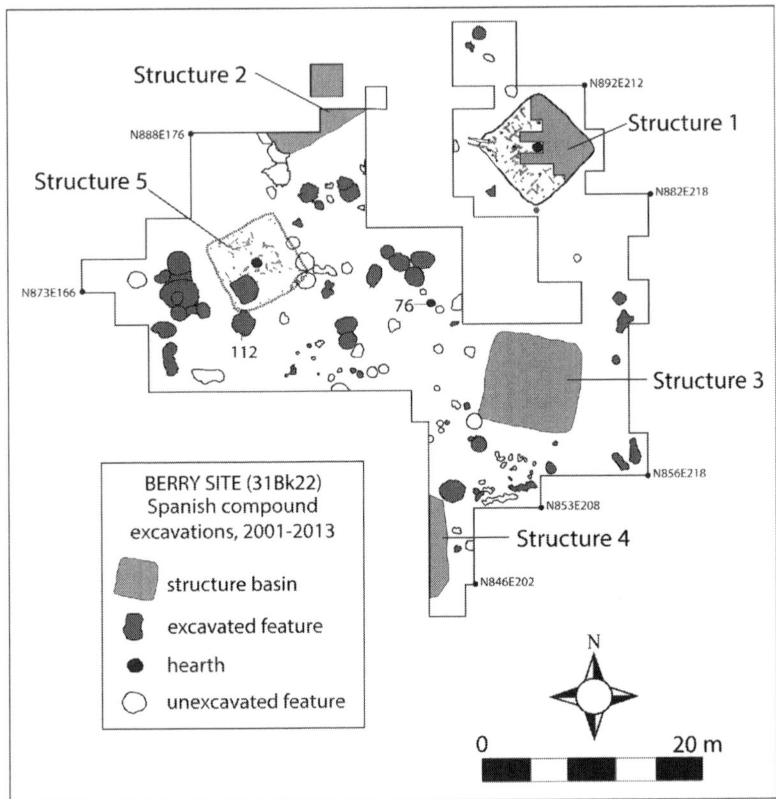

Map of identified features and structures of the Spanish compound at Fort San Juan, located at the Berry Site (31BK22) (Map by chapter authors)

real, but impermanent, differences between groups of people. There were six nonnatural factors that were thought to impact a person's humors: exercise, sleep, evacuation (menstruation and bowel movements), emotions, climate, and food, though climate and food were considered the most transformative.[53] To be European, then, was not a permanent state based on where a person was born or solely on one's lineage but instead a state that needed to be maintained. And to be Spanish meant one must live in a Spanish climate and act in a Spanish manner, with the most important manner being the consumption of Spanish foods. To be Spanish was to eat a meal that frequently began with a salad followed by wheat bread with olive oil, fresh lamb (or chicken or beef), and red wine (consumed in moderation), all foods

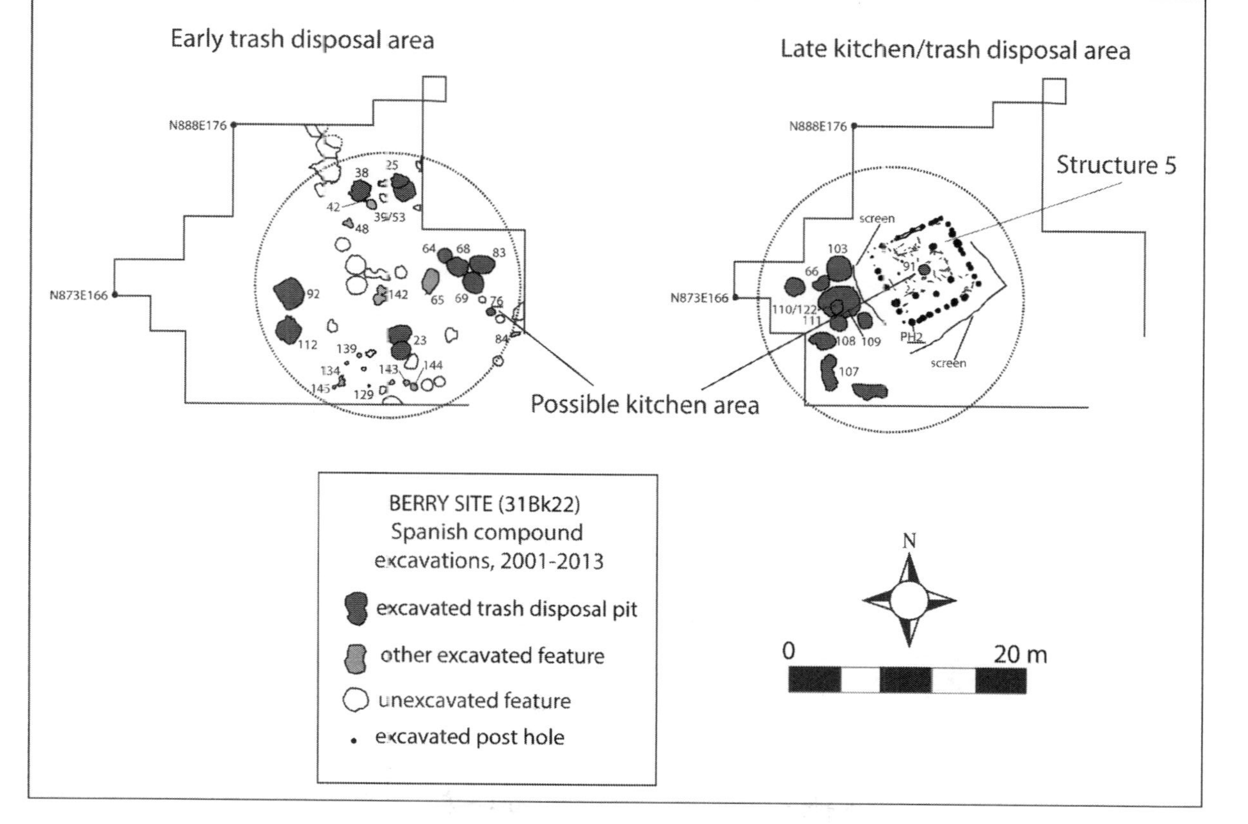

The early open-air kitchen (Feature 76) and trash disposal area (left) versus the later enclosed kitchen area and obscured trash disposal area (right). A piece of jack plate iron was recovered from PH2, a posthole near the possible entrance of Structure 5. (Map by chapter authors)

that were largely unavailable in North America during the sixteenth century.[54] If the climate a Spaniard lived in changed, and if the foods the Spaniard ate also changed, then it followed that the Spaniard would change. At the mildest, the Spaniard might become sick and suffer from stomach ailments; at the most severe, not only was death a possibility (e.g., Christopher Columbus believed that *La Navidad* on Hispaniola failed because of the disagreeable climate and unfamiliar foods eaten by the colonists[55]), but the body itself would fundamentally change. Skin might become darker, stature taller, hair straighter, and the beard, the quintessential Spanish masculine signature, might fall out.[56] In other words, the Spaniard might become Native.

While climate was not a force European powers could control in their colonies, they could control what their colonists ate, or at least they could try. Consequently, one of the long-term efforts by Spanish colonists, as with other European colonial enterprises in the Americas, was to grow, cook, and have colonists consume European foods. This need was recognized early, mandating a secondary, but important, goal of all Spanish *entradas*: to introduce Iberian foods to the Western Hemisphere. Watermelons, peaches, cowpeas, and pigs were some of the first Iberian foods introduced to the Southeast, though only the first three products were incorporated into Native cuisines;[57] pigs, conversely, were resisted as a food source by numerous Native groups into the late eighteenth century, serving as an edible metaphor of Western colonialism.[58] Either through active encouragement or through natural adaptation, each food item proliferated in the Southeast, helping terraform the area to suit more "Spanish tastes."

Food security based on a diet of Iberian foods was one of the goals at each of the forts Pardo established, including Fort San Juan.[59] However, this goal was never realized, and for their brief existence, we have every reason to believe that soldiers garrisoned in the interior ate Native foods prepared by Native women. From the Spanish perspective, then, Native women were both essential for survival and were also constantly jeopardizing it by cooking and serving Native foods.

Food and Sex

If their power over food (and thus over Spanish bodies) was not threatening enough, through provisioning Spaniards, Native women gained access to various kinds of potential relationships, both consensual and otherwise. And unlike their European counterparts, Native women had the option to socialize with, and thus form various relationships with, whomever they chose. Further, from the Spanish perspective, Native women behaved in ways very different from the ways Spanish women behaved. Today, we understand these behaviors as manifestations of different social and cultural constructions of gender roles. In sixteenth-century Spain, however, all females were understood to embody femininity, and to be feminine was to be weak, soft, gullible, frail, and emotional but also manipulative and sinful. Some critics challenged this perception of women outright, suggesting that European women complemented and brought out the best in European men.[60] This somewhat kinder view, however, did not extend to Native women. From the Spanish gaze, Native women were feminine, but unlike their Spanish counterparts, they were also considered wild and unrestrained. All women were sexual creatures, but Native women, unlike Spanish women, were not seen as knowing how to control their impulses. This understanding of behavioral differences between the sexes, and between groups of people, had profound legal and social consequences including permitting sexual violence against Native women, a horrific but prevalent practice throughout the history of European colonialism and imperialism.[61]

Underwriting this misguided and misogynistic view, though, are important differences in the construction and practice of Spanish and Native gender roles. Again referencing Charles Hudson's ethnohistoric research, Native women had more control than their European counterparts over deciding with whom they had sexual and nuptial relationships, as well as with whom their partners had relations. Marriage was a familial negotiation that took place between the mothers and sisters of the intended parties, but a woman's consent was necessary for the arrangement to proceed. Upon marrying, a woman could dissolve her union if it proved unsatisfactory; further, she had the power to permit or deny her husband a second wife or even a more casual sexual relationship with another partner. Importantly, sex was not confined to nor began with marriage; sex before marriage was normal, and though adultery was discouraged, it was also common.[62]

Whether Native women exercised their sexual rights with Spanish soldiers in the sixteenth century is debatable. Our primary evidence for exploring this form of symbolic power comes from the Spanish records, which were written by men who were indoctrinated with Western ideas of gender, sex, and personal liberties. Complicating matters further, archaeologically, consent is difficult to identify. And yet there do seem to be indications that the Spanish soldiers at Fort San Juan were anxious, if not fearful, of the actions of Native women. Take the following command from Pardo at the town of Guatari, which Pardo issued to the men he had stationed at Fort Santiago, which was established one month after Fort San Juan was built at Joara. At Fort Santiago, he instructed the corporal in charge that "no one should dare bring any woman into the fort at night and that he should not depart from the command under the pain of being severely punished."[63] We do not know who Pardo was trying to protect in this statement—the women of Guatari or the Spaniards posted there. While it may seem strange that Pardo would feel the need to protect his men from the women of Guatari, consider the potential symbolic power that they possessed. Further, Teresa Martín's testimony contains indications that the Spaniards at Fort San Juan had "caused disorders" with Native women, a social transgression that—while seen as minor in sixteenth-century Spain if committed against a low-class Spanish woman and potentially permissible if committed against a non-Christian—was likely not tolerated by Native societies in the Southeast, where women had a higher degree of sovereignty over their fields, foods, and bodies.

While the intention of the above statements is ambiguous, what is less ambiguous is a sizable piece of jack plate iron recovered from a posthole in Structure 5 at Fort San Juan.

Fear the Native Woman

During the construction of Structure 5 in the Spanish compound, someone placed a piece of jack plate iron, originally part of a Spanish plate of armor, into the fill surrounding a wall post (see PH2, labeled in the map showing the kitchen and trash-disposal area in Berry Site).[64] This piece of iron served no functional purpose. The dimensions and position of this piece and its likely value suggest it was not used to shim the post nor that it simply fell in on accident. Who planted it? Based on the construction techniques evident, we believe this structure was built almost entirely by Spaniards with little to no help from the Joaran people, suggesting that a Spanish soldier planted this piece of iron in this posthole. Why did he do so? Robin Beck suggests the iron was intentionally included in the post fill as an apotropaic device, or one used to ward off magic.[65] Whose magic, then, was he afraid of? It would appear it was the magical capabilities of Native women he was hoping to repel.

Though considered more a superstition than a reality, myths of witchcraft were widespread throughout sixteenth-century Europe and their colonies. Women were believed to be the principal agents engaging in this craft, and Native women were strongly suspected of knowing and practicing magic.[66] Based on Spanish folk knowledge at the time, by placing the piece of jack plate iron in the posthole, it appears this soldier was hoping to prevent the women who would work and perhaps live in Structure 5 from practicing their magical craft.

And who exactly were these women working and perhaps living in Structure 5? We believe they were not local, Joaran women who had engaged with the Spaniards for the first part of their occupation at Fort San Juan. After being threatened by a chief, probably from a Chisca village in northeastern Tennessee, Sergeant Hernando Moyano led a contingent of twenty Spanish soldiers and an unknown number of Joaran warriors to attack the village.[67] During these attacks, a number of women were taken by Moyano and brought back to Joara.[68] Eight were enslaved and taken to Santa Elena, where they were freed that same year.[69] Others probably stayed at Fort San Juan, living and working in and around Structure 5. Whether they remained voluntarily or by force is unclear. As evidenced by the escape of the feminine chief Tali Mico, Spanish "imprisonment" was not as absolute in the sixteenth-century Southeast, where they often lacked the materials, might, and institutions to fully imprison or enslave Native peoples against their will for very long.[70]

Supporting evidence for the proposal that non-Joaran women used and potentially lived in Structure 5 comes from Feature 112, located just outside the southwestern corner of the building (see the map showing the kitchen and trash-disposal area in Berry Site). Feature 112 is a circular pit nearly two meters in diameter and eighty centimeters deep (See top photo on page 112). It was unusual both for its extraordinary quantity of hickory nuts and for its unique assemblage of Pisgah pottery, a style of pottery typical of the Pisgah phase located in the Appalachian Summit to the west and northwest of Joara.[71] Sherds from at least eight Pisgah-series cooking jars were recovered from Feature 112, comprising 36.8 percent of the feature's ceramic assemblage; compare this to the overall Berry Site ceramic assemblage that is attributable principally to the Burke series and Burke phase, with less than 1 percent of pottery attributable to the Pisgah phase (See bottom photo on page 112).[72] Because those villages attacked by Sergeant Moyano were likely to have been Pisgah-phase sites, and because he traversed areas of Pisgah-phase settlements between

Photo of south half of Feature 112 removed, with north profile facing south (Photo by chapter authors)

Burke phase ceramics (a and b) typical of the Berry Site, and two Pisgah-series jars recovered from Feature 112 (c and d) (Photo by chapter authors)

Joara and Chiaha, we therefore interpret the Pisgah pottery from Feature 112 as an indication of the presence of women from those areas in the mountains in the Spanish domestic compound at the Berry Site.[73]

Whether enslaved or not, what is clear is that these women were a source of anxiety for at least one very troubled Spaniard, as evidenced by the jack plate iron, but if the screens around the northeast and northwest portions of the structure and the distance of the structure from the rest of the compound are any indication, he was not alone (see the map showing the kitchen and trash-disposal area in Berry Site). Likely the reliance on nonlocal Native women was intended to relieve some of the anxiety around the growing dependence on Joaran women that the Spanish occupation was fostering; likely there was hope that new women would learn to prepare Spanish foods and perhaps even behave more like Spanish women. Despite these hopes, something was amiss, and relations between Fort San Juan and the Native groups within the area quickly deteriorated.

While the razed compound and fort are clear indications of this, one less apparent but potential signature for this deterioration comes again from Feature 112. The eight Pisgah jars mentioned above conform to our expectations for Pisgah-style jars in almost all ways—they have filleted rims with notched or punctated patterns and their bodies are rectilinear complicated stamped. However, while Pisgah jars were commonly grit tempered, the Pisgah vessels recovered from Feature 112 are soapstone tempered, a tradition that not only was practiced by the women at Joara but also necessitates acquiring a nonlocal resource, soapstone. We do not know why these jars were produced in the manner that they were, but the use of soapstone as temper suggests that these nonlocal women may have joined local potting communities, networking with and perhaps learning to soapstone temper from Joaran women in sustained, meaningful interactions.[74] If so, this suggests that any effort to isolate or control these nonlocal women on the part of the Spaniards, and perhaps to create real distance between the domestic compound and the people of Joara, was not very successful. Through their denial of the social system that fostered the symbolic power vested in Native women, and their attempts to disempower it, they may have committed unforgivable social transgressions, the answer to which was erasure.

The Face of the Hand That Feeds . . .

With the arrival of the Pardo expeditions in the mid-sixteenth-century Carolina Piedmont, the symbolic power of Native women came into sharp focus for the Spanish Empire—Native women were essential to any Spanish colonial endeavor, but their involvement through food preparation was dangerous. Native women were granted unprecedented access to the Spaniards stationed at Fort San Juan, access that may have not only led to the exchange of goods and the formation of close relationships but also permitted them access, in turn, to information, all of which they had the power to use for their own social purposes. While feeding the Spanish was clearly a burden, it was also an opportunity, and an opportunity the Spanish were likely anxious about. Were the women of Joara overburdened by and disappointed in the Spanish before the latter's raids on Chisca villages in 1567? Were the women of Joara offended, perhaps even shocked, when Moyano returned from the mountains with enslaved women who would work and potentially live in the Spanish compound? Were they tired of the transgressions, both social and sexual, that Spanish men took from them?[75] While we do not have the answers to these questions, we do know that Native women in the Carolina Piedmont exhibited a considerable range of influence and power, from chiefly to political to social, that has previously been unaccounted for in the course of Spanish colonial entanglements in La Florida. Further, we do know that at least some Spaniards stationed at Fort San Juan experienced real anxieties and fears toward Native women, as evidenced by the piece of jack plate iron placed in one of the postholes in Structure 5. We also know that Native women were in sustained contact with Spaniards during this time owing to the labor and practice of food preparation, as attested to by the cooking features in the Spanish compound at Fort San Juan. Finally, we know that all three documented survivors of the attacks on Pardo's Spanish forts were married to Native women. Native women controlled life, both biologically and metaphorically, and that power was potent and tangible not only within their own communities but among Spanish colonists as well.

This dependency defined not only Spanish colonial entanglements but also Western colonial entanglements more broadly. From the first moments that Europeans set foot in the Western Hemisphere, their survival was dependent on the knowledge, skills, and labor of Indigenous women. Yet providing the nutrients their bodies needed was not enough—being European was a perpetual performance that played out with every meal. While the gravity of this performance may have been most crucial in nascent or borderland Spanish missions, even after a Spanish or Western worldview was made manifest in the Western Hemisphere through the radical transformation of the social and natural landscape, the negotiation continued. And throughout this time, the brokers of this negotiation were Indigenous women.

Many histories end there, but it is important that they continue—as necessary intermediaries with potentially immense social power,

Indigenous women in the Carolina Piedmont, in the Southeast, and in almost every colonial entanglement throughout New Spain and the Western colonial world were not simply supplying food or filling a labor need within a Western world system but were acting according to their own, non-Western ideologies which, in many instances, made them powerful actors. Indigenous women were just that—*Indigenous* women. And though they may have gained entry to European residences, compounds, and even fortifications because they were needed to fulfill European ideals of femininity, they acted according to their own social and individual constructions of femininity. For this reason, it is imperative that we consider the powerful relationship between Indigenous women, power, and food in colonial entanglements. At the very least, Indigenous women made Spanish men anxious. Indigenous women also, at the least, resisted. But, likely, Indigenous women were also feared, emboldened by their own ideas of feminine, and human, potential. And while their actions may not have toppled an empire in the Western construction of history, they undoubtedly shaped the unraveling of colonial entanglements in ways too often ignored.

Notes

1. Robin A. Beck, Christopher B. Rodning, and David G. Moore, eds., *Fort San Juan and the Limits of Empire: Colonialism and Household Practice at the Berry Site* (Gainesville: University Press of Florida, 2016); Kathleen Deagan, *Spanish St. Augustine: The Archaeology of a Colonial Creole Community* (Cambridge: Academic Press, 1983); Charles Hudson, *The Juan Pardo Expeditions: Explorations of the Carolinas and Tennessee, 1566–1568*, rev. ed. (Tuscaloosa: University of Alabama Press, 2005), 14; John Worth, "Recollections of the Juan Pardo Expeditions: The 1584 Domingo de León Account," in Beck et al., *Fort San Juan and the Limits of Empire*, 58–80.

2. See the Ribas's testimony in this volume. Hudson, *Juan Pardo Expeditions*, 23.

3. Brooke Bauer, *Becoming Catawba: Catawba Indian Women and Nation-Building, 1540–1840* (Tuscaloosa: University of Alabama Press, 2022); Kathleen A. Deagan, "Mestizaje in Colonial St. Augustine," *Ethnohistory* 20, no. 1 (1973): 55–65; Mary Van Buren, "The Archaeological Study of Spanish Colonialism in the Americas," *Journal of Archaeological Research* 18 (2018): 115–201; Christopher B. Rodning, "Mortuary Ritual and Gender Ideology in Protohistoric Southwestern North Carolina," in *Archaeological Studies of Gender in the Southeastern United States*, ed. Jane M. Eastman and Christopher B. Rodning (Gainesville: University Press of Florida, 2001), 77–100; Ruth Trocolli, "Elite Status and Gender: Women Leaders in Chiefdom Societies of the Southeastern U.S." (PhD diss., University of Florida, Gainesville, 2006); Barbara Voss, "Gender, Race, and Labor in the Archaeology of the Spanish Colonial Americas," *Current Anthropology* 49, no. 5 (2008): 861–93.

4. Christina Snyder, "The Lady of Cofitachequi," in *South Carolina Women*, vol. 1, ed. Marjorie J. Spruill, Valinda W. Littlefield, and Joan Marie Johnson (Athens: University of Georgia Press, 2009), 11–25.

5. Hudson, *Juan Pardo Expeditions*; see Alejandra Dubcovsky, *Talking Back: Native Women and the Making of the Early South* (New Haven, CT: Yale University Press, 2023), 1–12.

6. Kent Lightfoot, *Indians, Missionaries, and Merchants: The Legacy of Colonial Encounters on the California Frontiers* (Berkeley: University of California Press, 2005); see also Van Buren, "Archaeological Study of Spanish Colonialism in the Americas."

7. Ruth Behar, "Sexual Witchcraft, Colonialism, and Women's Powers: Views from the Mexican Inquisition," in *Sexuality and Marriage in Colonial Spanish America*, ed. Asunción Lavrin (Lincoln: University of Nebraska Press, 1997), 178–206; Rachel V. Briggs et al., "Fear the Native Woman: Femininity, Food, and Power in the Sixteenth-Century North Carolina Piedmont," *American Anthropologist* 126 (2024): 32–46.

8. Native communities in the Southeast have been called "heterarchical" because of the dual, complementary paths for social achievement available to both men and women (and perhaps third genders as well). For a discussion of heterarchy, see Carole Crumley, "Heterarchy and the Analysis of Complex Societies," in *Heterarchy and the Analysis of Complex Societies*, ed. Robert M. Ehrenreich, Carole L. Crumley, and Janet E. Levy (Arlington, VA: American Anthropological Association, 1995), 1–5. For a discussion of the social power of Native women in colonial contact situations, see Trocolli, "Elite Status and Gender"; and Voss, "Gender, Race, and Labor," 861–93.

9. Anna Brickhouse defines "unsettling" as the literal ways of destroying or thwarting the European settlement of America by Indigenous groups, as well as the active attempts to discourage European settlement. See Anna Brickhouse, "Mistranslation, Unsettlement, La Navidad," *Publications of the Modern Language Association of America* 128, no. 4 (2013): 938–46.

10. While we have long thought Teresa Martín was from the town of Joara (see Hudson, *Juan Pardo Expeditions*, 176), the translations of Teresa Martín's testimony in this volume encourage us to reconsider possibilities that she may have originally come from other areas traversed by members of the Pardo expeditions, even if she spent some time in Joara or in the Spanish colonial town of Cuenca. See note 47 (page 85) of the testimonial translations in this volume.

11. See Beck et al., *Fort San Juan and the Limits of Empire*, 15–16; Hudson, *Juan Pardo Expeditions*, 176.

12. Robin A. Beck, *Chiefdoms, Collapse, and Coalescence in the Early American South* (Cambridge: Cambridge University Press, 2013); Chester B. DePratter and Marvin T. Smith, "Sixteenth Century European Trade in the Southeastern United States: Evidence from the Juan Pardo Expeditions (1566–1568)," in *Spanish Colonial Frontier Research*, ed. Henry F. Dobyns (Albuquerque: Center for the Anthropological Studies, University of New Mexico, 1980), 67–77; Charles Hudson, *Knights of Spain, Warriors of the Sun: Hernando de Soto and the South's Ancient Chiefdoms*,

rev. paperback ed. (Athens: University of Georgia Press, 2017); Charles Hudson et al., "On Interpreting Cofitachequi," *Ethnohistory* 55, no. 3 (2008): 465–90; Janet E. Levy, J. Alan May, and David Moore, "From Ysa to Joara: Cultural Diversity in the Catawba Valley from the Fourteenth to the Sixteenth Century," in *Columbian Consequences, Volume 2: Archaeological and Historical Perspectives on the Spanish Borderlands East*, ed. David Hurst Thomas (Washington, DC: Smithsonian Institution Press, 1990), 153–68; Kathryn Sampeck, Jonathan Thayn, and Howard H. Earnest Jr., "Geographic Information System Modeling of de Soto's Route from Joara to Chiaha: Archaeology and Anthropology of Southeastern Road Networks in the Sixteenth Century," *American Antiquity* 80, no. 1 (2005):46–66; see also Hudson, *Juan Pardo Expeditions*.

13. Trocolli, "Elite Status and Gender."

14. Robin A. Beck and David G. Moore, "The Burke Phase: A Mississippian Frontier in the North Carolina Foothills," *Southeastern Archaeology* 21, no. 2 (2002): 192–205; Robin A. Beck, David G. Moore, and Christopher B. Rodning, "Identifying Fort San Juan: A Sixteenth-Century Spanish Occupation at the Berry Site, North Carolina," *Southeastern Archaeology* 25, no. 1 (2006): 65–77; Robin A. Beck, Christopher B. Rodning, and David G. Moore, "Limiting Resistance: Juan Pardo and the Shrinking of Spanish *La Florida*, 1566–1568," in *Enduring Conquests: Rethinking the Archaeology of Resistance to Spanish Colonialism in the Americas*, ed. Matthew Liebmann and Melissa S. Murphy (Santa Fe, NM: School for Advanced Research Press, 2011), 19–39; Robin A. Beck et al., "The Politics of Provisioning: Food and Gender at Fort San Juan de Joara, 1566–1568," *American Antiquity* 81 no. 1 (2016): 3–26; David G. Moore, Robin A. Beck, and Christopher B. Rodning, "Pardo, Joara, and Fort San Juan Revisited," in *The Juan Pardo Expeditions: Explorations of the Carolinas and Tennessee, 1566–1568 (Revised Edition)*, ed. Charles M. Hudson (Tuscaloosa: University of Alabama Press, 2005), 343–49; David G. Moore, Christopher B. Rodning, and Robin A. Beck, "Native Material Culture from the Spanish Compound," in Beck et al., *Fort San Juan and the Limits of Empire*, 341–67; David G. Moore, Christopher B. Rodning, and Robin A. Beck, "Joara, Cuenca, and Fort San Juan: The Construction of Colonial Identities at the Berry Site," in *Forging Southeastern Identities: Social Archaeology, Ethnohistory, and Folklore of the Mississippian to Early Historic South*, ed. Gregory A. Waselkov and Marvin T. Smith (Tuscaloosa: University of Alabama Press, 2017), 99–116. See also Beck et al., *Fort San Juan and the Limits of Empire*.

15. Pierre Bourdieu, "Symbolic Power," *Critique of Anthropology* 4, no. 13–14 (1979): 77–85.

16. Rebecca Earle, *The Body of the Conquistador: Food, Race, and the Colonial Experience in Spanish America, 1492–1700* (Cambridge: Cambridge University Press, 2012).

17. Beck et al., *Fort San Juan and the Limits of Empire*, 5–6; Hudson, *Juan Pardo Expeditions*, 14.

18. Beck et al., *Fort San Juan and the Limits of Empire*, 8.

19. Hudson, *Juan Pardo Expeditions*, 23–46.

20. Ibid., 176; See also Christopher B. Rodning et al., "Women and Power at Joara, Cuenca, and Fort San Juan," in *Mississippian Women*, ed. Rachel V. Briggs, Michaelyn S. Harle, and Lynne P. Sullivan (Gainesville: University Press of Florida, 2024), 247–71; Worth, "Recollections of the Juan Pardo Expeditions."

21. Hudson, *Juan Pardo Expeditions*, 176; see Teresa Martín's testimony in this manuscript, and note 49 on page 85.

22. Beck et al., *Fort San Juan and the Limits of Empire*.

23. Beck, *Chiefdoms, Collapse, and Coalescence*, 25–34.

24. Hudson, *Juan Pardo Expeditions*, 63; Trocolli, "Elite Status and Gender," 127.

25. Trocolli, "Elite Status and Gender," 195. See also Elizabeth Coonrad Martínez's chapter, this volume.

26. Crumley, "Heterarchy and the Analysis of Complex Societies."

27. Trocolli, "Elite Status and Gender," 189–94.

28. Ibid., 183.

29. Hudson, *Juan Pardo Expeditions*, 62.

30. Cordelia Fine, *Testosterone Rex: Myths of Sex, Science, and Society* (New York: W.W. Norton, 2017).

31. Charles Hudson, *The Southeastern Indians* (Knoxville: University of Tennessee Press, 1976).

32. Ibid., 260–67; see also Bauer, *Becoming Catawba*, 11; Theda Perdue, *Cherokee Women* (Lincoln: University of Nebraska Press, 1998).

33. Bauer, *Becoming Catawba*, 50–51; Hudson, *Southeastern Indians*.

34. "Beloved woman" refers to a broad class of women in Southeastern Indian groups who distinguished themselves in various ways and earned social respect and recognition within their communities. Some were previous leaders, and others served as counselors. See Hudson, *Southeastern Indians*, 186–87.

35. Paula Gunn Allen, *The Sacred Hoop: Recovering the Feminine in American Indian Traditions* (New York: Open Road Integrated Media, 1992); Wilma Mankiller, *Every Day Is a Good Day: Reflections by Contemporary Indigenous Women* (Golden, CO: Fulcrum Publishing, 2001), 95–96; Sarah Nickel and Amanda Fehr, eds., *In Good Relations: History, Gender, and Kinship in Indigenous Feminisms* (Winnepeg: University of Manitoba Press, 2020); see also Bauer, *Becoming Catawba*.

36. Mankiller, *Every Day Is a Good Day*.

37. Jodi A. Byrd, "What's Normative Got to Do with It? Toward Indigenous Queer Relationality," *Social Text* 38, no. 4 (2020): 105–23; See also Allen, *Sacred Hoop*; Trocolli, "Elite Status and Gender"; Voss, "Gender, Race, and Labor."

38. Dubcovsky, *Talking Back*, 3.

39. For Spanish provisioning, see Beck et al., *Fort San Juan and the Limits of Empire*; Beck et al., "Politics of Provisioning"; Hudson, *Juan Pardo Expeditions*; Rodning et al., "Women and Power." For a discussion of the transformation of raw foods into culinary products by Native women, for hominy see Rachel V. Briggs, "The Hominy Foodway of the Historic Native Eastern Woodlands," *Native South* 8, no. 1 (2015): 112–14; Rachel V. Briggs, "Cooks, Cooking, and Cooking Pots: A Landscape of Culinary Practice and the Origins of Moundville, AD 1070–1200,"

in *Mississippian Women*, ed. Rachel V. Briggs, Michaelyn S. Harle, and Lynne P. Sullivan (Gainesville: University Press of Florida, 2024); for acorn porridge, see Rachel V. Briggs, "The Civil Cooking Pot: Hominy and the Mississippian Standard Jar in the Black Warrior River Valley, Alabama," *American Antiquity* 81, no. 2 (2016): 316–32; and for kunuchee, see Gayle J. Fritz, "People, Plants, and Early Frontier Food," in Beck et al., *Fort San Juan and the Limits of Empire*, 237–70.

40. Beck et al., "Politics of Provisioning"; Beck et al., *Fort San Juan and the Limits of Empire*; Deagan, *Spanish St. Augustine*.

41. Rachel V. Briggs, "Detangling Histories of Hominy: A Historical Anthropological Approach," in *Baking, Bourbon, and Black Drink: Foodways Archaeology in the American Southeast*, ed. Tanya Peres and Aaron Deter-Wolf (Tuscaloosa: University of Alabama Press, 2018), 160–74; see also Briggs, "Hominy Foodway."

42. Pierre Bourdieu, "Social Space and Symbolic Power," *Sociological Theory* 7, no. 11 (1989): 14–25.

43. Briggs, "Hominy Foodway."

44. See both Teresa Martín's and Luisa Menéndez's testimonies in this volume. Both women bring up food twice.

45. Indeed, these comments may have a second, complementary intention as well—to indicate that in 1600 in the colony of St. Augustine, Spanish and other Indigenous women were "not good at being women," because they were unable to sufficiently provide for the colony.

46. Hudson, *Juan Pardo Expeditions*, 186; see Teresa Martín's testimony.

47. Beck et al., "Politics of Provisioning"; Beck et al., *Fort San Juan and the Limits of Empire*.

48. Beck et al., "Politics of Provisioning"; Beck et al., *Fort San Juan and the Limits of Empire*.

49. Beck et al., "Politics of Provisioning"; Beck et al., *Fort San Juan and the Limits of Empire*, 20–21.

50. Abra Johgart, "Native American and Spanish Ancillary Structures: An Analysis of Postholes at the Berry Site" (Unpublished BA thesis, Warren Wilson College, Swannanoa, NC, 2011).

51. Beck et al., "Politics of Provisioning"; Beck et al., *Fort San Juan and the Limits of Empire*; Johgart, "Native American and Spanish Ancillary Structures."

52. Earle, *Body of the Conquistador*.

53. Ibid., 26–27.

54. Ibid., 55.

55. Ibid., 1.

56. Ibid., 24–25.

57. Kristen J. Gremillion, "Adoption of Old World Crops and Processes of Cultural Change in the Historic Southeast," *Southeastern Archaeology* 12, no. 1 (1993): 15–20.

58. Rachel V. Briggs and Heather G. Lapham, "Edible Metaphors of Bear and Pig in the Native Eastern Woodlands" (presentation, 88th Annual Society for American Archaeology Conference, Portland, OR, March 29–April 2, 2023).

59. Hudson, *Juan Pardo Expeditions*; Beck et al., *Fort San Juan and the Limits of Empire*.

60. Theresa Ann Smith, *The Emerging Female Citizen: Gender and Enlightenment Spain* (Berkeley: University of California Press, 2006), 19.

61. Ibid.

62. Hudson, *Southeastern Indians*, 197–99.

63. Hudson, *Juan Pardo Expeditions*, 285.

64. Robin A. Beck, "The Iron in the Posthole: Witchcraft, Women's Labor, and Spanish Folk Ritual at the Berry Site," *American Anthropologist* 118, no. 3 (2016): 525–40.

65. Ibid.

66. Ibid.; Behar, "Sexual Witchcraft."

67. Hudson, *Juan Pardo Expeditions*, 27–29.

68. While we do not know for certain, it is possible that Luisa Menéndez was among those taken captive. Further, if Teresa Martín was not from the village of Joara, then she, too, may have been among these captive women. As such, there is a possibility that both women may have worked and lived in Structure 5 and may have even used and/or made the Pisgah jars represented in figure 5.

69. Hudson, *Juan Pardo Expeditions*, 28; see note 19, p. 197.

70. Snyder, "Lady of Cofitachequi."

71. Roy S. Dickens Jr., *Cherokee Prehistory: The Pisgah Phase in the Appalachian Summit Region* (Knoxville: University of Tennessee Press, 1976); Bennie C. Keel, *Cherokee Archaeology: A Study of the Appalachian Summit* (Knoxville: University of Tennessee Press, 1976); Trawick H. Ward and R. P. Stephen Davis Jr., *Time before History: The Archaeology of North Carolina* (Chapel Hill: University of North Carolina Press, 1999); Thomas R. Whyte, "Household Ceramic Diversity in the Late Prehistory of the Appalachian Summit," *Southeastern Archaeology* 36 no. 2 (2019): 156–64.

72. Beck and Moore, "Burke Phase"; Moore et al., "Native Material Culture," 359–60.

73. Beck et al., *Fort San Juan and the Limits of Empire*; Moore et al., "Native Material Culture."

74. John Worth, "What's in a Phase? Disentangling Communities of Practice from Communities of Identity in Southeastern North America," in *Forging Southeastern Identities: Social Archaeology, Ethnohistory, and Folklore of the Mississippian to Early Historic Souths*, ed. Gregory A. Waselkov and Marvin T. Smith (Tuscaloosa: University of Alabama Press, 2017), 117–56.

75. Hudson, *Juan Pardo Expeditions*, 176.

3

How Indigenous Women Created History in La Florida, 1600

Miriam Melton-Villanueva

Sixteenth-century documents survive from what is now included in the southeastern United States, mostly in Spanish. It is well known that friars wrote and archived most of the surviving written materials from this time. They preserved records they considered important, like journals of important men, letters to the king, and letters between high-ranking clerics. While those types of official records filled colonial archives, it is important to recognize that they represent the point of view of colonial power. In those records, women are generally ignored, as if women did not contribute to the creation of the colonies. But the La Tama document is different; it records the words of Indigenous women.

What Kind of Record Is the "Account of La Tama"?

This chapter engages the question of who included two Indigenous women, Teresa Martín and Luisa Menéndez, in this investigation of La Tama, and why these women gave their testimonies to what happened. The short answer lies in the kind of document at which we are looking and the nature of notarial records such as the "Relación." In general, notaries wrote documents for everyone, not just for the king or other cultural elites. What makes this particular "Relación," or "Account," special is that it appears to contain a broader sample of people and more details about daily life than would normally have been included in a response to the letter written by the king to the captain general of La Florida asking for the investigation.

Juan Jiménez was not a witness, so you might not even notice his name—it only appears at the bottom of the testimonies and at the very end of the whole report. Our document about the Indigenous region of La Tama named a diverse set of witnesses. However, Juan Jiménez is central to the story of the investigation. Juan Jiménez was the notary, the writer that took down everyone's testimony for the governing captain general. Jiménez signed his name at the end of the report, using ink on paper, writing everything by hand. Notice he spells his name with a J or an X interchangeably—spelling had not yet been standardized, so it might look funny to us, but back then both were correct. He was licensed to certify the accuracy of the record. The captain general of La Florida, Gonzalo Méndez de Canzo, led the investigation, so he made the interviews happen by the power and command of the king of Spain. But it was Jiménez who wrote down every word and even the last word. The first signature at the end of the document reads "G. Mendes de Canzo," the name of the captain general producing the investigation. Below the cross, the final signature is that of Juan Jiménez, the *escribano público* or notary public.

Centering Jiménez and his work as notary allows us to enter into the document itself with a critical eye and a better understanding of who he is. Jiménez reveals to us some of his process, allowing us to see him as an otherwise unseen writer, expert in documenting other people's ideas. In this line of work, he emerges as an interstitial figure, along with the people whose interviews he records; working in between differing cultures of status and literacy. "He stands as an intermediary between" those interviewed "and the broader historical record,"[1] allowing their words to be preserved and used to write a history of the United States that includes the voices of everyday people, not just kings, bishops, and governors.

How Historians Find Less Documented Voices

As an ethnohistorian, my favorite genre of documents is notarial records because notaries often recorded details that church or royal documents did not. Chronicles, official correspondence, and legal code were the official records historians once exclusively relied on to craft history. They are official, so they were also accessible (originals kept in archives and maintained). They are also easy to interpret because they were generated by the bureaucracy of a familiar, dominant culture; written in a common tongue about a colonial culture with which we are familiar. Conversely, notarial records remain less accessible and less understood.

However, writing history based solely on "easier to find and use" official documents today would be like interpreting school rules against using your phone to mean that no students ever used their phones at school. Social historians realized, *Hey, the laws we are using to describe historical events might actually be getting broken—on a regular basis.* This idea allowed historians to question claims by officials in their letters and laws. One way to do that is to think in terms of *prescriptive* versus *descriptive* language. The Spanish Royal Edicto XV of 1770 ruled that "only Castilian be spoken" in the Americas "as has been ordered by repeated laws, Royal decrees, and orders."[2] That edict prescribed a behavior (like a pharmacist might prescribe medicine) that was in large part wishful thinking about plans to eliminate Indigenous languages, because it did not describe what was actually happening on the ground, in practice. This means that even something considered as "neutral" as a law might actually be trying to prescribe how those in power want us to behave (no speaking in Nahuatl) but may not describe what we actually do (i.e., speaking and writing in Nahuatl). See, for example, the language of another law, Pastoral V of 1769, which tells us, "And whereas the decree that the Indians should learn Castilian . . . has been urged on the two dominions and has been one of the most saintedly and justly *repeated decrees of the laws* of these kingdoms, its execution, instead of being moved forward, *every day seems more impossible.*"[3]

The language of the decree itself explains why the Crown kept ruling the same thing over and over, year after year. Despite all the laws handed down over time that gave the expressed intent to make people speak Spanish, the actual practice of Indigenous languages was not slowing. Therefore, we can say that some laws or official attitudes had little effect on how people chose to live their lives. This is important because historians use documents, and if the only documents they use are "official," then the history they write will be from the point of view of people controlling the structures of colonial power. "The non-existence of Spanish artisans, merchants, and women . . . was presumed from their near absence in the bare military narratives of conquest."[4] Being able to write a complex story requires integrating a good cross section of society. Even in the present time, this goal to include the excluded can require great effort and intentionality, but it poses a special challenge in older periods. Easy-to-use royal records are all considered excellent primary sources, yet they exclude nearly all women and people of color. This problem of erasure can be spoken of in terms of racism, forced labor, misogyny, rape, and genocide; important decolonial concepts are being refined to speak of that which we, until recently, have not had words.[5] Thought of as a cycle of sources, erasure can also be approached as a methods problem.[6]

All documents can have limitations, but precolonial and colonial records written by notaries have the distinct advantage of representing a large cross section of society in regions of the world with a strong notarial tradition.[7] Colonial-era notarial/parish records survive in abundance everywhere Spanish, French, and Portuguese groups reached into the Americas. Archives in Louisiana, for example, house notarial records in Spanish, French, and English "filled with people who have not yet entered the historical record of the United States."[8] Such is the case of our notary's report about La Tama, where we get to read the testimonies of an interesting mix of people: illiterate Spaniards living in the garrison; a literate Irishman who gave information about the English; a low-ranking officer (second lieutenant, or *alferez*) who could sign his name; and two Indigenous women whose stories we investigate below.

What is not well known is that Indigenous nations also kept extensive records *before* the arrival of Columbus. In South America, a region with few surviving written records, textiles held histories and accounts.[9] In what today is Mexico, many written records survived. What the Spanish and Mexica Indigenous notarial systems had in common was a class of writers, the notaries. The precolonial notary, *tlacuilo* in Nahuatl (women participated as notaries before conquest), continued their writing traditions under colonial rule. They continued their work keeping local meeting records, getting integrated into Indigenous cabildo town councils and fiscalía church offices. Postcolonization, Mexica, Maya, Mixtec, Zapotec, and other communities left extensive records and trained their own Indigenous notaries to keep local records, even though they were required to use Roman lettering.[10] In this way *escribanos* can be seen as members of vibrant native social structures that thrived after conquest, supporting their communities' interests.[11] In some Indigenous *altepetl* municipalities, notaries continued to keep their own municipal records, in their own language, beyond the 1810 era of independence from Spain.[12]

Juan Jiménez, our star notary, uses the word *escribano*, which means notary in Spanish, to describe himself. Notaries would write down nearly anything: land sales, wills, apprentice agreements, even the contents of dowries. Thus this document that we are studying, the report about La Tama, falls into this category of notarial records, meaning written by notaries, and the kind of colonial records that record a broader sample of the population. While Juan Jiménez's ethnicity has yet to be established, it is within the realm of possibility that he is of Indigenous descent. John H. Hann found evidence of literacy among the Timucua and Apalachee who signed their names Lazaro Chamile Holatama and Don Bentura Ybitachuco, holahta, respectively.[13] However, the fact that Jiménez is working for the captain general of La Florida, not within a Native community, and that he does not use the title *cacica* for Luisa Menéndez, suggests Spanish ancestry.

Women Leaders (*Cacicas*) and the Lack of Men (*Caciques*) in the "Account"

Juan Jiménez, the notary, repeated the king's letter exactly and by hand, in order to explain the purpose of the interviews he was recording. Dated November 9, 1598: "I charge you and command you to become well informed about the disposition of that land through **caciques and Indians**."[14] Cacique male, *cacica* female, and caciques plural are what the Spanish called all Indigenous leaders, without respecting their actual language or culture group. This is an important clue to why these two Indigenous women became part of the La Tama historical record: from her own testimony, we know that at least one of them, Luisa Menéndez, was a leader in her community.

In other words, the king told the governor specifically to interview Indigenous leaders about La Tama. Given that Castilian Spanish genders male to designate mixed groups, he probably did not mean to limit the scope of interviews by gender. So even though today we might assume the king only asked to hear from male Indigenous leaders, *cacicas* are actually common in the vast colonial record that included La Florida.[15] This study, *Teresa Martín & Luisa Menéndez*, is a testament to how researchers continue to find *cacicas* in the archival documents throughout the Americas (see the last section in this chapter, on women in the Mexican colonial record). As Castilian Spanish did not have a word for Indigenous leaders, the Spanish adopted the term, and its political idea, from the first language they encountered, Taino, the most common language among Caribbean nations at the moment Columbus arrived. The Spanish subsequently used these two terms to identify all local leaders throughout the American continent—regardless of the radically different languages and political cultures they encountered.[16] It is of note, then, that Hann found documents in which the Spanish used Guale equivalents *mica* and *mico*, titles for specific women and men leaders in La Florida, which means the Spanish were working exceptionally hard in La Florida to communicate and understand the local nations' languages and structures of leadership—and considered their political status unique.

The term *cacique*, the term for male Indigenous leader, remains in the current Mexican vernacular and has evolved in Mexico today to mean a local political boss. But it is used now exclusively in its masculine form, a practice that fosters false assumptions about how gender worked, as if no women led Indigenous nations in the past. In fact, the opposite is true, many *cacicas* and other Indigenous women populate the colonial record; even surviving precolonial books, called codices, represent women.[17] Despite being born in Mexico City, I had never heard the word *cacica* until graduate school, first learning how common *cacicas* were in colonial documents from my adviser at UCLA, Kevin Terraciano. This shocking erasure of Indigenous women's history is another issue to which the La Tama record speaks. Because the colonial record is filled with *cacicas* and other female Indigenous leaders, we can say their silence is an artifact of a lack of engagement with notarial records in various languages other than English.

Since historians use written records for their craft, it is important to ask who wrote the documents or what their position of power was within the colonial system. According to the Lockhart school in which I was trained, best practices for ethnohistorians in so-called new philology prioritize Indigenous-language texts. In the case of La Tama, even though his ethnic identity is unclear, Juan Jiménez's report centers a Spanish point of view: notice how he, the notary, calls Teresa Martín "Indian," without naming her community or her role as a witness. Although Martín and Menéndez are entered into the notary's records, the kind of information we can glean from the La Tama account is limited in important ways that lead us to further research questions.

By way of comparison, in my article "Cacicas, Escribanos, and Landholders: Indigenous Women's Late Colonial Mexican Texts," I use notarial records to show how Indigenous women still exercised authority in their communities beyond these earliest years of conquest, as Otomí, Matlatzinca, and Mexica women gathered to make decisions for their community, contracted with money lenders to access the cash value of land, legally divided land between themselves, covered their husbands' debts, and owned as much land as men. Contrary to the argument that *cacicas* were just the wives of caciques, I demonstrated that *cacicas* held titles of leadership in their own right, not simply through marriage.[18] My argument centered on complicating the theory of decline in Indigenous women's status. If we apply this idea to the Martín and Menéndez, we see their roles within a larger time period within which Indigenous women were important to colonization. Learning to find the voices of those underrepresented in history makes our vision of the past more complete. In order to bring these events about women's lives into history, notarial records create a successful path.

That said, there are also many drawbacks to using notarial records. One is that the information becomes disjointed as it is gathered and many different points of view are integrated. This could explain why the Spaniards had different views about Indigenous women's status that had to change according to where they were. With the exception of the Calusa nation, which "stood apart" in having a patrilineal inheritance of leadership, North Florida and the Georgia coast's people showed matrilineal leadership patterns, and "ruling caciques and cacicas were usually succeeded by nephews or nieces, the offspring of their eldest sister."[19] Women's leadership was even "more prevalent" in what is now the Carolinas, in comparison to the larger context of southeastern nations.[20] Snyder tells us that the Spaniard Juan Pardo, from 1566 to 1568, interviewed women leaders. In Guatari, a woman led rulers of thirty-nine nation-states near what is today called Salisbury, North Carolina. In Joara, just north of what is now Morgantown, Pardo encountered shared leadership between a man cacique and an older woman *cacica*. And among all the leaders of governments with which Soto met in his four years pillaging the Southeast, "The Lady of Cofitachequi was among the most powerful." She spoke a language in the Muskogeean family common among Indigenous nations in the South; "her subjects included speakers of Catawban and Cherokee languages" and she ruled a "multiethnic, multilingual" polity.[21]

After all, the "Relación" is hardly the first time Indigenous women were recorded as being central to colonization. When Hernando de Soto arrived May 1, 1540, he and his armed men came expressly looking for Cofitachequi; they had already heard about the Indigenous nation with fabled wealth and power ruled by a woman. They expected Cofitachequi would be the next Mexico or Peru: large, wealthy Indigenous urban nations from which the Spanish were extracting enormous mineral and labor wealth. Of note, Soto was a veteran of Pizarro's infamously brutal plunder of the Inca. In search of the ruler and riches of Cofitachequi, Soto captured a group of local men in Hymahi, then burned them alive, one by one, because they refused to tell him how to find her.[22]

The presence of two Indigenous women from the interior in the "Relación" highlights the absence of Indigenous men. As the La Tama record shows, colonizers held local men against their will in a servitude of forced labor; this oppressive relationship could certainly have played a role in either their absence of presence in St. Augustine. Note 35 on page 67 of the "Relación" tells us a backstory in the town of Escamacu, where men had been kidnapped and enslaved as laborers at the garrison in Santa Elena. In Juan de Ribas's testimony, he says, "Some Indian laborers . . . fled," so Moyano was sent to recapture them. But they were not laborers in the way we think of compensated work. This phrasing softens what happened all along coastal towns in the Americas: European migrants brutalized and enslaved Native people.[23] They expected Indigenous Peoples to work without compensation. Ships were under pressure to extract wealth to avoid bankruptcy from the great costs of cross-Atlantic sailing. Ship captains (*armadores*) even shared a common tactic: to scoop up entire coastal villages and sell them into enslavement in order to fund return voyages. The brief narrative about Escamacu speaks directly to these histories of attempted enslavement and Indigenous resistance.

Another way to extract labor was to build a mission next to a garrison, and something happened that further reveals important context for La Tama. In 1592, twelve Franciscan missionaries arrived at St. Augustine to establish various missions throughout the area and develop instruction. One of the friars, Father Francis Panja, called the "Mexican," may have been Indigenous himself—he translated religious doctrine into the local language of the Yamasees. The "converts" at the mission at Talomato (St. Augustine's "Indian village" in the northwest end) rebelled due to never-ending work and punishments, destroying several missions, and assassinating clergy, saying,

> They prevent us from having our balls, our banquets, feasts, celebrations, games, and contests, so that being deprived of them,

> we lose our ancient valor and skill which we inherited from our ancestors . . . for everything they reprimand us, injuriously treat us, oppress us, lecture us, call us bad Christians, and deprive us of all the pleasures which our fathers enjoyed, in the hope that they would give us heaven; by these frauds subjecting us and holding us under their absolute control And what have we to hope except to be made slaves? If we now put them all to death, we shall destroy these excrescences, and force the governor to treat us well.[24]

These rebellions happened in the years immediately preceding the interviews for the account of La Tama and must have been foremost in the governor's mind during the inquiry. Most narratives identify a young Guale man as the cacique that led the resistance movement, whereas Francis and Kole's impeccably researched book incorporates unpublished accounts and notarial records that required transcribing original manuscripts to get at a more inclusive and expansive historical record.[25] In turn, this brings us to another drawback of these more local records: they can be difficult to interpret, because they require negotiating various language groups.

Even the interviews with Teresa Martín and Luisa Menéndez could be described as intentionally brief, circumscribed, as if the women were uncomfortable with the procedure. They choose their words carefully, offering little social detail about their communities. Instead, they focus on what the Spanish most wanted to hear: about gold, pearls, and landscapes of abundance. Luisa Menéndez and Teresa Martín's long-standing association with the garrison would have made the Indigenous women well aware that the king sought military intelligence about their land, information that could ultimately cause their nations to undergo even more suffering.

As we learn about the social and economic contexts behind the research, we cannot lose sight of a primary reason for the La Tama account to exist: that this was an investigation into a violent revolt against the occupation, the burning down of Fort San Juan by the Catawba nation. Overall, we learn colonial records paint a different picture than the commonly repeated "peaceful coexistence" narrative used to characterize relationships of conquest between Indigenous and colonizing leadership.[26]

More Was Said and Left Unsaid: Luisa Menéndez and Teresa Martín

The La Tama investigation first introduces us to Luisa Menéndez, Yuchi/Chisca *cacica* (Indigenous leader) of Guanaytique, when the governor interviews her husband, Juan de Ribas. He said that as a teenager he was sent inland on one of the Pardo expeditions to learn Indigenous languages,[27] making him one of the inquiry's ideal interview subjects. Toward the end of his testimony, he explicitly refers to Menéndez as his wife, which implies a priest and a church wedding, whether in Joara, Santa Elena, or St. Augustine. In turn, this suggests that a document recording the marriage still might exist somewhere in the colonial archives.

Most significantly, Juan de Ribas described his wife as a Yuchi/Chisca *cacica*, "su mujer, era la *cacica* de aquella tierra que llaman Guanaytique," emphasis added.[28] We only learn about her social status through her husband's testimony, which demonstrates to us that he understands the structures of governance in local communities. Since she was young when she was taken from her family, a hereditary component to her title seems likely; perhaps she was trained in diplomacy within a ruling Yuchi/Chisca family. Even if she were one of the eight enslaved women (see "Indigenous Women and the Un/making of Spanish Men in Northern La Florida, 1540–1568," in this volume), given her training, she may have understood her marriage to Juan de Ribas to have been on some level a strategic personal if not cultural alliance. Hann, for example, describes the "political bonding through marriage" of women and men in the region, noting that among the Calusa (one of the few patrilineal nations in the region), "the practice included the chief's heir once he had been so designated and he reached puberty."[29] In other words, though her work for the Spanish may have amounted to the labor of an enslaved person for a time, it is not out of the realm of possibility that, for her part, Luisa Menéndez's marriage was intentional.

Testifying before the captain general must have been terrifying, since Menéndez's specific Yuchi/Chisca township, Manaytique, was one of the towns destroyed by Moyano.[30] It is interesting that she, a trained Yuchi/Chisca *cacica* who grew up in the interior region, expressed doubts that she could possibly say anything more than her husband already said about her community's land. In her eyes, Juan de Ribas is a Spaniard, or she at least uses that word to describe her husband. Perhaps Luisa Menéndez was thinking geopolitically and used his association with the Spanish to give themselves legal protection in this investigation. More than just a deferral to her husband, which one might consider uncharacteristic for a *cacica* from a matrilineal culture, she seems to acknowledge that a Spanish account of the wealth of their land would be very different from her own. For example, if the Yuchi/Chisca concept of leadership was anything like that of the Mexica, the definition of a town could not be represented as objects (homes, walls) but rather by lives, the people and ecology of the town, an eye-opening characteristic of many early Indigenous maps in México.[31] When asked to describe that interior region to the king, what she described was food in abundance: corn, chestnuts, beans and squash, turkeys and ducks and birds. It may have been difficult for Luisa Menéndez to bear witness to the devastation of her Yuchi/Chisca people, of her land, in a way that would not offend her interviewers.

The investigators extracted information in her testimony about the buildings that Luisa Menéndez's community built and lived in. The motivation for this comes from the widely lucrative conquest of cities like the Mexica capital of Tenochtitlan, present-day Mexico City. It is important to note that the word *Mexico* comes from the word *Mexica*, the name of the Indigenous nation that ruled the region, with a locative -co added at the end, which tells you it is land, a place. *Mexico* thus means "land of the Indigenous Mexica nation." Luisa Menéndez remembered her Yuchi/Chisca town was very large with wood houses covered by chestnut branches, which likely contrasted sharply with Spanish desires to find another vast empire awash in gold and possessing a large and permanent infrastructure.

It should also be understood that Luisa Menéndez, as a Yuchi/Chisca woman and *cacica* hereditary leader, had access to a wide network of knowledge that eased her husband's life in the colony. As seen in the chapter here by Briggs, Rodning, Beck, and Moore, while stationed at Fort San Juan, Spanish men like Ribas would have been largely dependent on Indigenous women for basic sustenance. Menéndez's cultural knowledge of the region would have meant access to wealth in terms of valued possessions like food and other necessities like medicine, tools, and a knowledge of local animals (friendly and dangerous) and the land, and technologies like "using fire to make salt in great abundance with water from those springs," a technology Teresa Martín also described.[32]

While Menéndez testified about going to a large river "with many other women and men" to take out many large clams with pearls which they gave to Moyano, she clearly stated that her community did not know how to mine silver or gold.[33] Instead, she recommended that the Spanish should go up to the Chisca mountains, that there they could extract wealth in gold. She was certainly sending them away, farther along. She also carefully noted that what she remembered as a girl might not actually correlate to what she would consider important now as a grown woman (implying both that she had nothing to do with past events and that she now better understands the motivations of the Spanish). That clever phrasing exonerates her from any inaccuracies in her witness testimony. Luisa Menéndez, thus, with the exception of the pearl diving, deferred any further specific social detail about her community to her husband and did not divulge it at this investigation. Instead, she sent her listeners to look into the hill country, to seek riches among other nations.

Teresa Martín also testified about the event surrounding the death of Moyano—in relation to his thirst for pearls. Teresa Martín remembered Moyano receiving cases of pearls and his being killed when he returned to Escamacu. Her narrative therefore *almost* sounds like a veiled threat. To understand this, let us look at a translated excerpt of Las Casas's experience of seeing the tortures and atrocities committed on whole Indigenous communities by all the ship captains that roamed the coasts. He testified before the court in Spain that pearl extraction was the most inhuman (standardized orthography added):

> There is nothing more detestable or more cruel, then the tyranny which the Spaniards use toward the Indians for the getting of pearl. Surely the infernal torment cannot much exceed the anguish that they endure, by reason of that way of cruelty; for they put them under water some four or five ells deep, where they are forced without any liberty of respiration, to gather up the shells wherein the Pearls are; sometimes they come up again with nets full of shells to take breath, but if they stay any while to rest themselves, immediately comes a hangman row'd in a little boat, who as soon as he hath well beaten them, drags them again to their labour.[34]

In short, both Juan de Ribas's and Teresa Martín's testimonies hint at the larger cruelty of a new labor system being imposed on an unwilling populace, a society with a preexisting structure of governance with whom the aggrieved sought shelter.

Like Luisa Menéndez, Teresa Martín also encouraged the Spanish to look elsewhere, to take the "four-day journey" to the mountain ranges called Chisca. Yet she also reported more social information than Luisa Menéndez, the Yuchi/Chisca *cacica* leader, did. During the questioning, Teresa Martín contrasted her people with the communities that live nearer the coast by describing coastal people's more nomadic lifestyle, moving with game and not building large settlements. She characterized them as unpredictable in comparison to her own polity. The main description she gave for her society is that they are "settled and they live in permanent towns, with children and grandchildren and great-grandchildren" (page 72).

In her testimony about the first time Pardo passed through their township with infantry, Teresa Martín witnessed her relatives give Pardo gifts and large quantities of their own food. When Pardo withdrew, she said he left behind soldiers, saying he would return for them in three or four moons, meaning that he was externalizing the overhead expense of his troops to the Catawba. She reports, in phrasing that implies rape, that the soldiers began to "cause disorders." But she also denied knowing what ended up happening to the men from the garrison.

Overall in their testimonies, witnesses included details about what the king wanted to know: where to find precious metals and pearls. But the witnesses, Luisa Menéndez and Teresa Martín, made a point of sending the Spanish westward toward the mountains. They did not, however, downplay the abundance of their land in terms of food production, which Teresa Martín associated with permanent architecture. Their large township attracted the Spanish men, for whom a settled population translated into a large labor pool to grow and process the food they desperately needed out on the sandy coast.

Being invited to join this *Teresa Martín & Luisa Menéndez* project was so exciting, an opportunity for me to learn about notarial records about a *cacica* in Florida circa 1600. The histories of Indigenous women and their centrality to the colonial project have not yet been adequately studied and are not well known in the English-language scholarship. Returning to La Tama allows us to question why we, today, assume that Indigenous women were voiceless and powerless. The records' action and context add to these data about how women and men of Indigenous nations, by voluntary or involuntary means, led to the success of colonial powers in the Americas, most significantly through their scientific knowledge and much-needed labor. Because we found multiple points of evidence about Indigenous women serving as leaders and influential actors in La Florida, we can also say that Indigenous women played an important role in the success of the garrisons, missions, and the construction of colonial Florida.

This translation of the La Tama records serves to show English speakers the treasures in colonial Mexican archives: abundant notarial records survive in Spanish that add Indigenous voices to US history. Notwithstanding the king's request to interview caciques, the fact that the captain general interviewed Indigenous women shows the colonial system relied on their expertise in various ways. The Catawba and Yuchi/Chisca women's carefully worded testimonies that sent the Spanish looking elsewhere for treasures gives us a glimpse of the strategic power they wielded from within the Spanish presidio/garrison system. And Catawba men protected their women with their lives. Let us commit to integrating local voices into our "expanding archive"[35] with these rich notarial documents.

The colonial record does amaze, and it undermines the stereotype of Indigenous women's powerlessness. But more stories of Indigenous women remain hidden in Spanish, French, and Portuguese-language archives in the United States and abroad. Their spoken and unspoken stories of splendor, tragedy, and resistance also await the discovery of their rightful place in the historical narrative of the United States.

Notes

1. I thank our anonymous readers for this phrasing.

2. Shirley Brice Heath, *Telling Tongues: Language Policy in Mexico, Colony to Nation* (New York: Teachers College Press, 1972), 220.

3. Ibid., 207, emphasis added.

4. James Lockhart, "The Social History of Early Latin America: Evolution and Potential," in *Of Things of the Indies: Essays Old and New in Early Latin American History* (Stanford, CA: Stanford University Press 1999), 30.

5. Kerwin Lee Klein's *Frontiers of Historical Imagination* (Berkeley: University of California Press, 1997) lays out the theoretical structure underpinning historical erasure in European conquest narratives in a way that is useful for students to learn to critique common concepts.

6. For a discussion on less documented voices, see Miriam Melton-Villanueva, *The Aztecs at Independence: Nahua Culture Makers in Central Mexico, 1799–1832.* (Tucson: University of Arizona Press, 2022), 154–57; and Sheila Bock and Miriam Melton-Villanueva, "Collaboration, Multivocality, and the Unfinished Story of a Tale Collection," *Journal of American Folklore* 132, no. 523 (2019): 61–73.

7. The classic text that situates Indigenous precedent in notarial records is James Lockhart's *The Nahuas after the Conquest: A Social and Cultural History of the Indians of Central Mexico, Sixteenth through Eighteenth Centuries* (Redwood City, CA: Stanford University Press, 1994). Kathryn Burns's *Into the Archive: Writing and Power in Colonial Peru* (Durham, NC: Duke University Press, 2010) gives concrete examples for colonial Peru.

8. For notarial records as an untapped resource, see Melton-Villanueva, *Aztecs at Independence*, 156; Damon B. Akins and William J. Bauer Jr., eds., *We Are the Land: A History of Native California* (Berkeley: University of California Press, 2021) is a recent favorite for students to learn the difference in narratives when notarial records are used; each chapter ends with a brief discussion of the sources.

9. Katherine Davis-Young, "The College Student Who Decoded the Data Hidden in Inca Knots," Atlas Obscura, December 15, 2017, http://www.atlasobscura.com/articles/khipus-inca-empire-harvard-university-colonialism.

10. See Matthew Restall, Lisa Sousa, and Kevin Terraciano, eds., *Mesoamerican Voices: Native Language Writings from Colonial Mexico, Yucatan, and Guatemala* (Cambridge: Cambridge University Press, 2005), as it offers a large collection of documents, all translated from the original languages and very accessible for students. Mark Z. Christensen's *Nahua and Maya Catholicisms: Texts and Religion in Colonial Central Mexico and Yucatan* (Redwood City, CA: Stanford University Press, 2013) allows a view into notarial records that give "unofficial" versions of Catholicism.

11. For extensive examples of Indigenous women's political and economic lives through notarial records from the late colonial and Independence periods, see Miriam Melton-Villanueva, "Cacicas, Escribanos, and Landholders: Indigenous Women's Late Colonial Mexican Texts 1703–1832," *Ethnohistory* 6, no. 2 (2018): 297–322.

12. Melton-Villanueva, *Aztecs at Independence*, 45–83.

13. John H. Hann, "Political Leadership among the Natives of Spanish Florida," *Florida Historical Quarterly* 71, no. 2 (1992): 199.

14. Gonzalo Méndez de Canzo 1600, 141–42.

15. Lisa Sousa's *The Woman Who Turned into a Jaguar, and Other Narratives of Native Women in Archives of Colonial Mexico* (Redwood City, CA: Stanford University Press, 2020) covers a wide variety of notarial records about women from the early colony of New Spain.

16. Robert Stephen Haskett, *Indigenous Rulers: An Ethnohistory of Town Government in Colonial Cuernavaca* (Albuquerque: University of New Mexico Press, 1991).

17. For the foundational study of Indigenous women's colonial records, see Susan Schroeder, Stephanie Gail Wood, and Robert Stephen Haskett, *Indian Women of Early Mexico* (Norman: University of Oklahoma Press, 1997). For working with precolonial writing, see Elizabeth Hill Boone's works, *Cycles of Time and Meaning in the Mexican Books of Fate* (Austin: University of Texas Press, 2013) and *Stories in Red and Black: Pictorial Histories of the Aztecs and Mixtecs* (Austin: University of Texas Press, 2010).

18. This is a study of late colonial and nineteenth-century notarial records; see Melton-Villanueva, "Cacicas, Escribanos, and Landholders," 300–305; my research represents the first ethnohistory to find and use a large collection of Indigenous documents from the nineteenth century.

19. Hann, "Political Leadership," 195, citing Antonio de Argilelles, visitation of Guale and Mocama, 1677.

20. Christina Snyder, "The Lady of Cofitachequi: Gender and Political Power among Native Southerners," in *South Carolina Women: Their Lives and Times*, vol. 1, ed. Joan Marie Johnson, Marjorie Julian Spruill, and Valinda W. Littlefield (Athens: University of Georgia Press, 2009), 14.

21. Ibid., 16.

22. Ibid., 11.

23. See Andrés Reséndez, *The Other Slavery: The Uncovered Story of Indian Enslavement in America* (Boston: Mariner Books, 2017), for wide-ranging examples of events and records.

24. George Rainsford Fairbanks, *The History and Antiquities of the City of St. Augustine, Florida, Founded A.D. 1565: Comprising Some of the Most Interesting Portions of the Early History of Florida*. (New York: C. B. Norton, 1858), 114–18.

25. See J. Michael Francis and Kathleen M. Kole, *Murder and Martyrdom in Spanish Florida: Don Juan and the Guale Uprising of 1597* (New York: American Museum of Natural History, 2011) for a fascinating play-by-play about the Guale Rebellion.

26. For complex reasoning as to the causes for violence, see the documents and analysis in Francis and Kole's *Murder and Martyrdom*, 22, 25, 38, 45, 47, 96, 97, 116–17, 120, 128, 132–33, 141.

27. "An Account of La Tama and Its Land, and the English Settlement (1600)," in *Teresa Martín & Luisa Menéndez: Indigenous Women from Appalachia in the Spanish Colonial Record*, eds. Melissa D. Birkhofer and Paul M. Worley (University Press of Kentucky, 2025), 66–67.

28. "Relación de la Tama y su tierra, y de la población de ingleses (1600)," in *Teresa Martín & Luisa Menéndez: Indigenous Women from Appalachia in the Spanish Colonial Record*, eds. Melissa D. Birkhofer and Paul M. Worley (University Press of Kentucky, 2025), 52.

29. Hann, "Political Leadership," 193.

30. "An Account of La Tama," 86, n. 70.

31. Barbara E. Mundy, *The Mapping of New Spain: Indigenous Cartography and the Maps of the Relaciones Geográficas* (Chicago: University of Chicago Press, 1996).

32. "An Account of La Tama," 72, 79.

33. "An Account of La Tama," 77.

34. Bartolomé de Las Casas, *The Tears of the Indians; Being an Historical and True Account of the Cruel Massacres and Slaughters of above Twenty Millions of Innocent People: Committed by the Spaniards in the Islands of Hispaniola, Cuba, Jamaica, etc.; as Also in the Continent of Mexico, Peru, and Other Places of the West Indies, to the Total Destruction of Those Countries*, trans. John Phillips (Stanford, CA: Academic Reprints, [1656] 1953), 86, https://catalog.hathitrust.org/Record/102073506.

35. See Chadwick Allen, *Trans-Indigenous: Methodologies for Global Native Literary Studies* (Minneapolis: University of Minnesota Press, 2012), xvi–xvii, for theoretical movements toward inclusion of diverse sources in trans-Indigenous methodologies.

4

Making the "Yaa" to the Governor in the Méndez de Canzo "Account" and in Today's Florida

Dolores Flores-Silva and Keith Cartwright

Certain narratives challenge us and seem to speak from gulfs between us. They speak from a time beyond our accustomed timelines and from a space and set of perspectives outside our maps. These narratives pull us into unacknowledged pasts, have us listening to submerged histories and voices, pointing out otherwise unimagined futures. The Méndez de Canzo "Account of La Tama and Its Land, and the English Settlement" (1600) is such a text . . . in which three Spanish soldiers, an Irishman, and two Indigenous women are summoned to "say and declare what they know" about La Tama—not simply the land around the Indigenous town of Altamaha (in contemporary middle Georgia) but the vast interior of a land the Spanish claimed as La Florida—spaces mapped today as Tennessee, Virginia, North Carolina, South Carolina, and Georgia.

What do we bring to our readings of such a text? One of us, a native Spanish speaker from the Gulf state of Veracruz in Mexico, teaches in Virginia at Roanoke College (named after the English settlement that stirs some of the anxiety behind this relation). The other teaches at the University of North Florida and is descended from settlers of the Holston River Valley, which appears to have been home to Luisa Menéndez, whose notarized witness in this account is one of the earliest Indigenous voices on record from lands now occupied by the United States.[1] If Juan Pardo's expedition of 1566–1568 into the Appalachian interior had succeeded in its overambitious task of navigating an overland route between La Florida and the silver mines of Zacatecas in New Spain, Mexican and Indigenous history would have taken different turns regardless of whether an Estados Unidos de la Florida came into existence. Two things are clear, however, as we read the Méndez de Canzo "Account of La Tama" with imaginative lenses: (1) the futures of all of us living on land territorialized as the United States and Mexico remain a frontier of open possibilities, and (2) we inevitably bring the concerns and anxieties of our moment to interactions with archival pasts.

The Méndez de Canzo "Account" was a summons by the governor of La Florida (in response to a request for information from the Spanish Crown) to compile testimony about the Florida interior and its possibilities for colonization. Two Indigenous women were called to testify and share valuable information about their homes in the vast interior of La Florida. Our reading of their testimony—their resistance and their guarding of autonomy—began to change and gather a more charged sense of recognition when the governor of contemporary Florida, Ron DeSantis, hailed one of us down an administrative line of hailings and demanded an accounting of the ways in which diversity, equity, and inclusion (as well as concepts of critical race theory [CRT]) were funded and put into the curriculum across the Florida university system. The signed reports were sent forward to Tallahassee from the presidents of the various institutions across the state in an accounting for the public record that preceded the outlawing of state expenditures in the areas of diversity, equity, and inclusion, along with authoritarian intrusions into what could be read and taught in the state's classrooms. And in this moment of a Florida governor's desire to own the narrative of who we are, who we have been, and who we aspire to be together, we feel that a forgotten document taking in the testimony of a diverse cast of witnesses resident in colonial St. Augustine may be of compelling interest.

Between the Cross and the Sword—Remembering the Juan Pardo Expedition and Making the "Yaa" in La Florida

What do you do when the governor of Florida demands an accounting of you, under law as his subject, seeking information, records, a true report? For the six Florida subjects whose testimonies are recorded in the Méndez de Canzo "Account," we encounter a rare performative moment. Two Indigenous women, one likely a Catawba speaker and the other likely a speaker of Yuchi from a rival chiefdom,[2] an Irishman with knowledge of the ill-fated English Roanoke colony, and three Spanish soldiers (including the husband of one of the Indigenous women who testifies) give their accountings. They speak of the earliest Spanish settlements in the interior of the present-day United States. They speak under oath and are offered a chance to correct any errors when their testimony is read back for correction and affirmation. Neither of the two women can sign her testimony, and it is the governor who signs for them in his own name. Only one of the three Spanish soldiers can sign his own testimony. The gulf between spoken word and the notarized archive is duly recorded, with assurances that this gulf does not obscure testimonial truth. Presenting their "Relación" as a documentary production responsive to the Crown's call for information, the governor and scribe's "Account" contains what may be the earliest Indigenous voices to speak—more or less directly—in the settlers' archives from lands claimed now by the United States. Together, they speak from a set of relations bound up with the Juan Pardo expedition and its charge to blaze a route to the silver mines of New Spain.

The Juan Pardo expedition aimed to settle the interior of the Gulf and Atlantic basins of a land the Spanish had named *La Florida*, and Pardo was charged with establishing an overland connection with New Spain. Beginning with a renewed search for mineral and precious metal wealth in what was assumed to be an Appalachian *El Dorado*—as Kimberly Borchard has pointed out in a recent book and in her contribution to this volume[3]—the expedition was also charged with negotiating or enforcing Indigenous provisioning of a series of corncribs to be set aside for Spanish sustenance along the route they sought to open to Zacatecas.[4] We get a sense of Pardo's coercive work in a speech recorded by the notary early in the expedition on September 8 (1567) to a paramount chief of GuiomaE: "In the obedience which is owed to His Holiness and to His Majesty, it was fitting that he and the Indians who were subject to him should become Christians and, in addition to this, that he should gather a certain amount of maize and have a house built where it might be put."[5]

One week later, the expedition arrived in Otari (present-day Charlotte, North Carolina), where leaders from other locations had gathered to meet the Spanish, including the *cacicas* "Guatari Meco and Orata Chiquini," female rulers whose voices are recorded in the notary's attestation: "The captain . . . made them the customary speech through the interpreter. Having understood it, they said 'Yaa,' which means that they are ready to do it, which I, the notary, attest."[6] With each "yaa" of response to "the customary speech," the archive of Spanish authority, claimed lands, and supply lines—real or imagined—grew, as "the cacicas declared that they have authority over thirty-nine caciques" and vowed "to collect and have collected two rooms (camaras) of maize in performance of what is due to His Majesty, which I, the notary, attest."[7] In return for their yaa, Bandera writes, "I, the notary, attest how the captain gave to the cacicas, to each one of them an axe."[8]

Throughout Pardo's journey across the Appalachians, it is carefully recorded how the captain "said the customary speech" to the leaders he encountered, and how, one after another, "the cacique having heard and understood, replied 'Yaa,' which means that he is ready to do what is commanded now and for all time."[9] In TocaE, where the expedition had stopped for four hours, readers hear how one leader traveled seventeen days across the mountains from the west "in order to carry out and do that which was suitable to His Majesty's service . . . and to everything he made the 'Yaa,'" for which he was given "a small wedge and a large knife and a large conch shell and a little green taffeta, with which the cacique was very content, which I, the notary, attest."[10] The evangelistic "yaa" continues in the four-hour stop in TocaE as "four other caciques from the neighborhood of the place, who were called Enuque Orata, and Enxuete Orata, and Xenaca Orata, and Atuqui Orata. . . . all four together made the 'Yaa'" and received their gifts. At least three of these leaders came to Joara on Juan Pardo's return trip from rescuing Moyano and his men in the Tennessee Valley, coming with eighteen others "to make the 'Yaa,' which is obedience," receiving additional gifts from Pardo from November 6 to November 20.[11] It was also in TocaE on the return trip that Juan Pardo meets up with the Cauchi Orata, who had "taken certain captive Indian [women] to Joara by the command of the captain."[12] It is likely that Luisa Menéndez (the last of the six informants of the Méndez de Canzo "Account") was among this group of captive women taken from Moyano's raids on Maniatique and Guyapere. An article published in 2023 in *American Anthropologist* offers evidence that these women captured in Moyano's raid appear to have been enslaved by the Spanish in Fort San Juan (within or on the cusp of Joara), where they cooked for the Spanish garrison and were regarded with suspicion for potential witchcraft.[13]

"Making the yaa" is rendered by the Spanish as an Indigenous mode of social alliance and vassalage demarcating the rule of small towns, chiefdoms, and paramount kingdoms across the societies through which the Spanish traveled. Robin Beck writes that relations with the Spanish provided "some native leaders—especially those such as the Joara Mico and Guatari Mico who probably lacked regional stature during the time of the Soto expedition—the opportunity to improve their relative positions at a regional scale."[14] As Juan Pardo moved through these rulers' realms, making his speeches "to give understanding to the Indians how they live in error and that they should be under [obedience to] His Holiness and His Majesty," the violent power-show (as enacted by Soto and by Cortés) remained a clear alternative.[15] Of course, these yaas to the Spanish held up only as long as the violent threat of Spanish coercion held efficacy, with all five forts built there by the Spaniards falling and no more than three survivors (all married to Indigenous women) returning to Santa Elena after Pardo and Moyano left the interior.[16] What the Bandera account and Juan Pardo's own testimonial report narrate, however, is a string of successes, with Pardo recounting how "I made the speech," "I made them the customary speech," and "made the same speech" continuing "on the way to Zacatecas" until arriving at Satapo in the Tennessee Valley where "the cacique refused" and rather than making the yaa, the assembled warriors "did not reply anything but rather laughed."

Luisa Menéndez's Account

The testimony of Teresa Martín is the more complexly rendered and detailed of the testimonies from the two Indigenous women who were summoned before the governor, but we will focus here on Luisa Menéndez, in part because we have little to add to the reading of Teresa Martín's words offered by this collection's editors and other contributors but also because of how Menéndez's testimony may be shaped and summoned by that of her Spanish husband Juan de Ribas, and because of how Teresa Martín, who spoke of "disorders" caused by the Spanish soldiers "with the Indians and their women," may have spoken on Luisa's behalf in an assertive act of protest. We believe Luisa Menéndez carried a similar and even greater burden of trauma. Perhaps it is a certain reticence from Luisa herself, but at minimum, the governor and his notary seem to bring a reticence of their own to their interview with her—whether this comes from fatigue with the whole process of the account or from the effort to avoid undesirable information.

The editors of the collection *Fort San Juan and the Limits of Empire* imagined Luisa in Joara/Fort San Juan as "a captive among her [Catawba] enemies and the [Spanish] strangers who had befriended them" on the eve of her departure for Santa Elena with Pardo's soldiers.[17] There in Joara, "the anger and pain still sharp" from the slaughter of her loved ones amid their torched homes, "she silently called down on them all, old foes and new alike, the fires that had consumed Maniatique."[18] All of the Spanish forts in the interior, including San Juan, would be burned within the year, their garrisons slaughtered, and Santa Elena itself would be burned in a Guale Uprising in 1576. With some of the backstory taken into account, we turn to Luisa Menéndez's testimony, which begins as a rather oblique captivity narrative: "The General Gonzalo Méndez de Canzo made appear before him Luisa Menéndez, an Indigenous woman from the interior, specifically a town called Manaytique, to which Lieutenant Moyano had made a foray." The scribe offers little detail about Luisa and the form of her oath, and at the end of the testimony, he offers nothing on Menéndez's age except what she says, that "as she was a young girl when she left her homeland she cannot give as much information about the land as she would be able to say now that she is a grown woman. She says that her husband Juan de Ribas can better say what is in her land than she can, as he is a Spaniard." There is much to suss out here, but let us start with her hometown of Manaytique into which "Lieutenant Moyano had made a foray."

A 1584 account by Domingo de León, a translator who accompanied the Pardo expeditions, asserts that Chisca sources of gold may have been behind Sergeant Moyano's devastating foray in 1567 since "they find the gold in a river next to some of the towns that Moyano, the sergeant of Juan Pardo, destroyed, which are called Maniatique and Guapere, and from these two towns there are Indian women in the fort of St. Augustine, now Christians married with Spaniards, who relate there is gold in the river in great pieces and in many forms."[19] According to Beck, Maniatique was likely a rival town to Joara and was one of the two Chisca towns attacked by Moyano after Juan Pardo left him in charge of the fort at Joara. Moyano wrote to Pardo, notifying him that he had attacked and defeated "a cacique . . . named Chisca," killing more than a thousand of the town's inhabitants and burning fifty dwellings.[20] This would be Maniatique, Luisa Menéndez's home, and she likely fell into Moyano's control as a captive from this devastating attack, which she witnessed as a young girl. Following this offensive, Sergeant Moyano claims to have received a threat from "a cacique of the mountains" promising to eat the Spaniards and "a dog the sergeant had."[21] A four-day march across the mountains placed Moyano and nineteen Spanish soldiers (along with an unnamed number of Indigenous warriors, probably from Joara) at the high-walled palisade of his enemy, where, after gaining contested entrance through its heavily guarded gate, he claims to have killed 1,500 people and to have torched the entire town.[22] Even as most scholars believe that Moyano exaggerated the casualties inflicted on these two Chisca towns, the devastation of Maniatique and Guapere should not be underestimated. Neither the scribe nor Menéndez have much to say about this, aside from mention that she hails from Maniatique, one of the sites of Moyano's "foray."

Luisa Menéndez states that she was too young to remember much when she left her homeland and that her husband is a better source "as he is a Spaniard." Her reticence here may come at face value. If Teresa Martín was estimated at "forty years old, more or less" and would have been as young as seven years old at the time of Juan Pardo's expedition into her home of Joara, Luisa Menéndez may have been even younger. However, the Spanish may have overestimated the age of Indigenous girls (for their own purposes) and underestimated the age and wisdom of mature Indigenous women. We believe that Luisa Menéndez experienced firsthand the "disorders" that her *comadre* Teresa Martín mentioned. "Luisa" (before she was baptized as Luisa) would have been a victim of these assaults when Sergeant Moyano's men entered Maniatique and slaughtered and burned its defenders, and she may have experienced these disorders afterward, back at the Spanish base at Joara/Fort San Juan. The Spanish soldiers had every reason to "fear the Native woman" (or girl) as Briggs et al. have suggested in discussing the piece of iron planted in the enclosed kitchen of Fort San Juan "to ward off magic" or suspected witchcraft of the Chisca women/girls housed as captive cooks there.[23] The Juan Pardo relation offers a possible narrative for how she made her way to Joara if she did not accompany Moyano to the attack on Guapere and follow him on his circuitous return trek to Joara. In Chiaha, along the Tennessee River on November 1, 1567, after Pardo's second expedition had rescued Moyano from being pinned in by a brewing revolt, [Tocahe] Cauchi Orata arrived in the Spanish camp: "He had taken certain captive Indian [women] to Joara by the command of the captain."[24] Luisa Menéndez has little to say about any of this and defers to her husband, passing responsibility for the tale onto him while also recognizing his more secure standing in the colony.

In fact, the brevity of the Luisa Menéndez testimony appears odd in multiple ways. We suspect that the governor and his notary may have tired of the report process and were ready to wrap things up. Menéndez is the last to give her testimony and may not have been included had her husband, Juan de Ribas, not stated to the governor two days earlier that "the wealth of previously discovered lands cannot compare" and that "his woman could talk about this and much more, since she is an Indigenous woman from the area." Her loquacious husband seems confident she could say much, but she defers and claims to have little to say. Luisa Menéndez does not seem eager to revisit the source of her childhood trauma. It is her husband who spins tales of La Gran Copla, a mountain of diamond, and potential wealth beyond measure and who seeks to spark interest in further forays along the routes traveled by Juan Pardo and Moyano, and earlier by Soto. What Luisa Menéndez has to say is mostly rote: summarizing what the others have said, a minimal and perhaps obfuscating (or obfuscated) testimony.

We get the same Mississippian/Mesoamerican three-sisters narrative of abundant food staples: "She said what she knows and remembers is that her land is very good and fertile with lots of food, like corn, chestnuts, beans and squash, and nuts, and a large quantity of deer and cows and wild turkeys and ducks, and many flocks of birds that can be hunted for food." Like the others, her testimony mentions that "the Indians have golden nose adornments" (from trade with Chisca in the mountains), and—as in the testimony of Teresa Martín—we get the strange assertion that "the Indians there are white and blue-eyed with red hair." One wonders whether the expedition's quest to find Spaniards on the other side of these mountains—the desired proximity to the silver mines of Zacatecas—has much to do with this testimony. Luisa Menéndez's response to the governor's questions and to "being asked about the content of the above section of the letter and the acts" almost follows the form of the yaa that the Spanish expected in response to the customary speech demanding allegiance and loyalty to the king and pope upon entering Indigenous towns. Luisa Menéndez seems to give the yaa: "In her opinion there is a lot of gold and silver in those lands, but as she has stated, the Indians do not know about them." She tells a seemingly well-rehearsed story: "They got many pearls and gave them to Lieutenant Moyano, and likewise the Indians gave him gold nose adornments," adding that "if the Spanish went they would get a lot of wealth" and "regarding food, there would be no lack of it." In effect, we get "yes, yes, and yes." We are, however, unconvinced that she is eager to see this expedition undertaken or—especially—to assist with it as a translator and Native guide, in spite of her husband's obsessions with gaining wealth there.

Given that Luisa Menéndez identifies herself as a native of Maniatique and says that in her land there is "a spring there with three or four heads of salt water" that serves as a source for salt production and that "in all of that land there is no other salt water," we get a location for her home and for the town that Moyano devastated. Maniatique, as Beck writes, "was probably located along the North Fork of the Holston River near modern-day Saltville, Virginia."[25] Saltville was one of the key salt sources (or "brines") in the south and positioned at a crossing of an "Indian path" linking the upper Holston River (and the whole Tennessee Valley) with the upper Catawba Valley through Joara.[26] Teresa Martín had spoken earlier of these saltworks and had mentioned in even more detail how salt was rendered (by boiling the water down over a fire). If Teresa Martín was, as she appears to state, native to Joara or from elsewhere in the region, she could have known about the workings of the salt trade from Maniatique to Joara. But given the thirty-plus years that Menéndez and Martín interacted in Santa Elena and then St. Augustine as confidants and *comadres*, Teresa Martín had ample opportunity of hearing all of this from Menéndez, and it was Martín who offered her testimony first. What we get from Luisa Menéndez is less than what Teresa Martín narrated but remains a marker for Luisa's home and her traumatic experience with the Spanish.

Maniatique and Guapere did not give the yaa. Beck identifies the second of the towns destroyed by Moyano as being located "along the upper Nolichucky or Wataugua rivers" in East Tennessee, from which Moyano and his nineteen men traveled four days to a heavily fortified town of Chiaha where they built their own fortification and awaited Juan Pardo's arrival with reinforcements.[27] Ultimately, none of the inhabitants of "La Tama" abided by the yaa any longer than necessity demanded or opportunity provided. Their yaa was always strategic and situational. It was a yaa under duress, and we read Luisa Menéndez's account in this manner. Truly we might read the whole chain of response here—from the Crown to the governor's yaa, that of his scribe, the Spanish and Irish soldiers, and Teresa Martín and

Luisa Menéndez—as giving a differently situated witness to the King's demand for an account. There is one group of inhabitants of the St. Augustine garrison, however, that is not included in this accounting, and this population bore considerable witness to Spanish and Indigenous interactions, serving as go-betweens and interpreters between groups. This is the African and Afro-Creole population of La Florida, whether free or enslaved. And it is a silenced accounting that calls for attention.

Making the Yaa to a New Florida Governor

In January 2023, Florida governor Ron DeSantis tasked state universities with making a report of the resources supporting diversity, equity, and inclusion initiatives on state campuses, as well as any curriculum that addressed CRT, positioned by DeSantis as a divisive concept of leftist indoctrination.[28] As the legislature followed up with bills banning public expenditures in these areas and began a set of intrusions into what could be read and taught in the state's classrooms, teachers across the state were told the error of their "woke" ways in speech after speech. According to Florida lieutenant governor Jeanette Nuñez, "The policies they advocate are based on hate and based on indoctrination."[29] Books have been pulled from Florida classrooms. The governor has affirmed that "Florida is where woke goes to die," and universities across the state, often as reticently as possible, have made the yaa.

This is a good time and setting from which to consider the stakes of reading the Méndez de Canzo "Account," made under oath in St. Augustine in the year 1600. There, in an outpost of the Spanish Empire, three Spanish soldiers, an Irishman, and two Indigenous women—likely Catawba and Chisca (or proto-Yuchi)—were charged with telling what they knew of the wealth and resources in the interior of the country. The fortress-town of St. Augustine included a population of free and enslaved Africans and Black Creoles, as well as communities of Timucuan, Mocama, and Guale peoples living outside the walls. Like much of Latin America, St. Augustine was a diversely populated Catholic outpost, one that solemnized marriages and baptisms across racial or ethnic lines and that—in spite of its hierarchical structures and ruthless foundational violence—accorded its subjects certain inclusive human rights. It was a civic pattern different from what would develop in Anglo-America, and it precedes narratives enshrined as national stories of unalterable destiny: from Jamestown, Virginia to the Plymouth Rock Puritans.

The 1619 Project, first published by the *New York Times* in 2019, stirred attention for its supposed historical revisionism and its attentiveness to an unfree African presence at the heart of the British colonial project. There was nothing exceptional, however, about such an enslaved presence in American colonies. The Africans who ended up in Jamestown in 1619 were, in fact, intercepted from a Portuguese slaver bound for Veracruz,[30] the key port in giving New Spain what was already the second largest enslaved population in the Americas.[31] The earliest presence of enslaved Africans in a colonial settlement in the present-day United States was neither in Jamestown nor in St. Augustine but in San Miguel de Gualdape (1526), the first town established by the Spanish in La Florida somewhere near Sapelo Sound along the mouth of the Altamaha River ("La Tama"). Shortly after the death of the settlement's leader, Lucas Vásquez de Ayllón, enslaved Africans set fire to the place, escaping toward the Indigenous Guale, and becoming Florida's earliest maroons.[32] Fray Antonio de Montesinos, whose sermon of 1511 had marked him as the first European to denounce the enslavement and abuse of Indigenous people—famously denying confession to slaveholders and asking from the pulpit, "Don't you understand? How can you live in such a lethargical dream?"[33]—helped to lead the settlers' escape from San Miguel de Gualdape to Santo Domingo with around 150 survivors.[34] "Woke" as Montesinos may have seemed to be in Hispaniola, he was still a Dominican evangelist on the wrong end of an Indigenous and African revolt in the first European settlement in the present-day United States.

If, as Florida's current governor, Ron DeSantis, insists, "the divisions in our society are . . . about foundational principles,"[35] with "the major divide . . . the issue of wokeness,"[36] then perhaps what he calls this "woke dumpster fire"[37] goes back deeply in time, say to 1526, when enslaved Africans set fire to San Miguel de Gualdape and allied with Indigenous Guale. Among those African maroons would have been Wolof speakers who marked "open-eyed" persons of wide-awake spiritual and ideological perception as *hippikat*—foundational ancestors of our hipcats, hipsters, hippies, and their disparaged countercultural vision. Foundational realities and coerced "yaa-makings" have long been contested in Florida and across the Americas. Indigenous groundings of vision, articulated as *kab'awil* or "double gaze" by Chacón,[38] and African American "double-consciousness," as conceptualized by Du Bois,[39] have worked to navigate gulfs between peoples across American contact zones.[40] Teresa Martín and Luisa Menéndez certainly display modes of "inventive adaptation," as Gina Caison shows in her chapter in this volume.[41] We know that Africans also took part in these inventive adaptations, accompanying Ponce de León, Cortés, Narváez, and Soto, and the colonial record reveals how an enslaved Black man from Soto's 1539 expedition aided the *cacica* of Cofitachequi in escaping the Spanish, accompanying her back to her home near present-day Camden, South Carolina.[42] Some accounts attest to the two of them marrying.[43] We do not know if enslaved and/or free people of African descent took part in the Pardo expedition, but it would be against the pattern of these expeditions and of colonial Florida demographics if they did not, even as Africans posed a risk of flight and alliance with Indigenous Peoples. Enslaved Africans, "probably fewer than fifty," as Jane Landers writes, played a role in the founding of St. Augustine in 1565,[44] and Africans would have been included among the garrisons of Florida's interior fortifications. To get a sense of the Black population of St. Augustine around the time of the Méndez de Canzo "Relación" (1600), we turn to Landers's assertion that in 1606, "there were one hundred black slaves in Florida, including forty belonging to the Crown."[45] During the eighteenth century, Florida would become a southern border destination for Africans escaping enslavement in Carolina and Georgia, since they were welcomed and armed by the Spanish Crown. Spanish reliance on free Black subjects and Indigenous Peoples in Florida was greater than in most of the Spanish Empire as the British colonies and early US republic pressured the border. Africans possessed of the tenacious courage to be free migrated steadily across that border.

Florida governor Ron DeSantis has attacked CRT as a divisive concept of indoctrination spreading racial hate. But CRT, examining legislative and judicial formations of race, can be an extraordinarily effective tool for civic understanding and remediation. The establishment of a sharply divided populace, split along binary lines between white and Black, free and enslaved, with Indigenous people subject to removal, was the work of the Florida legislature shortly after Spanish cession in 1821. Despite the Adams-Onis Treaty's citizenship guarantees to all free persons residing in the colony at the time of Spanish cession, Florida's constitution made it clear that only whites would be citizens. Anglo-Floridians established an explicitly white supremacist state. Daniel Schafer writes that the "relatively liberal race laws of Spain" changed rapidly under US control, leaving "no place for free blacks" and little place for Indigenous communities.[46] Florida's territorial government "limited the right of free blacks to assemble, carry firearms, serve on juries, and testify against whites," while children of mixed-race couples were "ineligible to inherit their parents' estates," and "severe penalties" were imposed "on white men found to be involved in sexual liaisons with black women."[47] The Seminole War of 1835–1842 heightened every anxiety harbored by Florida planters. Calls for Indigenous removal and the removal of Black freemen (as a demographic possibility), intensified.

It is always dangerous to collapse space and time when speaking comparatively of almost five centuries of history in a space as fluid and variously charted as La Florida has been, but we sense tenacious patterns of resistance, autonomy, and navigation of authoritarianism circulating within the spaces that have been mapped as Florida. Today, as Florida's governor stokes contemporary settler-(retro)colonial anxieties and boasts of how his regime has "prohibited the teaching of toxic racial ideologies" and paved the way for "education, not indoctrination,"[48] we look to history and to what has been included, excluded, or recently retrieved from the archives. We conclude our reading of the "Account of La Tama" with a counter-*relación* informed by Luisa Menéndez as well as by applications of CRT, a mode of understanding currently outlawed in Florida public education and denigrated as "a perversion of basic American principles," a "crackpot ideology" that has been "smuggled into the classroom."[49] We admit to being Veracruzan-Virginian /Floridian smugglers of banned goods of understanding: a foundational occupation and activity in the spaces from which we hail.

We must underscore here some of the stakes of reading this document from Florida as we point to truly crackpot indoctrination in new teaching standards approved by the Florida Board of Education in July 2023. These newly established Florida standards (and we fear their ideological and legislative contagion across state lines) insist on teaching the upside of enslavement: "How slaves developed skills, which in some instances, could be applied for their personal benefit."[50] This bizarre focus on historic job training sounds much like Joel Chandler Harris (of Uncle Remus fame) writing, in 1897, of how "though they came here as savages," Africans were "so lifted up that in two centuries they were able to bear the promotion to citizenship that awaited them" and thus "in their bondage here" can be seen "the scheme of a vast university in which they were prepared to enjoy the full benefits of all the blessings which have been conferred on them."[51] That is where we find ourselves positioned: in a "vast university" system that invokes colonial affirmations of how the colonized (and unsettled) benefit from being resettled colonial subjects. Lesson plans along these lines might turn to Andrew Jackson's 1830 State of the Union Address to assert the benefits to Indigenous Peoples of forced removal from their homelands . . . or to the job skills developed by Luisa Menéndez in Fort San Juan, Santa Elena, and St. Augustine. All of this is likely the result of a larger national declension narrative fueling the Make America Great Again (MAGA) movement. Florida has become, again, a pioneering space: this time for civics-based curricula grounded in "American exceptionalism" and "originalist opinions."[52] As Gina Caison insists, Teresa Martín's and Luisa Menéndez's voices remain with us, in "the perpetual here, now."[53] But some undead something else—some settler-colonial Lost Cause—has been perpetually and cyclically relaunching its furious last stand and "cover-ups," as Caison's *Red States* (2018) has helped us see.[54]

Rather than making the yaa, our own "Relación" turns to Florida's civic truth: Article I of the state's founding Constitution (1845), which begins with the recognition "That all freemen, when they form a social compact, are equal," while the vote is restricted to "Every free white male person of the age of twenty one years and upwards," followed by the assertion "that the free white men of this State shall have a right to keep and to bear arms for their common defence."[55] Article XVI clarified that the legislature would not have power to pass laws of emancipation of slaves and could not interfere with the importation of "persons as may be deemed slaves," but guards every power to block entry into the state of "free negroes, mulattoes, and other persons of color."[56] These seem like remarkably clear founding principles. And we can see that equity and inclusion have a long history of being outlawed concepts. The state legislature made life progressively difficult for Floridians of color, ruling in its second general assembly (1846–1847) that any assembly of "slaves, free negroes and mulattoes, consisting of four or more, met together in a confined or secret space, is hereby declared to be an unlawful meeting."[57] In 1848, the legislature further strengthened the law calling for free people of African descent to be required to find guardians, leading to the logical end of this legislation in an 1859 law encouraging free Black Floridians to choose masters and to re-enslave themselves voluntarily.[58] The legislature banned books that were critical of enslavement (1859) and silenced all opposition.[59] We recognize patterns in this listing of founding civic facts. And while teachers of history, literature, and civics may be compelled to make the yaa in response to executive requests for information and legislative edicts, many educators do so reticently and from a position that encourages open-eyed readings of the damage done (and gulfs widened) by recurrent patterns of white supremacy, by originalist opinions of the courts, and by daily forms of coercive power. We imagine ourselves doing and being much better than this.

The Florida legislature, in 1853, made it "unlawful for any Indian or Indians to remain within the limits of this State."[60] Seminole—and other groups who remained sequestered and unconquered in the Everglades and elsewhere across the state—held on, outside of the full reach of Florida law and in contempt of it. Black residents of Ocoee, Florida, were massacred and run out of town for their efforts to vote in 1920, and during the Jim Crow years, Florida led the nation in lynchings per capita.[61] The state was so full of racial hatred that Martin Luther King noted in a 1964 *Southern Christian Leadership Conference Newsletter* article titled "400 Years of Bigotry and Hate," that St. Augustine presented "the most corrupt coalition of segregationist opposition outside of Mississippi."[62] Ironically, the civil rights movement was seeking rights that had been accorded centuries prior in Florida under Spanish rule. Knowledge and acknowledgment, rather than old patterns of reactionary indoctrination, provide essential means of fostering investment in a "we the people," a functionally inclusive society that has yet to exist fully in Florida or the nation. Voices that open us up to different relations of knowledge—accessed here in the Méndez de Canzo "Account of La Tama" through the words of Teresa Martín and Luisa Menéndez—tell a story beyond what we have studied and imagined together. In the documents presented in *Teresa Martín & Luisa Menéndez*, we can hear some of the earliest Indigenous voices recorded in colonial Florida. Bearing first-person witness that is alternately reticent and assertive, Teresa Martín and Luisa Menéndez carefully negotiate speaking into the record of an authoritarian system that aims to colonize and occupy their homelands. Reading their words to the Florida governor in the context of their times and experiences can help us reassess our long pasts, our contested moment, and our potential for reimagined futures.

Notes

1. Melissa D. Birkhofer and Paul M. Worley, "Introduction" to this volume, p. 1 (Note 2).

2. John H. Hann, *The Native American World beyond Apalachee* (Gainesville: University Press of Florida, 2006), 80, 151.

3. Kimberly C. Borchard, *Appalachia as Contested Borderland of the Early Modern Atlantic, 1528–1715* (Tempe: Arizona State University Press for the Arizona Center for Medieval and Renaissance Studies, 2021), 1; and "Spanish Appalachia: The Canzo Inquiry in the Context of La Florida" in this volume, p. 25.

4. Melissa D. Birkhofer and Paul M. Worley, "Introduction" to this collection, p. 10.

5. Charles Hudson, *The Juan Pardo Expeditions: Explorations of the Carolinas and Tennessee, 1566–1568*, rev. ed. (Tuscaloosa: University of Alabama Press, 2005), 259r.

6. Ibid., 262–63.

7. Ibid., 263.

8. Ibid.

9. Ibid., 266.

10. Ibid.

11. Ibid., 277.

12. Ibid., 276.

13. Rachel V. Briggs et al., "Fear the Native Woman: Femininity, Food, and Power in the Sixteenth-Century North Carolina Piedmont," *American Anthropologist* 126 (2023): 32–46.

14. Robin Beck, *Chiefdoms, Collapse, and Coalescence in the Early American South* (Cambridge: Cambridge University Press, 2013), 83.

15. Hudson, *Juan Pardo Expeditions*, 311.

16. Briggs et al., "Fear the Native Woman," 12.

17. Robin A. Beck, Christopher B. Rodning, and David G. Moore, eds., *Fort San Juan and the Limits of Empire: Colonialism and Household Practice at the Berry Site* (Gainesville: University Press of Florida, 2016), 233.

18. Ibid.

19. Quoted in John E. Worth, "Recollections of the Juan Pardo Expeditions: The 1584 Domingo de León Account," in Beck et al., *Fort San Juan and the Limits of Empire*, 71.

20. Beck, *Chiefdoms, Collapse, and Coalescence*, 76.

21. Ibid.

22. Ibid.

23. Briggs et al., "Fear the Native Woman," 10.

24. Hudson, *Juan Pardo Expeditions*, 276.

25. Beck, *Chiefdoms, Collapse, and Coalescence*, 76.

26. Ibid., 76–78.

27. Ibid., 78.

28. Emma Pettit, "A Florida University Is Quickly Assembling a List of Courses on Diversity. Why? DeSantis Asked," *Chronicle of Higher Education*, January 3, 2023,

https://www.chronicle.com/article/a-florida-university-is-quickly-assembling-a-list-of-courses-on-diversity-why-desantis-asked.

29. Divya Kumar, "Florida Plans to 'Curb' Diversity Efforts at Colleges, Universities, Nunez Says," *Tampa Bay Times*, January 24, 2023, https://www.tampabay.com/news/education/2023/01/24/florida-plans-curb-diversity-efforts-colleges-universities-nunez-says.

30. Olivia B. Waxman, "The First Africans in Virginia Landed in 1619. It Was a Turning Point for Slavery in American History—But Not the Beginning," *Time*, August 20, 2019, https://time.com/5653369/august-1619-jamestown-history.

31. Herman L. Bennett, *Africans in Colonial Mexico: Absolutism, Christianity, and Afro-Creole Consciousness, 1570–1640* (Bloomington: Indiana University Press, 2003), 18.

32. Jane Landers, *Black Society in Spanish Florida* (Urbana: University of Illinois Press, 1999), 12–13.

33. Bartolomé de las Casas, *History of the Indies*, trans. and ed. Andrée Collard (New York: Harper and Row, 1971), 183.

34. Paul E. Hoffman, *A New Andalucia and a Way to the Orient: The American Southeast during the Sixteenth Century* (Baton Rouge: Louisiana State University Press, 1990), 61, 80.

35. Ron DeSantis, *The Courage to Be Free: Florida's Blueprint for America's Revival* (New York: Broadside Books, 2023), 250.

36. Ibid., 156.

37. Ibid., xiii.

38. Gloria Elizabeth Chacón, *Indigenous Cosmolectics: Kab'awil and the Making of Maya and Zapotec Literatures* (Chapel Hill: University of North Carolina Press, 2018), 15.

39. W. E. B. Du Bois, *The Souls of Black Folk* (New York: Penguin Books, 1903; repr. Bantam, 1989).

40. Dolores Flores-Silva and Keith Cartwright, *Gulf Gothic: Mexico, the US South and La Llorona's Undead Voicings* (New York: Anthem Press, 2023), 1–5.

41. Gina Caison, "Here, Now: Mapping Southeastern Indigenous Literature across Time," 185–186.

42. Landers, *Black Society in Spanish Florida*, 10–13.

43. Ibid., 13.

44. Ibid., 15.

45. Ibid., 19.

46. Daniel L. Schafer, *Anna Madgigine Jai Kingsley: African Princess, Florida Slave, Plantation Slaveowner* (Gainesville: University Press of Florida, 2003), 61.

47. Ibid., 62.

48. DeSantis, *Courage to Be Free*, xviii.

49. Ibid., 127, 156, 132.

50. Brenda Álvarez, "Florida's New History Standard: 'A Blow to Our Students and Nation,'" *neaToday*, August 3, 2023, https://www.nea.org/nea-today/all-news-articles/floridas-new-history-standard-blow-our-students-and-nation.

51. Joel Chandler Harris, *Aaron in the Wildwoods* (Boston: Houghton Mifflin, 1897), 153.

52. DeSantis, *Courage to Be Free*, 14, 100.

53. Caison, "Here, Now," 197.

54. Gina Caison, *Red States: Indigeneity, Settler Colonialism, and Southern Studies* (Athens: University of Georgia Press, 2018), 222.

55. Acts and Resolutions of the General Assembly Archives, 5, 15, 7, accessed December 21, 2022, https://onlinebooks.library.upenn.edu/webbin/serial?id=flactsres.

56. Ibid., 22.

57. Ibid., 44, https://archive.org/details/actsofgen46flor/page/44/mode/2up.

58. Ibid., 27, 13, https://archive.org/details/actsofgen47flor/page/26/mode/2up; https://archive.org/details/actsofgen58flor/page/12/mode/2up.

59. Ibid., 96–97, https://archive.org/details/actsofgen59flor/page/96/mode/2up.

60. Ibid., 133, https://archive.org/details/actsofgen52flor/page/132/mode/2up.

61. Equal Justice Initiative, *Lynching in America: Confronting the Legacy of Racial Terror*, 3rd ed. (2017), https://eji.org/reports/lynching-in-america.

62. Martin Luther King Jr., "400 Years of Bigotry and Hate," *Southern Christian Leadership Conference Newsletter*, special St. Augustine Issue II, no. 7 (1964): 7.

5

Native American Women's Roles and Leadership in the 1500s–1800s

Elizabeth Coonrod Martínez

European explorers arriving on the Eastern Seaboard or through the Mexican Gulf discovered nations small and large, sophisticated governing societies, and communities that relied on farming, fishing, and seasonal hunting, who displayed a practice of generous hospitality and were governed by male and female leaders. As the Dutch, followed by the English-speaking, explorers negotiated with Native communities in the Northeast, they observed the governing system of the Haudenosaunee/Iroquois Confederation, a six-nation, multistate system of individual town governance and central representation.[1] Interacting with the Delaware/Ojibwe peoples and, in the Southeast, the Catawba and Cherokee nations, they observed similar democratic systems with council-style government, which at the time did not exist in Europe. These Native systems of debate and discussion influenced the creation of the US Constitution.[2]

Participation and rights for women, however, were not included in the important US document, despite the fact that the newcomers had observed the same. Women in the United States would not be able to have decisive roles or to vote, as women in Native nations had had for centuries. Native American women carried responsibilities for the agricultural process and community livelihood and also served as negotiators and interpreters at crucial junctures; they oversaw local community councils and served as chiefs and as warriors in defense of their nations. When colonists moved into their regions, they established and managed trading posts, and women advisers determined whether to go to war or not. Just the act of listening and participating in discourse by a chief's wife was viewed, for her penetrating mind, as the equivalent of warrior.[3] Their most important roles were ceremonial duties, for the good of the community.[4]

In the Haudenosaunee system, women settled issues arising from alliances, appointed male representatives for governing councils, recalled them if needed, and retained the right to speak. For the Iroquois and Cherokee, the clan mother selected and advised the chief, issuing a warning if he did not proceed with the community's welfare in mind; after three warnings, he was removed. Smaller community councils were headed by women, deliberating matters of physical and spiritual needs. In terms of workload, women met as a group, "pooling their knowledge, resources, and labor power." Fields were planted and harvested as a community, but women managed food storage and preparation.[5] In the winter, they oversaw communal arrangements at the Longhouse. Native women received "far greater respect, status and control than did European or colonial women."[6]

At first, when the Spanish, then the English, encountered female Native chiefs, they labeled them princesses, or royalty. Later on, Europeans were not as content to have to respond to them and left their status and names absent from records. Upon entering villages, Europeans could witness women directing activities, ensuring the community's welfare. At busy times, such as planting and harvest, men worked alongside the women;[7] otherwise, they left to hunt and fish. French traders in the lower Mississippi Valley initially dealt only with men, in trading for animal skins, but soon they understood that men were the hunters and women the keepers of the clan, deciding marriage unions and adoption of members from other clans, constructing and repairing their homes, teaching and caring for the children, and providing food. A universal value among Native nations was never to deny anyone food,[8] but in times of scarcity, food was rationed.[9]

Once the US colonies solidified, colonists chose to ignore a key concept observed in Native societies: that all members performed in their respective callings and voted equally, that women were decision-makers in a community of equals. Matilda Joslyn Gage, who worked with Elizabeth Cady Stanton to create the National Woman Suffrage Association in 1869, wrote a set of precepts for women's rights, based in Haudenosaunee principles.[10] Her home a station on the Underground Railroad, Gage was also an advocate for Native American rights and worked closely with the Wolf Clan of the Mohawk Nation. As new members became involved in the association, Gage felt that the original ideas were being diminished, and she withdrew. Leading a protest at the unveiling of the Statue of Liberty in 1888, she declared it was hypocritical to represent liberty as a woman when US women were being denied political and social rights. Gage recognized in Native societies the importance of women's participation. But the US women's suffrage movement left important Native tenets aside.

The 1500s

Spanish ships whose men plundered small islands in the Caribbean and captured Indigenous people for enforced enslavement in the search for gold were the earliest Europeans to survey the Georgia, Carolinas, and Virginia coasts, mapping rivers, bays, capes, and other geographical features. In 1521, they made landfall near the mouth of the Santee River and captured sixty people, including a young boy they trained to be an interpreter. Lucas Vázquez de Ayllón was commissioned to take settlers to the coastal region, and arrived in 1526 to set up the first, though short-lived, Spanish colony near the Sapelo Sound in Georgia. In the North just two years earlier, Giovanni de Verrazano visited Narragansett Bay and described seeing a large Native population living by agriculture and hunting.[11] The De Soto expedition came next, entering from the Gulf of Mexico in 1539, as the ill-fated Pánfilo de Narváez expedition[12] had done ten years earlier. Having heard of a rich land of *Apalache* from the survivors, and having seen pearls brought by members of the Ayllón expedition, De Soto docked in the Panhandle and traveled in the Southeast region. His company later turned west and headed back toward the gulf along the Mississippi River.[13] "Cordially received and given food" in each village, De Soto responded by taking hostages.[14] When he and his men traveled up a small river in the present-day Carolinas, they were met by a female dignitary in a large canoe, with eight handmaidens, and called her the (Señora) Lady of Cofitachequi. She could have been on the river for other reasons, but De Soto decided it was to welcome him. The Catawba are river people, the women were associated spiritually with the rivers and worked from canoes to find precise herbs and make curatives; men fished and carried trade goods in their canoes and transported tall canes used in their houses and for tools. Over a century later, in 1701, English explorer John Lawson observed how deftly both men and women handled canoes to quickly reach other villages.[15]

After De Soto's group enjoyed hospitality and consumed food in the Lady's community for twelve days, he was told there was no more. He proceeded to take the Lady hostage, and dug up "200 pounds of pearls and an abundance of deerskins" from sacred burial sites, an act he would repeat in the next community.[16] Thinking her powerful and influential, assuming she commanded a vast territory called Cofitachequi,[17] De Soto wanted to use her as leverage in the search for gold and more pearls, but she soon escaped. Other self-governing communities showed her respect, perhaps as clan mother, for Catawba kinship networks formed through marriage with members of other communities, while they remained identified by the mother's line.[18] Those traveling with De Soto suggested a matrilineal society, referring to her as a *cacica*, female rendering of *cacique*, an Arawak term for chief picked up by the Spanish in the Caribbean. Later, Spanish chroniclers romanticized the encounter, with only one mentioning that De Soto kidnapped, "enslaved, tortured, and killed" Indigenous people along his journey.[19] None bothered to record the Lady of Cofitachequi's actual name.

Fidalgo de' Elvas and Gonzalo Fernández de Oviedo,[20] neither of whom traveled with De Soto, wrote that the Lady removed pearls from her neck to place around his, and alternately, that she sent the necklace with a niece. Oviedo: "She returned to her village, leaving our Spaniards very satisfied and enamored of both her fine wit and her great beauty, which was perfect in the extreme; and they were so enthralled with her that neither then, nor afterwards did they learn her name. Rather, they were happy to call her 'Lady,' and were right to do so, because a lady she was, in all things." Based solely on reports and other writings, in 1605, the chronicler "El Inca" Garcilaso de la Vega published an account describing the Lady of Cofitachequi's arrival in a canoe with female attendants, in a manner much like the Roman story of Cleopatra's arrival to receive Marc Antony.[21]

Earlier in the 1500s, the four survivors of the Narváez expedition who washed up on the Texas shore received directional information and aid from women after escaping earlier capture. Heading southwest,[22] they tried to find other Spaniards. They applied the power of suggestion and basic techniques to help people heal, which they had learned in Native communities in order to present themselves as healers. They often had followers travel with them from one Native community to another, and Álvar Núñez Cabeza de Vaca, who wrote an account about the fated journey, references four women, without naming them, who accompanied them for some distance and tended to their needs.[23] Later, resting at a small village in 1535, seven years after their shipwreck, Cabeza de

Vaca and his three cohorts were anxious to continue west and needed a guide. Men in that town refused to travel because they feared being killed in outer enemy territory. Two women offered to guide them, one of whom was originally from the town *Junta de los R*íos, at the confluence of the Río Conchos and Río Grande.[24] After a safe and uneventful journey, she took them to her father's home for rest and food. [25] These expert, confident, unnamed women made it possible for the Spaniards to head south and find rescue.

Spanish chronicler Gaspar Pérez de Villagrá, accompanying Juan de Oñate in 1598, also remarked on Native peoples' hospitality: "At a fine pueblo, well laid out, / To which they gave the title of San Juan / . . . Here all the Indians with pleasure / Did share their houses with our folk."[26] The appointed chronicler of the colonists' journey to New Mexico, he documents how they struggled in the Chihuahua Desert, desperate for water, when a group of Native people helped them locate the Río Grande. After crossing the river, they took some of the men hostage, to keep as guides. As they traveled, Villagrá describes Polca, who wanted to rescue her husband Milco, following them on foot for miles, her baby on her back: "We all saw, coming toward our post, / A furious, gallant, barbarian woman."[27] Making references to other brave women, in the Spanish assault on the town of Acoma, he describes Luzcoija, a "noble" and "beauteous barbarian, [with] great beauty and novel air, . . . reverenced and respected" by all, who conferred with the remaining captains, and they determined to stand ready at dawn.[28] Assessing the purpose of Villagrá's chronicle being to honor Oñate, scholar Phil Jaramillo finds that his descriptions instead are about the deeds of everyday, common Spanish foot soldiers and the pioneering settlers, portraying them as heroic figures.[29] This could include the Native women Villagrá describes, significant characters of their societies, making choices and decisions.

Another important decision-maker decades earlier was Malintzin, a young woman who became Hernán Cortés's interpreter.[30] Mexican popular culture calls her Malinche, castigating her for betraying "the Indian,"[31] and yet her actions were typical of Native matrilineal society. Fluent in several languages, she quickly learned Spanish and aided Cortés in negotiations as he advanced to Tenochtitlan, now Mexico City. Likely born circa 1500, upon Cortés's victory over the Mexica/Aztec regime in 1521, she was able to secure a better life and opportunities.

Historian Camilla Townsend pored over early colonial accounts and texts in Nahua, preserved in Mexico City archives, to study the nature of women's communal work: a workforce in Maya and Nahua populous communities, comprising women of a lower strata or social level. Townsend argues that because Malintzin was witnessing rapid changes and understood Native societal strata, she "bargained for a husband and an encomienda" (large property) in payment for her services as interpreter, doing so confidently.[32] Having first borne a son with Cortés, once released from interpreter duties, she married a different Spaniard and had two more children and managed her own life until her death in 1528. In matrilineal practice, decisions were made for the best outcome and to benefit children. Townsend's in-depth review of Malintzin's children's pursuits after her death, in colonial court records, shows they prevailed in securing rights to concessions and properties Malintzin set up through colonial law.[33]

In the 1970s and 1980s, US Chicana writers reevaluated this historic figure, pointing out Malintzin's intelligence and decisiveness, how she made choices for her own and her children's future, leading to feminist Chicana literature and theory. Chicano male writers who preferred the popular culture version considered the new vision of Malintzin too feminist and called Chicanas "Malinches or *vendidas*," sellouts to Mexican culture. But they were voicing "their own lack of representation."[34]

The European gaze conceived of women as noble and lovely when in a lofty position but primarily meant to be subservient; in one of the earliest portraits of a "New World" woman by artist John White in 1585, titled *Seminole of Florida*, a nameless woman attired in a thin cloth of long fringes barely covering her lower personal area, her breasts exposed and tattoos on her arms, sustains eye contact with the viewer while she smiles and offers two bowls of food.[35] When women's conduct fell outside the European frame, Native women were seen as sexual, promiscuous, and, especially, aggressive, when defending territory and villages. Oviedo stated that "fierce" women were prepared to use both sex and violence to regain their freedom. De Soto's practice of taking women by force was documented only when the woman fought back: a man named Herrera, alone behind some of his companions, guarding a captive, was surprised when she suddenly grabbed his genitals and "had him in such a fatigued and exhausted state that if other Christians had not happened to pass by and rescue him, the Indian woman would have killed him . . . she hoped to free herself, and flee."[36] Chroniclers chose to ignore the woman's plight, and none bothered to record the woman's name or fate.

The 1600s

The earliest English settlement, led by Francis Drake in 1585, had disappeared by the time English ships returned to the Eastern Seaboard in 1590. A new community called Jamestown was set up in 1607; while scouting the land and building lodging, they were saved from starvation by the nearby Powhatan Confederation.[37] Wahunsenacawh, paramount chief of the Powhatan, sent children, including his daughter, Amonute/Matoaka, the playful one, with food. Known today as Pocahontas,[38] born around 1595, she played with the colonists' children and learned English. Determined to control Native communities by tricks of friendship, the colonists fomented relationships with children. When Pocahontas became a young woman, she chose a husband, Kocoum, and they had a baby. Because of growing concern about the intentions of the English, with settlements rapidly expanded, she was sent further inland to her husband's village; her father also relocated his own village to the west. Knowing of his love for his daughter, the English wanted to use Pocahontas for leverage over the Powhatan nation. Traveling upriver to make contacts, in 1613, the English ship captain Samuel Argall coerced a young couple from that village to bring her with them and visit the ship. The friend wanted to go aboard and insisted Pocahontas accompany her; she was reticent at first but, under pressure, agreed and boarded for a tour. Her friends left, and Pocahontas was held captive.

Argall took her to Jamestown, a ransom requested from her father was delivered, but she was still kept confined; a female relative was allowed to visit, and Pocahontas told her she had been raped on the ship and was pregnant. Forced to convert to Christianity and baptized with an Anglo name, after the baby was born, she was married to a widower, the older tobacco planter John Rolfe.[39] In 1616, accompanied by a few Powhatan representatives, they boarded a ship for England; she was introduced as Lady Rebecca Rolfe, *civilized savage*. As they planned their return trip, Pocahontas took mysteriously ill and died in 1617. She was buried in England, and her son, Thomas, was left behind with Rolfe's relatives. Hearing this, her father died the next year.[40] In US popular culture, Pocahontas is portrayed as a princess, much like the Lady of Cofitachequi. But the ugly story of her kidnapping, forced marriage, and early death is missing. The English took her liberty and choice. Had Pocahontas remained near her people and in the Powhatan region, with her Native spouse, her life would have been very different.

In December 1620, the *Mayflower* arrived at Provincetown, they dug up a burial ground, took the corn offering to eat, then moved on. Finding a deserted site on good defensive ground, they called it Plymouth. The next day they were surprised when Tisquantum, whom they called Squanto,[41] arrived speaking English; he told them it had been his village, Patuxet. He taught them where to fish and how to prepare the soil for planting with dead fish. In typical generous practice, the Wampanoag provided the newcomers with food. A long-standing confederation of unified communities,[42] each with a chief, in Martha's Vineyard (originally *Noepe*, "land between the streams") and Nantucket they were women. The paramount chief was Massasoit. In 1623, colonist Edward Winslow took a Wampanoag interpreter and marched into a Pocasset town, heading straight for the council house, where a meeting was in process about diseases overtaking their community. Treated hospitably by the female *sachem*, he expressed disappointment not to find Chief Corbitant, and in his notes called her the chief's wife. He did not bother to learn her name, yet he stated she was the person he raised his gun toward the previous spring, when he pursued false rumors that Corbitant killed Squanto.

Like the Spanish, the English felt no respect for Native women leaders. They diminished their actions and ceremonial roles and refused to recognize their command over the agricultural process, livelihood, and welfare of their communities. Early colonists remarked on "what seemed to them a woman's high degree of freedom over personal matters, including choosing a husband and even, in some instances, making the decision to end a marital relationship. [But] . . . the structure of native society led to the high degree of respect and freedom that Native American women experienced."[43] Although a *saukskwa* (female chief) was at times referred to as "queen, but more often dismissed in passing,"[44] they could not conceive of a woman governing.

The most important *saukskwa* after the English arrival was Tatapanum/Weetamoo, an observant young woman born in 1635, wondrously competent and strong, serving as adviser and chief. The daughter of Corbitant and the unnamed *saukskwa* whom Winslow disrespected, she is known in only two ways: for being a female who inherited her father's role and for her four husbands. Her sister married Metacomet, Massasoit's son, and Weetamoo married his brother, Wamsutta, who succeeded Massasoit as Wampanoag paramount chief. Weetamoo prominently managed Pocasset agriculture and quickly learned how the English created deeds to secure plots. In 1651, she cleverly outsmarted the English in resolving her own community's deed with oral agreements and witnesses; this "Indian deed" with her mark has survived.[45] In 1659, Winslow walked the outer boundaries of the Plymouth settlements bordering the Pocasset, marking as "uninhabited" the lands left vacant to honor those who died from disease and as "overgrown" what were obviously Native fields in high agricultural growth, then he created a new deed.[46]

Increasing rapidly, the English colonists took more Native lands, disrupting local practice, which was to head inland to winter longhouses built for some twenty families, returning in the spring to their homelands near the coast, where they lived in wigwams or *wetus*. Now when they returned, those spaces were taken up by colonists, and the Wampanoag pushed to reclaim them. The trickery increased: In 1662, a deed produced by Rhode Island colonist Peter Tallman encompassed part of Weetamoo's Pocasset territory and nearly all Sakonnet lands, stating it had been "freely" given him by Chief Wamsutta, who died that year, after being jailed by the Plymouth Court and likely poisoned. The document was more a bond than a deed. Joining in protest before the court, the sister *saukskwas* pressured for resolution, and the lands were placed in a "protectorate," granting Native residence under Plymouth supervision.[47] Tensions continued to escalate, and all-out war began in 1675, after a group of Puritan militants massacred the residents of a Narragansett winter longhouse: mostly women, children, and old men. Called "King Philip's War" for the name the English gave Wamsutta's brother, Metacomet, it endured for three long years. The Wampanoag, allied with the Narragansett, tried to defend Native territories,[48] but the English bore down harshly: thousands of Native peoples were killed, and thousands more were shipped to the Caribbean, enslaved, and sold.[49]

An important warrior, Weetamoo lost her first husband in war, and the second died after a meeting with the English; she married again, but that husband plotted with the English, so she divorced him. Continuing to defend her own and other communities, she was helping lead families away from an English assault on her village in 1676, when she drowned in the Taunton River. The English removed and mutilated her body, putting her head on a pole, as they did with Metacomet's head.[50] Her new husband was shipped to a Bermuda market of enslaved persons.[51] Weetamoo's bravery makes her a standout in history, which seldom includes her.

Awashonks, born in 1640, was an important negotiator who came of age as tensions escalated before the war. As Sakonnet chief, for her community's safety, she tried to maintain friendly relations with the English even while being supportive to other Wampanoag. In 1675, the colonist system threatened that if she helped Metacomet, her people would be enslaved. Even so, after the war ended, she was arrested and not released until an extensive amount of Sakonnet land was taken and her community subjected to English rule. In English legal records of subsequent years, she was brought before the Plymouth Court to account for deeds by her adult children; the last mention of her name, in 1683, was about her daughter Betty, charged with fornication because she gave birth to a child out of wedlock. The English were surprised to find decisive women who chose their own partners and handled the process of sexual relations themselves, leading to descriptions of Native women as living "a free, if not libertine, existence."[52] In the 1660s, German adventurer John Lederer traveled through Apalache and toward the coast, stating there were "strong, cunning natives and fierce warrior women" to be found; he claimed to have learned of an island with "a polity of bellicose women and 'effeminate and lazie' men from a native chieftain whose language he did not speak."[53]

Not only was Native women's command over their communities ignored but their leadership in treaty negotiations both baffled and angered Europeans. Women's presence at negotiations was mostly left out of history texts; a rare account in 1830 indicates seven elder Choctaw women among the councilmen who listened to discussions by US commissioners for a new treaty to take over their land. Hundreds of Choctaw and a few US spectators sat in the outer circle. After the

Choctaw council voted not to sell, people left and traveled home, but the few men remaining were pressured to sign the treaty.[54]

The 1700s

For some colonists, trade opportunities improved and diversified when they took an Indigenous wife: they gained access to land and received protection from her clan. Native women usually chose their mate, the exception being when a woman was captured. Marrying outside one's cultural group was not uncommon. "Initially, it was probably not much more exotic for a Creek woman to cohabit with a white Carolinian than for her to marry a Chickasaw or a Cherokee."[55] In the upper part of what is now New York state, British Indian Affairs agent William Johnson found convenience in common-law marriage with Molly Brant (1736–1796), from a mixed-blood, Christianized Mohawk Iroquois family. They lived with her clan near the Mohawk River. At the outset of the Seven Years War with the French in 1756, Johnson recruited Iroquois warriors for battle, and the English victoriously seized Fort Niagara with their help. But without their awareness, Johnson acquired Iroquois land under English law. After his death in 1774, Brant continued overseeing her community as clan mother, her eight children's education, and that of other children. "It came as a shock to traders toward the end of the eighteenth century when their wives refused to let them send their sons to be educated in Charleston or Savannah. . . . As many European fathers would find to their astonishment, they had little control over the education of any *metis* (half Indian) children—even teaching sons the arts of war and hunting was a role for the mother's brother or another close male relative within the mother's clan. Indian wives and their clan expected to remain in charge of the children's education and upbringing."[56] As English populations increased, such unions were discouraged; children born to one Native parent began to be called by the derogatory term *half-breed* and assigned lesser status.[57] Brant, as a Loyalist, supported the English during the US Revolutionary War, and after her community lost their lands, she had to take refuge in Kingston, Canada.[58]

Coosaponakeesa, also known as Mary Musgrove (1700–1763), was raised in the Wind clan in Coweta, capital of the Creek nation.[59] Daughter of a Muscogee-Creek mother and an English trapper from the province of Charles Town, in 1716, she married an English fur trader and had three sons. They lived in her community until 1732, when they moved to set up a trading post on the Savannah River. Since Creek women owned land and possessions separate from their spouse, her lands followed where she lived. For years, she served as an interpreter for newly arrived colonists; she was, in fact, essential to the new colonists of Georgia and highly respected by both the Creek and the English colony.[60] Her husband died in 1735; she married again, set up a different trading post, and widowed again in 1742.

In 1744, she married an English clergyman named Bosomworth. As the English colony expanded, she was told that under English law she had to pay back taxes on her Creek properties. She and her husband traveled to London in 1755 to present her claims before the Board of Trade, but they referred her back to the Georgia courts. After pressure against her, the colony reached a compromise with Coosaponakeesa, granting title only to St. Catherine Island.[61] For many years she expertly straddled two cultures, but in time, the newcomers wanted her out of the way: "Mary Bosomworth's Indian ancestry was used increasingly to explain her deficiencies—her frequent temper tantrums, her obesity, and her occasional drunkenness were examples of an excess of freedom and her failure to control herself." After the mid-1700s, there would be no more accounts of Indian "princesses and their virtues."[62] Native women's rights had become a nuisance.

During the rapid movement south by colonists, an important adviser among the Cherokee was Naanyehi, née Nancy Ward (1738–1822). As new colonists pushed, she led warriors in counterattacks, continuing as a warrior even after her husband was killed in battle. To the end of her life she urged the Cherokee not to give up their lands.[63] Sequoyah (born c. 1770) studied the differences between the two languages, diligently identifying Cherokee sound patterns, to create a syllabary with letters as the English used. He isolated eighty-five distinct sounds to make syllables, put in a printing press, and published the first bilingual newspaper and printing press for the Cherokee Nation.[64] Raised by a single-parent mother who taught him to conduct trade in order to make a living, later he also served on the US side in the War of 1812. The Cherokee syllabary had to be done in his spare time; it was his young daughter Ah-yo-ka who continued working on the project, having learned the syllabary by age six. She would help him promote and continue teaching the system not only in his own community but later in Arkansas, Alabama, and

Oklahoma. Despite trying to live in concert with the colonists and their newly imposed laws, the Cherokee community was removed by force.

Heading West

After the United States acquired Louisiana, the Lewis and Clark expedition was organized and received key assistance from a knowledgeable young woman, Sacajawea (Bird Woman), who served as interpreter and negotiator. Born circa 1788 in the Lemhi Shoshone community,[65] she and other girls were captured in a raid on her village by the Hidatsa Sioux[66] when she was twelve, and she was later sold, with another girl, to a much older French-Canadian trapper. A pregnant teenager when she met the explorers in late 1804 in North Dakota, her baby was born while the company waited to construct their Fort Mandan. Sacajawea had already mastered several languages and became especially effective during their travels, managing dialogue and interactions with leaders from various nations; at one point, the chief they met was her brother, who provided horses and a guide to reach the Bitterroot Mountains. Sacajawea withstood abuse by her husband, made the perilous journey carrying her baby, and died young, in 1812.[67]

A woman Lewis and Clark never met, Watkuese, of the Nez Perce/Nimiipoo ("salmon eaters," in the Oregon-Washington-Idaho region), helped save their lives. Born likely in the early 1770s, also a girl when kidnapped by a Blackfeet hunting party, traded to the Cree and to the Chippewa from the Great Lakes region, she eventually escaped with her baby on her back. Heading west on foot, she survived mainly on berries. Her child died along the way, and she had to bury him. She was barely alive herself when a Salish hunting party found and took her to her village. As she recovered, Watkuese recounted her experiences, adding that she had seen many white people headed west; she described them physically and said they were powerful. The villagers were surprised, some thought she had lost her mind. But when people matching that description arrived in 1805, they warily provided food to the exhausted and starved strangers and watched them eat greedily, becoming very sick. Out of fear, there was talk of cutting them down in their weakened state. But Watkuese, still in a frail state and near death, heard the talk and implored they be spared, because kind people had helped her. Sacajawea visited Watkuese, but the explorers never even knew. Her story is known today through Nez Perce oral accounts.[68]

As US expansion pushed beyond the original colonies, Native nations were removed again and again. The Lenape-Delaware, originally from the Hudson and Delaware Rivers area, pushed out to the Ohio and nearby rivers; then after the arrival of Quaker colonists and the 1782 "mob killing of ninety Delaware men, women, and children in Gnadenhutten, Ohio, . . . Christianized Delawares [who] were slaughtered and scalped after hymns and prayers,"[69] they fled for their lives to Spanish territory, Missouri, or "Indian land," which later became part of the United States. They were a matrilineal society with various *sachems*, which US authorities disliked having to sit with and wanted them to appoint "a king." Between 1829 and 1831, they were moved again, to the area of the Missouri and Kansas Rivers, where they were able to make income with trade posts and ferries and as government scouts. After the US Civil War, they were pushed out again, to Oklahoma; some remained and were required to renounce Native heritage and the matrilineal system in order to remain on their land.[70] Over a century later, Kansas poet laureate Denise Low searched for traces of her ancestors in the region along the Kaw River, where 320 acres of land belonged to the Delaware. Searching through land deeds, she found that by the late 1860s, all portions were transferred to the railroads and wealthy farmers. The only markers of former Delaware presence were a string of railroad stations carrying the names of leaders: Fall Leaf, Lenape, Tiblow, Secondine.[71]

The Cheyenne nation, inhabiting the upper Mississippi region, interacted first with French traders, but by the early 1800s they were pushed further west by new immigrants using scorched earth tactics, such as murdering and dismembering relatives of the leaders.[72] Continuing to defend their territories, Buffalo Calf Road Woman (1844–1879) fought courageously in the 1876 Battle of Little Big Horn and the subsequent Black Hills War; she saw her husband imprisoned, and she died of malaria. Pine Leaf (1806–1854), who although born in the Gros Ventres nation grew up with the Crows, was an excellent shot and horse rider and could expertly field dress a buffalo. She served as chief at a time when the US Army was forcing upper Midwest peoples onto reservations. Another warrior and Chiricahua Apache shaman in the southwest, Lozen (1840–1887), embarked on a hazardous journey across the desert to the Mescalero Apache Reservation to transport her mother and infant child away from danger and death. Honored by the Apache for her courage, endurance, and skill,[73] she was appointed to work with other leaders in negotiating a treaty with the army. But upon Gerónimo's surrender, she was imprisoned in Alabama and died of tuberculosis.[74] In remote western Texas, a child kidnapped, with her younger brother, in a raid on the Parker colonists' fort, grew up Comanche, married Chief Peta Nocona of the southern Comanche Penateka band, and preferred the name Nautdah to her original name of Cynthia Ann Parker. Her oldest among three children, Quanah, became the last Comanche warrior. In the early 1850s, traders from San Antonio reported seeing a white woman in front of her teepee with two boys playing at her feet; they asked if she wanted to leave with them, and she did not. In 1864, federal troops working with Texas rangers killed Peta Nocona and captured women and children, among them Nautdah and her infant daughter. Taken to Fort Worth and left under the care of Parker relatives, she was terribly upset, more so after her daughter died of influenza; she never spoke again but only stared out to the forest and kept trying to escape. She died in 1871.[75]

Recent Native Women's Leadership

When war against Mexico in 1846–1848 brought victory for the United States, new territories opened in the Southwest and greater West and were soon filled by hundreds of wagon trains. The first explorer to enter the region in 1846, John Frémont, enjoyed Paiute hospitality: a feast of roasted trout, as described by Sarah Thocmetony (Shell Flower) in her memoir. Her father, Paiute/Numu Chief Winnemucca, would continue to host many newcomers. "The chiefs do not live in idleness. They work with their people, and they are always poor for the following reason. It is the custom with my people to be very hospitable . . . when people visit them in their tents, they always set before them the best food they have, and if there is not enough for themselves they go without."[76] Her grandfather, Chief Truckee, traveled with other Paiute men and the US troops to California to help in the war.

Born in 1844, Sarah witnessed a variety of journeys along the Great Basin Indian trail through the mountains: the most reckless, she says, was the Donner party, which destroyed and burned her community's winter store of food, weeks before their journey up into the mountains. The first cohort of Mormon settlers arrived in 1851,[77] and although Chief Winnemucca offered his home, they were unfriendly and refused interaction.[78] Others were more ruthless. Wanting his daughters to learn English, Chief Winnemucca sent Sarah and her sister to a convent school in San Jose, California, but after a few weeks they were expelled: parents did not want Indian girls in the classroom. In Nevada, to protect them, they were sent to be servant-playmates in a private home, where Sarah quickly mastered English. Two Native girls had been raped and killed by white men shortly after silver was discovered in 1859, and Paiute warriors took up arms, starting a short Pyramid Lake war. More clashes followed, and many deaths from diseases like smallpox ensued. Describing an incident where a newcomer known to be carrying a large sum of money struck out through the mountains and was found later robbed and killed, Sarah says they knew that the arrows sticking out from the bullet holes were placed there to accuse Indians. The military asked her father whose arrows they were, that band of Washoe was called to account, and several Native men were accused of murder and shot.[79]

Like other nations, the Great Basin peoples moved between winter and summer homes; now when they returned to the lowlands, their land was often occupied. In the mid-1860s, Chief Winnemucca's community was pushed out of the Pyramid Lake region; the northern Paiute, Bannock, and western Shoshone were sent to a reservation at the Nevada-Oregon border. They nearly starved because the federal agent pocketed funds for their provisions; groups sought relief at Fort McDermit near the Quinn River, there to protect the stagecoach route; others returned to their original lands. New waves of miners and ranchers flocked to northern Nevada, southern Idaho, and Utah, and competition for resources soared. In 1872, President Ulysses Grant designated the Malheur Reservation in southeast Oregon, with forced, massive relocations. This also was a failure, what with the great distance from traditional hunting grounds and because the best lands of the reservation were being illegally appropriated by white settlers.

Sarah was hired as interpreter for the Indian agent Rinehart, whom she described as belligerent and harsh; he soon fired her, even banned her from the reservation for trying to communicate Native needs. In

1872, she married an army lieutenant who soon abandoned her; she sought a divorce and made gloves to earn a living, residing near Pyramid Lake. One day, a Paiute group visited her to request her help because their community was starving. She first fed the visitors, to whom "bread and meat tasted very good indeed. It put one to mind of old times when bread and meat were plenty,"[80] then she interceded for them at the military post.

War erupted in 1878 between the Bannock and a newly arrived military, which pursued them to Wyoming, killing 140 and rounding up over 1,000. A general hired Sarah as interpreter; she had to ride with the army to outer regions to consult with each band. Eventually 543 "Indians" and several Paiute residents were sent to the Yakima reservation in eastern Washington state, where they endured great deprivations and inhumane treatment. When she first arrived at the site with the general, she was horrified. Sarah began giving lectures in San Francisco about her people's dire conditions and was interviewed by the *New York Times*; she wrote letters to government officials and, in 1879, traveled to DC with her father and two other Paiute representatives to plead before the secretary of the interior. He sent a letter with her requesting the Paiute be allowed to return to Malheur. But the Yakima agent refused to let them leave,[81] and in time, the reservation was closed. Some Paiute began camping in small colonies in Nevada and small sites near Pyramid Lake and Duck Valley, which eventually became designated as reservations.

In 1882, Sarah was invited by women educators to give a series of talks in New England. Seeing that audiences on the East Coast were fascinated by her anecdotes, mimicry, and exposition skills, the women encouraged her to write an autobiography, which they published.[82] Back home, she married a lieutenant she met while working as interpreter at the Vancouver Barracks; he died three years later.[83] She set up a private school for Native children to study in their own language, but it was closed by the 1887 Dawes Act, which required English as the language of instruction.[84] She worked to quickly convert it to a technical training center, but the authorities closed the school in 1888, and the students were transferred to an Indian boarding school. Native American autonomy was ending.

Sarah Winnemucca witnessed extraordinary things, remaining always cognizant of the ways of her own community: "The chiefs do not rule like tyrants. They discuss everything with their people. . . . The women know as much as the men do, and their advice is often asked. The council-tent is our Congress, and anybody can speak, women and all."[85] Her book presents the invaluable direct words of a Native American woman who lived the transitions of the late nineteenth century, a woman who knew languages, worked as interpreter and negotiator, lectured, and wrote. She died in 1890 at age forty-seven, from tuberculosis.

Today there are many accounts by Native women relating the past, and their own journeys, philosophies, and histories: Chippewa Louise Erdrich; Chippewa/Creek Joy Harjo; Mojave Natalie Díaz; Chickasaw Linda Hogan; Cherokee Marilou Awiakta; Sioux Susan Power; Navajo Luci Tapahonso; Tohono O'odham Ofelia Zepeda; Laguna Pueblo Leslie Marmon Silko; Cree-Metís Lisa Bird-Wilson; Potawatomi Robin Wall Kimmerer, and others.

Traces of Native heritage can be found in everyday objects. What might seem simply Mexican (tapestries and shawls from the early colonial era, and Mexican regional dresses) or "midwestern" (Plains Indians cloaks in museums, and small images) represents Native history. Women's handiwork, embroidery and beadwork, can preserve not only the memories of Irish, German, and other immigrants but also Native matrilineal teachings: "I remember my mother teaching me to embroider simple scrolled designs. . . . Mother taught me to love the floral aesthetic, in all its inflections."[86] Contemporary Native American life is a life in limbo, says Denise Low, who researched her family roots from the early 1600s in Manhattan and New Jersey,[87] to Pennsylvania and Ohio, then Kansas, where her parents grew up and her grandparents remained after other family members accepted removal to Oklahoma in 1867. She hunted for old photos and documents in library archives, then visited cemeteries in Flint Hills, elatedly discovering the image her mother taught her to sketch as a child: on the gravesites of her grandfather's paternal relatives, people raised with the Ramapough band of Delawares, was "a band of entwined scrollwork, with a four-petaled, scalloped blossom at its center. No flower exists in North America with this shape. From beadwork designs I recognize it as the Ojibwa Rose, an Algonquin design. It is also the Medicine Wheel, a representation of stages of life, from birth to old age. The four divisions represent the seasons, from spring to winter, and winds of the four directions."[88] Other gravestones had Christian symbols, crosses, and Bible quotes; only a few had the Lenape Algonquin image.

Low's grandfather grew up in central Kansas, a town called Burns, near the original Delaware trading post. After the Ku Klux Klan arrived, his family moved to Kansas City, when he was sixteen.[89] "Pop being an Indian made him quite inferior in the pecking order," her older sister told her. "Indians had trouble getting good jobs and were poor. For most of his adult life he worked as a laborer, often at dangerous jobs,"[90] including a meatpacking plant, where he worked to start a union,[91] and as a railroad switchman for twenty years. "He was slow,"[92] her sister remarked, meaning other people did not talk the same way. Low remembers as a child playing cards with him, waiting patiently out of respect, during her grandfather's long pause relating a story. She contemplates the costs of suppressing one's heritage.

Typical foods and food preparation also carry Native heritage, such as *tamales* in Mexico[93] and *johnnycakes* ("journey" cakes). "My mother served corn in some form almost every day. . . . She kept alive recipes that were documented as early as 1654, when chronicler Edward Johnson described tamales: 'Delicious cakes baked by wrapping the moistened meal in husks of corn and baking them under the embers.' This was in Massachusetts. Johnson went on to describe a basic corn gruel, still a staple known as 'grits.'" The clan mother knew what to plant each season, kept the clan strong, and decided "how food will be apportioned."[94]

Women were associated with corn spiritually: Unknown Woman first brought corn to the people; field corn was prepared for consumption, boiled into hominy, and ground. Women among the Choctaw and other Southeast nations were responsible for handling medicines, performing high duties, and officiating in first harvests: the Green Corn Ceremony was "the heart of their social and ceremonial world, a time of renewal and forgiveness, of sharing and thankfulness, a time to feast and dance in celebration of the harvest, and to ensure success in hunting and warfare." If the ceremony were impeded, it impacted on Native life.[95]

"The Ojibwe understood women to represent an important political constituency within their communities"; their roles were indispensable. Clan mother Molly Brant noted in the eighteenth century that if a group of emissaries included women, it would be known they were about "'good business.' Diplomatic parties always included women as an immediately visible sign of the peaceful nature of their mission."[96]

Denise Low knew the Midwest was not an easy place to live: "As I grew up, I was made aware that everything could suddenly change forever." Those who remained in Kansas "kept quiet about Native connections"; there were still signs posted: "No Indians Allowed."[97] Her mother, her grandfather's daughter, was strong-willed, relentless in both caring for her family and getting an education, proud of becoming a medical stenographer. "Her family had taught her to be an active, assertive woman, in keeping with Native expectations. In school she received higher grades than most of the boys in her class . . . she saw them take leadership roles, while she had few choices of vocation, and it galled her."[98] It does not seem fair to Low, but she knew her grandfather was proud of her mother. The turquoise ring he always wore was treasured by her mother after his death. Turquoise was her favorite color, Low says; she had a wool Guatemalan jacket with bright tones of red and turquoise. Together with the Algonquin four petals, turquoise is a symbol of the original peoples.

Leslie Marmon Silko builds her memoir around turquoise, stating that in "the classic period of Teotihuacan, the Nahua empire sent out traders with macaws and feathers north along the turquoise trail to Arizona and New Mexico to bring back the turquoise so highly coveted. Turquoise exchange accounts for the well-traveled trade routes [later] followed by the Spaniards, guided by their Indian captives."[99] Since turquoise is not found in Kansas, Low wonders if her father acquired it during his travels for work by train, often to the Southwest. "Traveling, an elder once told me, is a Delaware tradition."[100]

A search for markers on the presence of Native peoples can lead to travel and a deeper understanding of the land, and reading books by Native women whose female ancestors were interpreters, guides, negotiators, chiefs, and keepers of family clans helps teach these valuable histories and philosophies.

Notes

1. The pre-US, Native governing system is visible today in the *pueblos* of New Mexico, with chiefs over the nineteen self-governing communities centrally represented in a headquarters at the Indian Pueblo Cultural Center in Albuquerque.

2. Discussed by a variety of sources: Jennifer Davis, "The Haudenosaunee Confederacy and the Constitution," *Library of Congress* (blog), September 21,

2023, https://blogs.loc.gov/law/2023/09/the-haudenosaunee-confederacy-and-the-constitution; Benjamin Franklin's interactions with Native groups, Livia Gershon, "The Native American Roots of the US Constitution," September 15, 2021, https://daily.jstor.org/the-native-american-roots-of-the-u-s-constitution; "Iroquois Constitution: A Forerunner to Colonists' Democratic Principles," *New York Times*, June 28, 1987, https://blogs.loc.gov/law/2023/09/the-haudenosaunee-confederacy-and-the-constitution/; a 2023 account on the History Channel, Becky Little, "The Native American Government That Helped Inspire the US Constitution," July 12, 2023, https://www.history.com/news/iroquois-confederacy-influence-us-constitution; the article, Renée Jacobs, "The Iroquois Great Law of Peace and the US Constitution: How the Founding Fathers Ignored the Clan Mothers," *Indian Law Review* 16, no. 2 (1991), https://digitalcommons.law.ou.edu/ailr/vol16/iss2/5; and books by Native American scholars: *An Indigenous Peoples' History of the United States* (2014), by Roxanne Dunbar-Ortiz; *Exemplar of Liberty: Native America and the Evolution of Democracy* (1991), by Donald A. Grinde; and the more difficult to find *Indians and the United States Constitution: A Forgotten Legacy* (1987), by Kirke Kickingbird and Lynn Kickingbird.

3. Michelene E. Pesantubbee, *Choctaw Women in a Chaotic World* (Albuquerque: University of New Mexico Press, 2005), 138–39.

4. Focus of book study by Michelene E. Pesantubbee; also see Brenda J. Child, *Holding Our World Together: Ojibwe Women and the Survival of Community* (New York: Penguin, 2012), chap. 1.

5. Rebecca Kugel, *To Be the Main Leaders of Our People* (East Lansing: Michigan State University Press, 1998), 71–75, 123–24.

6. Jacobs, "Iroquois Great Law of Peace and the US Constitution."

7. Pesantubbee, *Choctaw Women in a Chaotic World*, 115–16, 132–39.

8. Kugel, *To Be the Main Leaders of Our People*, 39–40.

9. Eirlys M. Barker, "Princesses, Wives, and Wenches: White Perceptions of Southeastern Indian Women to 1770," in *Women and Freedom in Early America*, ed. Larry D. Eldridge (New York: New York University Press, 1997), 44–61.

10. Sally Roesch Wagner, "How Native American Women Inspired the Women's Rights Movement," National Park Service, accessed February 25, 2025, https://www.nps.gov/articles/000/how-native-american-women-inspired-the-women-s-rights-movement.htm.

11. "Early History," Narragansett Indian Tribe, accessed February 25, 2025, https://narragansettindiannation.org/history/early.

12. A force of three hundred docked at Tampa Bay in 1528, traveling north to the Panhandle; along the way they treated Native peoples with hostility, and their resources became depleted. Not being able to locate their ships, in the Panhandle they constructed crude rafts and tried to sail across to Mexico (Texas), but ultimately only four members, not Narváez, survived.

13. Ayllón and De Soto, each enriched as slave raiders, plus De Soto, who acquired riches by accompanying Pizarro to conquer the Inca in Perú, never returned from these expeditions.

14. Robert J. Conley, *The Cherokee Nation, A History* (Albuquerque: University of New Mexico Press, 2005), 18.

15. Brooke Bauer, *Becoming Catawba: Catawba Indian Women and Nation-Building, 1540–1840* (Tuscaloosa: University of Alabama Press, 2023), 25–27.

16. Chester B. DePratter, "Cofitachequi: Ethnohistorical and Archaeological Evidence," *Anthropological Studies* 9 (1989): 133–56.

17. The Piedmont region, near Camden, South Carolina, and the Wateree River, called the Mulberry Mound.

18. Bauer, *Becoming Catawba*, 50–51.

19. The one exception was Fernández de Oviedo; see Kimberly C. Borchard, *Appalachia as Contested Borderland of the Early Modern Atlantic, 1528–1715* (Tempe: Arizona Center for Medieval and Renaissance Studies, 2021), 44; Conley, *Cherokee Nation*, 18.

20. A major chronicler of the early Spanish colonial enterprise, sent to Hispaniola in 1514 to supervise gold smelting, Oviedo studied the natural environment. Returning to Spain, he was appointed historian of the West Indies and prepared volumes titled *General y Natural Historia de las Indias*, with first mentions of pineapples, tobacco, barbecue, and the hammock. But his peer, also a major chronicler, Bartolomé de las Casas, is said to have stated Oviedo's writings contained as many lies as pages.

21. Borchard, *Appalachia as Contested Borderland*, 36n83.

22. The nomadic groups they encountered in south Texas subsisted on seasonal nuts, mesquite pods, and the *tuna* cactus, in periods they could not fish or find meat. Their lives were difficult. The Spaniards searched for towns and larger, sedentary communities.

23. Andrés Reséndez, *A Land So Strange, The Epic Journey of Cabeza de Vaca* (New York: Perseus, 2007), 183.

24. Currently the Ojinaga and Presidio border area. The extensive Mogollón culture flourished here, throughout northern Mexico and the US southwest. The *Junta* or Jumano Native Americans were absorbed and erased by the colonial system.

25. He described the town's spacious, mud-plastered homes with thick walls, built half underground to keep cool, similar to the historic site Paquimé. Fifty years later, the Mexico City merchant Antonio de Espejo, traveling with a group, stopped at Junta de los Ríos. The townspeople remembered the four castaways. A decade later, the ruthless Juan de Oñate crossed the Río Grande near this site, with a large company of colonists who established Santa Fe. See Reséndez, *Land So Strange*, 196–97.

26. Gaspar Pérez de Villagrá, *Historia de la Nueva México, 1610*, trans. and ed. Miguel Encinias, Alfred Rodríguez, and Joseph P. Sánchez (Albuquerque: University of New Mexico Press, 2004), canto XVI, lines 18–19.

27. Ibid., canto XIII, lines 20–21.

28. Ibid., canto XXVI, lines 20–24.

29. Phil Jaramillo, "The Heroic Image in Gaspar de Villagrá's *Historia de la Nveva México*," *Bilingual Review* 19, no. 1 (1994): 39–47.

30. Spanish colonial record states she was kidnapped or sold to merchants as a child in the Nahua Highlands and taken to a Chontal Maya city near the Gulf,

where she did communal work. After a group of Spaniards engaged the Chontal in battle and won, she was offered, in a group of women, to them as tribute.

31. Rendering all Native nations and communities the same entity, which is impossible.

32. Camilla Townsend, *Malintzin's Choices: An Indian Woman in the Conquest of Mexico* (Albuquerque: University of New Mexico Press, 2006), 154.

33. For additional important Native women figures in Latin America, see Margarita Ochoa and Sara V. Guenguerich, eds., *Cacicas, The Indigenous Women Leaders of Spanish America, 1492–1825* (Norman: University of Oklahoma Press, 2021).

34. Tey Diana Rebolledo, *Women Singing in the Snow* (Tucson: University of Arizona Press, 1995), 93–95.

35. Patrick Deval, *American Indian Women* (New York: Abbeville Press, 2015), 108.

36. Borchard, *Appalachia as Contested Borderland*, 37, quoting from Oviedo's *Historia General* 2:161.

37. At least thirty villages and some twenty-five thousand people.

38. It was the name of her mother, who died in childbirth; her father often called her by that name.

39. John Smith was never her betrothed. Exploring in the nearby forests (presumably for evidence of the lost Roanoke colony), a Powhatan hunting party took him to their community, where he pledged friendship. His life was never in danger.

40. See *The True Story of Pocahontas: The Other Side of History*, by Linwood "Little Bear" Custalow and Angela L "Silver Star" Daniel (2007); and *Pocahontas and the Powhatan Dilemma* (2004), by historian Camilla Townsend.

41. He and four other young men were kidnapped from the Maine coast in 1605 by an English sea captain; in England, he worked in households, mastering English. Nine years later, he returned but was kidnapped again, with twelve others, again by an English captain, who took them to Spain to sell as enslaved persons. Freed by monks, he hopped a ship to England and perhaps met Pocahontas, returning home in 1619, where his entire village had died (from European diseases); Massasoit welcomed him into his community.

42. The Aquinnah, Mashpee, Chappaquiddick, Niantic, Pocasset, and others.

43. Barker, "Princesses, Wives, and Wenches," 44.

44. Lisa Brooks, *Our Beloved Kin, A New History of King Philip's War* (New Haven, CT: Yale University Press, 2018), 1–3, 33–34.

45. Ibid., 27, 68.

46. Ibid., 39–41.

47. Ibid., 46–50.

48. https://narragansettindiannation.org/history/early/, and Eric B. Schultz and Michael J. Tougias. *King Philip's War: The History and Legacy of America's Forgotten Conflict* (Woodstock, VT: Countryman Press, 1999).

49. In *Understanding and Teaching Native American History* (Madison, WI: University of Wisconsin Press, 2022), authors Kristofer Ray and Brady DeSanti (Ojibwe) argue that the emergent Indian slave trade of the 1500s through the early 1600s challenges commonly held assumptions that North American slavery

began in 1619 or that slavery was African inclusive and South centered, showing that the Atlantic coast was equally part of the extension of Native slave trade and contributed thousands of workers to the Atlantic world's evolving labor market, thus creating a blueprint for the African trade.

50. According to the writings of the Puritan minister Increase Mather; see https://ourbelovedkin.com/awikhigan/pocasset.

51. Deval, *American Indian Women*, 104–105.

52. Barker, "Princesses, Wives, and Wenches," 56.

53. Borchard, *Appalachia as Contested Borderland*, 133–34, 141–43.

54. Pesantubbee, *Choctaw Women*, 1–2.

55. Barker, "Princesses, Wives, and Wenches," 49.

56. Ibid., 52.

57. Theda Perdue and Michael D. Greene, *Cherokee Women: Gender and Cultural Change, 1700–1835* (Lincoln: University of Nebraska Press, 1998), 107–108.

58. Deval, *American Indian Women*, 108–109.

59. The Muscogee-Creek territory extended from the Tennessee River to what are now the Alabama and Georgia flatlands. After they sided with the English during the War of 1812 and war by a small faction within their nation, the Tennessee general Andrew Jackson subdued them, and the US government took all their land and removed them to Oklahoma. Their Cherokee neighbors would suffer the same fate later, despite taking the US side in 1812, fighting squatters, and trying to retain their sovereignty by travel to DC to meet with officials in person, even gaining a Supreme Court decision in their favor. Once gold was discovered in their territory, they were forcibly removed to Oklahoma, their homes and possessions snatched up by the squatters.

60. Deval, *American Indian Women*, 109.

61. Previously Spain's northernmost outpost, from 1587 to 1680, after Spain had withdrawn from posts farther north. They shared *Santa Catalina* with a Guale community, founded a Jesuit mission, and considered making the site the colony headquarters instead of St. Augustine.

62. Barker, "Princesses, Wives, and Wenches," 55.

63. Deval, *American Indian Women*, 110.

64. See https://education.nationalgeographic.org/resource/sequoyah-and-creation-cherokee-syllabary/; and Theda Perdue and Michael D. Green, *The Cherokee Nation and the Trail of Tears* (London: Penguin, 2008).

65. Their homeland along what is now the Idaho-Montana border.

66. Inhabiting what is now North Dakota, near the Missouri River.

67. Her actual likeness unknown, the golden one dollar coin honors Sacajawea, with baby at her side, issued by the US Mint between 2000 and 2008. A French American sculptor created a statue of her possible likeness in 1910, with her granddaughter, Mink Woman, Fort Berthold Reservation, serving as model. Located in the North Dakota capitol in Bismarck, a replica was sent to Statuary Hall in the US Capitol building in 2003, the first of only two Native women represented there.

68. Transcription of an account by a Nez Perce interlocutor, published as "Watkuese and Lewis and Clark," by Ella E. Clark, *Western Folklore* 12, no. 3 (July 1953): 175–78.

69. Denise Low, *The Turtle's Beating Heart, One Family's Story of Lenape Survival* (Lincoln: University of Nebraska Press, 2017), 32, 58.

70. https://delawaretribe.org/services-and-programs/historic-preservation/removal-history-of-the-delaware-tribe/.

71. Low, *Turtle's Beating Heart*, 155–56.

72. Dunbar-Ortiz, *Indigenous Peoples' History of the United States*, 137–39.

73. Deval, *American Indian Women*, 169.

74. The military war on the Apache nation—once very strong—the longest (1850–1886) in US history; Dunbar-Ortiz, *Indigenous Peoples' History of the United States*, 150.

75. They were forced to surrender in 1875 in the Palo Duro Canyon, where his nation took refuge, after the army surrounded them and killed 1,500 of their horses; Quanah then helped people settle on the Oklahoma reservation. See *Empire of the Summer Moon: Quanah Parker and the Rise and Fall of the Comanches, the most Powerful Indian Tribe in American History* (2010), by S.C. Gwynne.

76. Sarah Winnemucca, *Life among the Piutes* (Boston: Cupples, Upham, 1883; Mount Pleasant, SC: Arcadia Press, 2017), 28.

77. They established Mormon Station, later renamed Genoa.

78. Winnemucca, *Life among the Piutes*, 11–13.

79. Ibid., 32.

80. Ibid., 63.

81. See Rosalyn Eves, "Sarah Winnemucca Devoted Her Life to Protecting Native Americans in the Face of an Expanding United States," *Smithsonian*, July 27, 2016, https://www.smithsonianmag.com/history/sarah-winnemucca-devoted-life-protecting-lives-native-americans-face-expanding-united-states-180959930/.

82. On the book cover, she was labeled a Paiute "princess."

83. His addiction to gambling depleted her savings.

84. Deval, *American Indian Women*, 162–63.

85. Winnemucca, *Life among the Piutes*, 28.

86. Low, *Turtle's Beating Heart*, 33.

87. The very first Indian reservation—in 1754, Brotherton, in southern New Jersey, apportioning just over three thousand acres—is a space now called Indian Mills.

88. Low, *Turtle's Beating Heart*, 32.

89. Ibid., 4.

90. Ibid., 11, 55.

91. In 1958, Kansas and other states, passed anti-union laws, now described as "right-to-work" laws.

92. Low, *Turtle's Beating Heart*, 12.

93. For more examples of ancient Native practices present in cooking, see the special issues of *Arqueología Mexicana*, "Cocina prehispánica mexicana." Heriberto García Rivas. Arqueología Mexicana. Panorama Editorial (Dic 2016), and "Cocina prehispánica: recetario." Cristina Barros y Marco Buenrostro. Arqueología Mexicana, Edición especial (Dic 2002). https://arqueologiamexicana.mx/ediciones-especiales/e12-cocina-prehispanica

94. Low, *Turtle's Beating Heart*, 107.

95. Pesantubbee, *Choctaw Women*, 152, 23, 117–19.

96. Kugel, *To Be the Main Leaders of Our People*, 71–72, 93n35.

97. Low, *Turtle's Beating Heart*, 32, 58.

98. Ibid., 96.

99. Leslie Marmon Silko, *The Turquoise Ledge: A Memoir* (New York: Penguin, 2010), 151.

100. Low, *Turtle's Beating Heart*, 20.

6

Here, Now

Mapping Southeastern Indigenous Literature across Time

Gina Caison

As I was beginning my work on this chapter, I sought a concrete item that might ground my consideration of "An Account of La Tama." The voices of the two Indigenous women who resonate from the text stand to shift numerous understandings of the history of Indigenous literature in the region currently called the US Southeast and of the timeline of written Indigenous literatures in the land mass currently known as North America. I read the text again and again, often with multiple maps displayed on my computer screen, attempting to track where these women's voices were coming from and where they called home. The distance seemed almost baffling. In tracing a route from present-day St. Augustine, Florida, to the ridges of the Appalachian Mountains and from present-day Morganton, North Carolina, to the southwestern border of Virginia, I was struck by the sheer expanse of space these two women had seen in their lifetimes and the knowledges they had carried. I pondered how we might hold the diversity of peoples, languages, landscapes, traditions, and legacies in view in order to make sense of what Teresa Martín and Luisa Menéndez were telling not only the colonial notary, and by extension the Spanish Crown, but also us—contemporary readers seeking to glean a better understanding of the history and futures of Indigenous literatures in the United States. This chapter, then, proposes ways we might engage the testimonies of Martín and Menéndez through a regional and temporal continuum of Indigenous literary traditions.

While staring at my own bookshelf that houses so many examples of this area of study, my eyes landed on a beloved item sitting atop a stack of books: a small clay turtle effigy molded by the contemporary Catawba potter and weaver, Faye Greiner. The turtle in question is relatively unassuming. It fits in the palm of one's hand. It is nearly black, with a sheen from the traditional firing process central to southeastern pottery. Engraved on its back is a small pattern with a tiny circle in the center from which radiate out six lines resembling a spider's web. From there, six more lines extend to the edge of its carefully rounded shell. From beneath its mounded back protrude six appendages: four legs, a slightly upturned head, and a delicate tail. This repeating pattern, more than simply an artistic interpretation of a turtle's shell, also gives us a map. There is a center and four cardinal directions plus two (above and below). And there is one more direction offered—the center circle—where one is: here, now. It offers a potential map to an understanding of how one might map a Catawba-centric world in the Southeast. It also works as a link in the temporal construction of a long southeastern Indigenous tradition of women as cultural leaders and knowledge keepers, as the Catawba scholar Brooke M. Bauer explains in *Becoming Catawba* (2023). For my present purposes, I wondered if this turtle was offering me a way into understanding "La Tama" within an Indigenous literary tradition, as a kind of companion text that both gestures outward and grounds a reader inward to where they are here, now.

The two women in "An Account" find themselves living among the Spanish in St. Augustine even though they each identify themselves as being from much farther inland. Martín may have been from what is identified as Joara, a town many sources identify as being connected to Catawba as well as Cherokee peoples, while Menéndez is identified as from Manaytique, which has been identified as likely from near the present-day borders of Tennessee, North Carolina, and southwestern Virginia. While present-day tribal delineations may not wholly account for these women's home community identities in the 1500s, it seems possible to conclude that we can understand their work in a southeastern Indigenous continuum that would include attachments to present-day nations such as the Catawba, Cherokee, and Yuchi. Their travels and interactions may have also been connected to Monacan, Mvskoke, or Timucua peoples. Thus, contextualizing their work requires we listen for the waves of connection across the region among tribal nations while also honoring a kind of regional specificity. It asks that we not upstream our present understandings of place and nation while also leaving room for imaginative connection based on our present knowledge. In being asked to record and account for their homelands in this document in 1600 La Florida, they enact perhaps the earliest instances of two key ideas within Indigenous literary studies: writing home and tribalography. As Choctaw scholar Michael Wilson explains, Indigenous authors have built on the idea of writing home, not only in the literal sense of writing a letter *to* one's home but also in the literary resistant sense, in that they write their homes into the literary realm in order to assert Indigenous presence over absence.[1] Even though Martín and Menéndez are not working within what many might imagine as a Western literary narrative tradition, they are nonetheless taking the powerful step to write home. In asserting the power, abundance, and organization of their home communities, they enact a kind of protoresistance that makes their homes actively present in the colonial archive. They do not allow the Spanish to engage in fantasies of *terra nullius*. Moreover, they engage in what Choctaw writer and scholar LeAnne Howe has termed "tribalography," whereby "native stories, no matter what form they take (novel, poem, drama, memoir, film, history) seem to pull all the elements together of the storyteller's tribe, meaning the people, the land, multiple characters and all their manifestations and revelations, and connect these in past, present, and future milieu. (Present and future milieus means a world that includes non-Indians)."[2] Martín and Menéndez do just this, bringing together not only their pasts in the homelands and the generous supplies of food and provisions their communities can provide but also a kind of present and future as they have built lives among the Spanish and traversed other southeastern Indigenous homelands in these travels. (Importantly, we cannot know under what pressures and conditions these life choices were made and the individual degree of consent exerted in marrying and living among the Spanish.) They demonstrate Howe's conception of tribalography that "comes from the native propensity for bringing things together, for making consensus, and for symbiotically connecting one thing to another."[3] They attempt to bring together communities and knowledges. As one example, such a view might even explain their seemingly odd references to red-haired, light-skinned, blue-eyed Native people. It is possible they are demonstrating an Indigenous-centric logic of incorporation that can build connections rather than delineate stark differences among people with varying phenotypic traits.[4] In this moment, they show that their worldviews already possess the conceptual logic to incorporate into their own cultures what others might see as different or "other." Ultimately, in their use of writing home and tribalography, the two women help initiate a new movement in the history of Indigenous literature of the Americas.

Working within this understanding of Martín and Menéndez as among the very earliest examples of Indigenous literature, we might then begin to think about how their work fits into a tradition that radiates out from where they are—the center of their turtle's back—spatially to the far reaches of the region and temporally into our own contemporary understandings of Indigenous literature. In this way, I think it is productive to jump forward to look at one of the more contemporary examples of a monumental undertaking to map Indigenous literature in the landmark poetry anthology *When the Light of the World Was Subdued, Our Songs Came Through* (2020) edited by Mvskoke poet Joy Harjo with the aforementioned LeAnne Howe and fellow Mvskoke poet Jennifer Foerster. This work presents the many and varied poetic expressions of Indigenous writers across time and the continent at large. Moving region by region, the editors work to outline how each region displays continuities and diversities among the people and their poetics. Speaking of the Southeast, Foerster writes, "For a person with indigenous roots in the Southeast who is looking for evidence of your homeland, you have to follow invisible maps. . . . When we look at maps of the Southeast, we do not see ourselves, we do not see our memories of place. But that doesn't mean we do not hold these memories and embody them, not only in cultural practices or ways of life, but in our poetics."[5] I assert that we might think of Martín and Menéndez as an early entry into this poetics of the Southeast across Indigenous communities that were connected even if they were occasionally in conflict. They offer a map that stretches from St. Augustine to Appalachia. Moreover, they initiate the earliest of records of what Foerster describes as "inventive adaptation," whereby writers and orators work to navigate the invasion and expansion of colonial forces.[6] This history of inventive adaptation continues across the centuries following Martín and Menéndez's *relación* of their homelands.

It is important to realize, however, that when I speak of Martín and Menéndez as a kind of "first," I am speaking of a first as defined by specific print Latinate alphabetic texts. Indigenous literatures demand that readers let go of Western conceptions of what constitutes the literary. Indigenous Peoples of the continent have numerous forms of literature, many of which continue today. These forms include, but are not limited to, glyph texts, material cultures and craftwork (including baskets, pottery, and beadwork), earthworks, and oral storytelling traditions.[7] All of these forms may include both narrative and poetic elements if the audience understands how to read them. As Kristina Bross and Hillary Wyss explain, "An overly strict definition of literacy unnecessarily restricts the full exploitation of all early American Literature, especially early Native literature."[8] Thus, while Martín and Menéndez are significant as one of the earliest appearances of Indigenous voices in the colonial archive, there exists a literary tradition on the continent of which their work constitutes but one small part. In his anthology of early Native poetry, Robert Dale Parker argues "that Native American literacy, broadly defined, goes back far before Columbus, and that, defined narrowly as alphabetic literacy, it has a far longer and wider history than people usually realize or take into account."[9] Rather than point to Martín and Menéndez as an "origin" of Indigenous literature in the region, we might more accurately think of their offering as an inventive adaptation of older traditions in order to participate in an emerging Latinate alphabetic print culture of the colonial era.

In some ways we might think of their contributions to the La Tama narrative as a kind of early instance of recording Indigenous oral literature, as we know their accounts of their homelands were transcribed by the colonial notary Juan Jiménez. We should exercise caution, however, in delineating a strict oral–written divide when we talk about Indigenous literature of earlier eras. As Bross and Wyss explain of New England, "Certainly stories, religious beliefs, and political exchanges were expressed orally and transmitted from one generation to another in a form that was highly ritualized and clearly central to preserving the immediacy and intimacy of communal life. At the same time, material objects played—and continue to play—a significant role in Algonquian communicative practices."[10] They go on to illustrate how "Burial goods basket patterns, pictographs, mats that line the interiors of wigwams, and even utensils reinforce oral exchanges with physical inscriptions whose functions, although quite varied, always communicate something to members of the communities in which they are produced."[11] So while Martín and Menéndez do participate in a kind of oral storytelling account of their homelands, we cannot simply assume that the history of Indigenous literatures on this continent is one of an exclusively oral tradition that eventually makes its way to the Western-inflected written works produced today. Additionally, the very fact that other non-Native people participate in the testimonies recorded for the La Tama document should also allow us to see how many peoples around the globe also possessed an idea of oral storytelling and accounts. Gaspar de Salas and David Glavid participate in the oral accounts given before Jiménez just as do Martín and Menéndez. As Bross and Wyss argue, "To insist on an oral/print cultural divide in the seventeenth and eighteenth centuries is nonsensical in any number of ways."[12] One key example would be that religious groups all over Europe regularly relied on oral practices in their sermons and sacraments. Simply put, we should not be so quick to draw such easy divides between oral and written traditions for any peoples.

In addition to participating in an early instance of the concepts of inventive adaptation, writing home, and tribalography, Martín and Menéndez also exemplify another often overlooked component of early Indigenous literature, which is the prevalence of women's accounts of their homelands and experiences. As Elizabeth Coonrod Martínez explains in her chapter, these accounts spread across the continent. Regarding early Indigenous literature, Bross and Wyss argue that "the written and material archive of early Native authors exists piecemeal and often overlooked in museum, manuscript collections, and protein from the colonial period. Too often, access to these works is limited by outdated archiving practices, the fragility of the materials, or a history of scholarly disinterest."[13] Along with Conrad Martínez, I add gender to this catalog of reasons why certain information about preinvasion Indigenous lifeways can be difficult to reconstruct. As Cutcha Risling Baldy explains of cultural bias of early anthropologists in California, such as Alfred Kroeber, their "training and cultural background [influenced] an active erasure of women's experiences, the roles of women in the culture and society, and also the epistemologies central to women in Native culture."[14] Similarly, when thinking of seventeenth-century Spanish La Florida, it is certainly possible (even likely) that many early colonial invaders and settlers did not recognize Indigenous women as knowledge keepers with valuable information. Additionally, it is possible (even likely) that scholars across the centuries have perpetuated a bias (implicit or not) against seeing women's contributions to early Indigenous literature as important pieces of the larger story of Indigenous literary history across the continent.

As scholars such as Bauer outline, women repeatedly appear in the archive, if one is receptive to the idea of their presence in document, object, and story. Understanding this presence is, as Ann Marie Plane argues, "precisely the dilemma that faces scholars who are interested in women's writing in general and Native American women's writing in particular."[15] Speaking of her own research, she explains, "Of the few documents that reveal aspects of women's lives in the seventeenth and eighteenth centuries, all but a handful were written by men. Of the documents that speak to the experiences of Native American women . . . not one was actually penned by a woman."[16] Rather than dismiss this work as not a part of a women's literary tradition, she argues that "although purists may wish to adhere to a strict definition of 'women's writing,' doing so both elides and erases women in general and Native women in particular from the pages of history."[17] When considering the circumstances by which Martín's and Menéndez's words come to us through Jiménez, we should not discount their contributions from an early Indigenous women's literary history simply because their recording secretary was a man. They participate, as Mishauna Goeman explains, in a process by which "Native women's literature presents ways of thinking through the contradictions that arise from the paradoxes and contradictions that colonialism presents and that Native people experience on a daily basis."[18] In Goeman's frame, this (re)mapping represents a spatial re-reckoning. Martín's and Menéndez's testimonies draw this space into their own tribal-graphs map that writes home both geographically and temporally. They (re)map a here and now.

In fact, I offer that we can see their work as a kind of early entry in the long tradition of Indigenous women's literature from across the continent. This tradition continues through the confession and conversion narratives of New England in the 1700s as well as the statements from California Native peoples regarding the uprising at San Gabriel Mission in 1785. Under a range of contexts, Indigenous women across the continent, including Sarah Pharaoh and Sarah Simon (both Narragansett), Katherine Garrett (Pequot), and Toypurina (Tongva), offered early testimonies about their lives while experiencing colonial occupation. Sarah Simon's three letters to her English schoolmaster Eleazar Wheelock from the 1760s offer one rare example of an Indigenous woman recording her own thoughts about her relationship to colonial education and religious struggles in her (non)conversion to Christianity. Regardless of the form or the place, Native women of the eighteenth century repeatedly point to similar themes regarding their struggles against colonial patriarchal systems such as those of the English and the Spanish.[19]

Moving into the nineteenth century, even more Indigenous women would begin to share their stories via both transcribed testimony and their own writing. One such example is the *Memoir of Catherine Brown: A Christian Indian of the Cherokee Nation* (1825), which was shaped and recorded by Rufus Anderson, working for the American Board of Foreign Missions. Brown's memoir bears many markers of the attitude of its scribe, as he records Brown's life from the perspective of one who wants to offer a tale of Christian salvation and redemption.[20] At the same time, Cherokee women would offer collective memorials and petitions against the Indian Removal Act and the forced removal of them from their homelands in the Southeast.[21] Meanwhile, in the Great Lakes region, Jane Johnston Schoolcraft (Ojibwe) began to compose a number of poems in both her Ojibwemowin language and English, many of which explore themes of her life as a woman negotiating motherhood and traditions among a changing cultural landscape.[22] As forced relocation and enrollment into boarding schools continued to affect Indigenous nations across the continent in the nineteenth century, there began to emerge more first-person written texts from Native women. These include Sarah Winnemucca (Northern Paiute) and eventually, at the end of the century, perhaps the most famous early Native woman writer, Zitkala-Ša (Yankton Dakota) whose work spanned into the early twentieth century.[23]

This early Indigenous women's literary tradition was indeed part of a larger history of Indigenous literature also offered by men. Some of these texts include the 1678 poem "In obit Viri verè Reverendi D. Thomas Thatcher, Qui Ad. Dom. Ex hâc Vitâ migrant, 18.8.1678," composed in Latin by an Indigenous Harvard student known only as Eleazar, as well as the recorded account of Seneca leader Thaonawyuthe's experiences in the US Revolutionary War. Thaonawyuthe's narrative *Chainbreaker's War*, like Martín's and Menéndez's testimony, is a transcribed account that nonetheless appears as relatively and plausibly accurate to the speaker's initial meaning.[24] In the Southeast, the Cherokee scholar and innovator Sequoyah developed and codified the Cherokee syllabary, giving Cherokee people a profound moment of literary sovereignty as they could now begin to read and write in their own non-Latinate script in their Native language. The syllabary motivated the formation of the first

Native American newspaper, *The Cherokee Phoenix*, which became a site of significant political writing as southeastern Indigenous nations fought against removal. Cherokee writers and political leaders of the 1820s and 1830s, including Elias Boudinot, John Ridge, John Ross, and David Vann, published treatises on Indigenous land and political rights in a number of English-language newspapers across the United States just as Cherokee women produced their collectively authored memorials in defense of their remaining in their homelands. In 1854, Cherokee writer John Rollin Ridge published what is considered by many to be the first Native American novel, *The Life and Adventures of Joaquin Murieta: The Celebrated California Bandit*.[25] As with Indigenous women's writing, the number and variety of Indigenous literary texts produced by men continued to increase during the late nineteenth and early twentieth centuries.

There is no reason, necessarily, to draw hard binaries between women's and men's literary histories outside of recognizing that the same factors that have affected non-Native women living under settler colonial patriarchy compounded to affect the (un)appreciation and (non)elevation of Native women's writings over the years. This fact makes the presence and reevaluation of Martín's and Menéndez's accounts of their homelands all the more exciting. Scholars working in Indigenous studies, particularly Indigenous feminisms, have long understood the central role women have played as knowledge keepers and leaders of their respective nations. As Bauer explains of Catawba women, "They were at the forefront of developing a shared social and political identity that became a nation."[26] To have the chance to hear from two Indigenous women from the Southeast during this time offers documentary insight into how women on the ground navigated their own lived experiences. Scholars of Indigenous literature should be particularly keen to bring Martín's and Menéndez's accounts to bear on their own understanding of how women chose to navigate their interactions with those colonial authorities who were searching for knowledge about land and agricultural matters.

Moreover, in addition to the narrative choices they make in their accounts, I posit that we might see a kind of poetics in their testimonies. Their statements are relatively short, oral accounts where they have the opportunity to emphasize particularly strong imagery of their homelands. Thus, in addition to seeing these statements as progenitors of Indigenous political, narrative, and biographical traditions, we might also think about how they relate to later Indigenous poetic works that build from similar themes of inventive adaptation, writing home, and tribalography. As Joy Harjo explains, despite the European misunderstanding of what constitutes literacy, "indigenous nations prized and continue to value *the word*. The ability to speak in metaphor, to bring people together, to set them free in imagination, to train and to teach, was and is considered valuable, more useful than gold, oil, or anything else the newcomers craved."[27] Martín's and Menéndez's verbal juxtaposition of the value of their own homelands in terms of agricultural bounty against what they recognize as the colonizer's craving of riches and jewels places them as poetic precursors of those who engaged in what Harjo calls the value of *the word*. In other words, from Martín and Menéndez's words spin out numerous other multifaceted traditions. Or as Harjo asserts, "Just as we have familial ancestors, so we have poetry ancestors."[28]

If we might indulge for a moment that there is something of an ancestral poetics in Martín's and Menéndez's recounting of their homelands, then we can begin to trace those who might be their poetic descendants. Three poets whose work I think aid in this tracing are Mvskoke author Chip Livingston, Monacan poet Karenne Wood, and Eastern Band of Cherokee poet Gladys Cardiff. These are not the only three writers that one could place into a genealogy of Martín and Menéndez. I chose to begin with Livingston because he is Mvskoke from Florida, placing us in proximity to the place from which Martín and Menéndez speak. Together the texts help exemplify a kind of inventive adaptation that spans across time. I move on to consider two women poets whose homelands are proximate to the homes that Martín and Menéndez write toward. As a Monacan poet from the southern Virginia highlands, Wood demonstrates a kind of writing home as she orients the reader through multiple directions. Finally, Cardiff demonstrates the propensity for making connections between past, present, and future milieus that Howe explains constitutes as a core component of tribalography. By comparing and building connections between contemporary Indigenous poets and Martín and Menéndez, I hope to illuminate how the two women's early accounts participate in an ongoing Indigenous literary tradition in the place we currently call the United States.

In his poem "Punta del Este Pantoum," Chip Livingston builds a bright image of one shoreline town, "Punta del Este," in present-day Uruguay, demonstrating inventive adaptation as he modifies the standard poetic form.[29] A pantoum is a form of poetry where interwoven repeating lines appear across a set of quatrains (four-line stanzas). The form requires repetition and connection as the writer builds on the poem's central images. The fact that Livingston writes this poem from Uruguay in South America calls up the interconnectedness of Indigeneity across the Americas, uniting the colonial invasion of the Spanish from Florida and points farther south. However, in this form defined by connection, Livingston offers repetition with a difference across the stanzas. The first stanza begins, "Accept my need and let me call you brother, / Slate blue oyster, wet sand crustacean, / In your hurrying to burrow, wait. Hover. / Parse opening's disaster to creation's"—notably ending with an enjambment that carries across to the second stanza, which, traditionally speaking, should begin with the second line from the first stanza.[30] Livingston offers this variation on the form instead: "Slate, to another blue-eyed monstrous sand crustacean, / Water-bearer. Hear the ocean behind me, / Pursued, asking to be opened, asking Creation / To heed the tides that uncover you nightly."[31] Whereas the first stanza's second line identifies our central figure as an oyster, "Slate blue oyster, wet sand crustacean," the line that should repeat has been modified to "Slate, to another blue-eyed monstrous sand crustacean."[32] In this way, Livingston connects the oyster to the speaker. In the first line, the speaker asks the oyster's permission to regard them as brothers in this watery landscape. Whereas the traditional pantoum form calls for repetition among the lines, Livingston adapts this to his larger point: Let the small crustacean and the human speaker be related as brothers. In this way, he participates in a tradition of inventive adaptation, taking one form and shaping it to his purposes to build connection. Such contemporary examples of inventive adaptation may seem far removed from the accounts provided by Martín and Menéndez. However, I argue that their very usage of taking what would have been a form they knew—the sharing and passing of oral knowledge about place—and adapting it to the written and recorded testimony before the Spanish scribe is itself a form of inventive adaptation.

In a similar vein, Karenne Wood's poem "Directions" demonstrates features of Martín's and Menéndez's orientation to their homelands. In each case, I see these works participating in the act of "writing home" that Wilson outlines. Wood's Monacan homelands in the Piedmont region of present-day Virginia would have likely constituted a neighboring nation to those of Martín and Menéndez. Nonetheless, rereading

Wood's poem in light of their testimonies, and then rereading their testimonies in light of Wood's poetry allows key ideas to emerge that might otherwise go unnoticed. In her poem, Wood writes and acknowledges the four directions: east, west, south, and north. She goes on to speak up to the sky and then to the earth beneath our feet. Lastly, she gives thanks to the place where we are now, thus mirroring the directions carved on Faye Greiner's Catawba clay turtle's back with which I opened this chapter. Poignantly, the poem closes with a reminder: "We who have loved you / grow as dark roots beneath your / toes. We touch you. Here. Now."[33] This closing reminds the reader of how homelands are also made by the ancestors under one's feet, reaching out to the here and now. One place where we start to see resonance across time from Martín and Menéndez to Wood is in the section regarding the earth. She writes, "What to say about the earth, whose / love lives like bright knives within us? / Like us, it is alchemy: chromium, / zinc, magnesium, copper. Like us, / a fire swirls within. Disordered, / too, the balance skewed."[34] Here, Wood links the precious metals and minerals of the earth to the very being of the people, like "alchemy." This imagery calls back to the recounting of metals that both Martín and Menéndez try to convey to the gold-greedy Spanish. Both women link the use of precious metals to ceremonial events, which might be read as a kind of subtle recognition of where any given item's value resides. The two women answer and acknowledge the questions about precious metal resources, but they each have their own kind of twist on this knowledge, privileging instead the abundance of their lands in agricultural rather than extractive mining resources. They create a vision of their home on their own scale of value, like Wood orienting the audience to a directional sense of where one is from and where one is now. They write home not as letters *to* but as the creation *of* where the Spanish fit within their own worlds, however distant those may be.

While Wood's poetry helps us think about the spatial poetics in Martín's and Menéndez's accounts, Gladys Cardiff's work offers us a way to think about the temporal value to placing the two women within an Indigenous literary tradition of tribalography. In her poem "Combing," Cardiff forwards the image of combing her daughter's hair: "Bending, I bow my head / and lay my hands upon / her hair, combing, and think / how women do this for each other."[35] She goes on in the next stanza to recount how in the past "I take her place. Beneath / my mother's hands I feel / the braids drawn up tight" and then she goes on to explain how her mother also "combed her grandmother / Mathilda's hair using a comb made out of bone."[36] In working across these three stanzas, we see Cardiff pull together strands of the past, present, and future milieus of tribalography. She closes the poem with this meditation, "A simple act / preparing hair. Something / women do for each other, / plaiting the generations."[37] This "plaiting the generations" is something we see if we zoom out and think about all of the Indigenous writers, and Indigenous women writers in particular, who emerge from the traditions of knowledge keeping that Martín and Menéndez initiate. It is similar to how Bauer explains the pottery process as one "Catawba women have followed for thousands of years, a tradition that passes to future generations and ties women together through kinship."[38] Martín and Menéndez make their own voices heard, calling from their own girlhoods and in perhaps subtle gestures pointing toward a future. They build connections between their homelands and their current place in St. Augustine, and they express a kind of incorporative hospitality whereby their homes are abundant and enriched enough to share with and support newcomers. And though it is but historical conjecture, one might pause on the imagery that Cardiff provides for us: women combing and braiding one another's hair. Did these two women, Teresa and Luisa—or even the now-unknown names they knew one another by in their own languages—sit together bowed under one another's hands as they combed and braided each other's hair? Could they have known the call they would ultimately send out to us—here, now?

Indeed, few people can tell the future. However, we do know that these two women witnessed profound changes in their lives and landscapes. While we cannot be entirely certain of what their present-day tribal national affiliation would be, they would have likely been heavily influenced by the overlapping Catawba, Cherokee, and Yuchi worlds of their homelands and the Muscogee cultural landscape they traversed on their way to St. Augustine. As Bauer has explained of Catawba women, "The effects of violence and other social disruptions caused by the rise of colonialism altered their lives and polities forever, but the people remained. The period transformed Catawba women's and their predecessors' lives, but the special turmoil did not destroy these resilient people. Instead, Piedmont Indian women responded to the historical stresses in ways that brought many people together through intermarriage, trade, and linguistics affiliations."[39] Women such as

Martín and Menéndez offer a glimpse into these conditions in the 1600s, and their voices leave a legacy that stretches into the present in Indigenous literary forms from the oral to the textual. As Bauer argues, "Between 1540 and 1840, dramatic transformations did occur for Catawbas and their ancestors. However, the change that dominated Catawba women's lives does not fit a simple declension model."[40] This refusal to simply tell some narrative of decline lies at the heart of how we might understand Martín's and Menéndez's accounts today. They claim their homelands as the bountiful, assertive, ceremonially responsive and community-oriented places that they were. They write home by telling their stories through the method of inventive adaptation, and in so doing they enact an ethos of tribalography whereby connection—even to the Spanish who question them—remains central to their futures.

Considering this, I find one particular image especially apt from each woman's account. Both Martín and Menéndez are asked about pearls in their homelands, and they each offer an account of gathering what we can only presume to be freshwater mussel pearls. As Martín explains, "there are pearls, which they harvest from a large river about a day's journey from her town and that a great quantity of pearls in leather pouches were presented to both said Captain Juan Pardo and Lieutenant Moyano. She remembers seeing Lieutenant Moyano with pouches filled with many large, white, round pearls." (page 70)[41] And Menéndez offers, "Asked if there are pearls in that land, this declarant said that with many other women and men, she went to a river where they took out many large clams, and they harvested many pearls and gave them to Lieutenant Moyano" (page 77)[42] The Spanish are certainly interested in pearls as a kind of gem that might produce a lucrative extraction economy. Martín's and Menéndez's responses are understandable and likely accurate, given the relative abundance of freshwater mussels in Appalachia and its foothills. In other words, we know that the women are correct in their assessments because we know that the region is home to one of the largest populations and diversity of freshwater mussels in the world.

However, there is something else provocative in the centrality of the pearl. Invertebrates such as freshwater mussels and saltwater oysters produce pearls when small, foreign objects become lodged inside their shells. If the animal cannot expel the small piece of debris from its shell, it begins to secrete layers of its own mother of pearl, or shell material, in order to soothe the irritation to its soft tissue. The animal creates layer after layer in order to blunt the effects that the small invader has rendered. Eventually, a pearl is formed. While neither woman offers the accounts of collecting pearls as a metaphor, from a literary studies point of view, the analogy is hard to ignore. What are these foreign invaders in Martín's and Menéndez's homeland if not unwanted debris? The Europeans have arrived, lodged, and settled inside the homes of Indigenous Peoples. When it becomes clear that explosion is not an option, Indigenous Peoples begin their own varied and multifaceted process of reducing irritation, smoothing over the irksome invaders. Importantly, this process should not be viewed as benign. It took great work, pain, and sacrifice for Indigenous Peoples to make pearls of survival from the debris of invading settlers. Nonetheless, what is a pearl if not a profound image of inventive adaptation? It renders something beautiful, priceless, illustrious from an invading and sometimes even fatal irritant. It in no way justifies or excuses the violence, sacrifice, or hardship, but nonetheless it exists as evidence of the attempt to survive.

The history of Indigenous literatures in written Latinate alphabetic script might be read like these pearls. The pressure to adapt their literary traditions to written Latinate script becomes an irritant lodged in the epistemological history of the continent. Indigenous people, however, through their propensity for generative connection and incorporation, begin the process of smoothing over this invader, making the foreign object something of their own creation—more illustrious than it started, more valuable than settler colonialism imagined. In other words, Indigenous authors across the centuries have made pearls from specks of dirt. When readers fail to see the ways that Native writers have done this throughout the centuries, they fail to appreciate the power of the work. As Foerster asks, "Why would we not have written in available and contemporary forms . . . to speak back to the language of the oppression? Positioned as we were at the crossroads, why would we not have also engaged the dominant language to stand up for our humanity, our rights?"[43] In other words, as Bauer offers, there is no declension narrative here. It is a layered process over time, adding shine, luster, and dimension to the collective traumas of invasion. It is the process by which Chip Livingston looks to the oyster in the water along Punta del Este and asserts kinship: "Heed this call of creation. Call me brother."[44]

To my ear, the work of Teresa Martín and Luisa Menéndez speaks forward in time to writers such as Gladys Cardiff, Jennifer Foerster, Joy Harjo, LeAnne Howe, and Karenne Wood, saying, "Call me sister."

Together they build a tradition across the years that continues, changing as it innovates, adding layers to the story of Indigenous literature on this continent. They speak to the directions on the Catawba turtle's back, carefully engraved and molded by Faye Greiner's hands. Returning to my opening meditation, this turtle, too, tells a story of Indigenous literary traditions. In its four directions, the turtle offers a map across space, just as Martín and Menéndez do. It also gestures the two more directions—up and down—just as Martín and Menéndez reference the ceremonial traditions of their homelands as well as the abundance of the earth beneath their feet. Most importantly, though, the center circle on the turtle's back calls upon the idea of where one is: here, now. Martín and Menéndez offer their testimonies on the fourth and sixth of February in the Gregorian calendar year of 1600, a calendar time that had only been in official use by the Catholic Church for eighteen years. We do not know for certain what year it was in their own Indigenous calendar systems. But we can know that on those appointed days, they showed up to speak their truths into the colonial record, thereby sending a letter forward to where we are now as we read their words. Harjo writes of her contemporary efforts in editing the *When the Light Was Subdued* that her editorial team's hope is "for you to open the door to each poem and hear a unique human voice speaking to you beyond, within, and alongside time."[45] It is these unique human voices that make up the chorus of Indigenous literary traditions on the continent. These voices emerge among the invisible maps and the engravings on the turtle's back. They call out to their poetic descendants, joining them in a refrain of the perpetual here, now.

Notes

1. See Michael Wilson, *Writing Home: Indigenous Narratives of Resistance* (East Lansing: Michigan State University Press, 2008).

2. LeAnne Howe, *Choctalking on Other Realities* (San Francisco: Aunt Lute Books, 2013), 31.

3. Ibid., 31.

4. Although there is no evidence for it, I also cannot help but wonder if they are playing a minor trick here on the Spanish—a kind of inside joke, if you will.

5. Jennifer Foerster, "Renewal," in *When the Light of the World Was Subdued, Our Songs Came Through*, ed. Joy Harjo, LeAnne Howe, and Jennifer Foerster (New York: W. W. Norton, 2020), 360.

6. Ibid.

7. See Caroline Wigginton, *Indigenuity: Native Craftwork and the Art of American Literatures* (Chapel Hill: University of North Carolina Press, 2022).

8. Kristina Bross and Hilary E. Wyss, "Introduction," in *Early Native Literacies in New England: A Documentary and Critical Anthology*, ed. Kristina Bross and Hilary E. Wyss (Amherst: University of Massachusetts Press, 2008), 5.

9. Robert Dale Parker, "The Garden of the Mind: An Introduction to Early American Indian Poetry," in *Changing Is Not Vanishing: A Collection of American Indian Poetry*, ed. Robert Dale Parker (Philadelphia: University of Pennsylvania Press, 2011), 3.

10. Bross and Wyss, "Introduction," 4.

11. Ibid.

12. Ibid.

13. Ibid., 1.

14. Cutcha Risling Baldy, *We Are Dancing for You: Native Feminisms & the Revitalization of Women's Coming-of-Age Ceremonies* (Seattle: University of Washington Press, 2018), 83.

15. Ann Marie Plane, "The Dreadful Case of Sarah Pharaoh: Finding Native Women's Voices in an Eighteenth-Century Infanticide Case," in Bross and Hilary E. Wyss, *Early Native Literacies in New England*, 88.

16. Ibid.

17. Ibid.

18. Mishauna Goeman, *Mark My Words: Native Women Mapping Our Nations* (Minneapolis: University of Minnesota Press, 2013), 8.

19. See the documents in Bross and Wyss as well as Steven W. Hackel, "Indian Testimony and the Mission San Gabriel Uprising of 1785," *Ethnohistory* 50, no. 4 (2003): 643–69.

20. Rufus Anderson and Catherine Brown, *Memoir of Catherine Brown: A Christian Indian of the Cherokee Nation* (Boston: Crocker and Brewster, 1825).

21. See Theda Perdue and Michael D. Green, *The Cherokee Removal: A Brief History with Documents* (Boston: Bedford/St. Martin's, 2005), 129–34.

22. See Jane Johnston Schoolcraft, *The Sound the Stars Make Rushing through the Sky: The Writings of Jane Johnston Schoolcraft*, ed. Robert Dale Parker (Philadelphia: University of Pennsylvania Press, 2008).

23. See Sarah Winnemucca Hopkins, *Life among the Piutes: Their Wrongs and Claims* (Boston: For Sale by Cupples, UPHAM, 1883); and Zitkala-Ša, *American Indian Stories, Legends, and Other Writings*, ed. Cathy N. Davidson and Ada Norris (New York: Penguin Classics, 2003).

24. See Eleazar in Harjo et al., *When the Light of the World*; and Chainbreaker, *Chainbreaker: The Revolutionary War Memoirs of Governor Blacksnake as Told to Benjamin Williams*, ed. Thomas S. Abler (Lincoln, NE: Bison Books, 2005).

25. For a Cherokee literary history, see Daniel Heath Justice, *Our Fire Survives the Storm: A Cherokee Literary History* (Minneapolis: University of Minnesota Press, 2005).

26. Brooke M. Bauer, *Becoming Catawba: Catawba Indian Women and Nation-Building, 1540–1840* (Tuscaloosa: University of Alabama Press, 2023), 14.

27. Joy Harjo, "Introduction," in Harjo et al., *When the Light of the World*, 1.

28. Ibid., 5.

29. Chip Livingston, "Punta del Este Pantoum," in *Sing: Poetry from the Indigenous Americas*, ed. Allison Adelle Hedge Coke (Tucson: University of Arizona Press, 2011), 252. Reprinted by permission of Chip Livingston.

30. Ibid.

31. Ibid.

32. Ibid.

33. Karenne Wood, *Markings on Earth* (Tucson: University of Arizona Press, 2001), 5. Reprinted by permission of the University of Arizona Press.

34. Ibid.

35. Glady Cardiff, "Combing," in Harjo et al., *When the Light of the World*, 386. Reprinted by permission of Gladys Cardiff.

36. Ibid.

37. Ibid., 387.

38. Bauer, *Becoming Catawba*, 122.

39. Ibid., 2.

40. Ibid., 14.

41. See p. 70.

42. See p. 77.

43. Foerster, "Renewal," 358.

44. Livingston, "Punta del Este Pantoum," 252.

45. Harjo, "Introduction," 3.

Contributors

Hannah Abrahamson is assistant professor of Latin American history at College of the Holy Cross. Her current book project examines the histories of Maya and Spanish women's respective roles as laborers and grantees in Yucatán, Mexico's encomienda system of Indigenous labor and tribute. She received her PhD from Emory University in 2022. Her research interests include household dynamics, gendered labor structures, and Indigenous bondage in the Atlantic World.

Robin A. Beck is professor of anthropology and curator of Eastern North American Archaeology at the Museum of Anthropological Archaeology, University of Michigan. Beck is the author of *Chiefdoms, Collapse, and Coalescence in the Early American South* (2013), editor of *The Durable House: House Society Models in Archaeology*, and coeditor, along with Christopher Rodning and David Moore, of *Fort San Juan and the Limits of Empire: Colonialism and Household Practice at the Berry Site* (2016). He has published numerous book chapters and articles in journals such as *Current Anthropology*, *American Anthropologist*, *American Antiquity*, *Historical Archaeology*, and *Southeastern Archaeology*.

Melissa D. Birkhofer is a settler scholar and teaching assistant professor in the English Department at Appalachian State University, where she teaches courses on Latine and Indigenous Literatures. In 2023, she and Worley won the *North Carolina Literary Review*'s John Ehle Award for their article, "She Said That Saint Augustine Is Worth Nothing Compared to Her Homeland: Teresa Martín and the Méndez Cancio *Account of La Tama* (1600)." Together with Paul M. Worley, she is cotranslator of Miguel Rocha Vivas's *Word Mingas* (2021), whose Spanish edition won Cuba's Casa de las Américas Prize in 2016. She was the founding director of the Latinx Studies Program at Western Carolina University and is a codirector of the journal *Label Me Latina/o*.

Kimberly C. Borchard earned her M.A. and B.A. from Ohio University and her Ph.D. from the University of Chicago. She teaches Until recently, she taught courses in Spanish, Latin American colonial literature, and

"Spanish for Social Justice" human rights issues facing Hispanic immigrant communities in the U.S. at Randolph-Macon College in Ashland, Virginia. Her first book, Appalachia as Contested Borderland of the Early Modern Atlantic, 1528–1715, has led to a new project research documenting the history of the Talimali Band of the Apalachee Indians of Louisiana and their efforts to maintain tribal sovereignty from the eighteenth century until today. She is soon to relocate to the Appalachian foothills, where she will focus on translation, writing, and raising chickens.

Rachel V. Briggs is teaching assistant professor of anthropology and the curriculum in archaeology at the University of North Carolina at Chapel Hill. Rachel is coeditor with Michaelyn Harle and Lynne Sullivan of the book *Mississippian Women* (2024) and has published several book chapters and articles on American Indian food and gender roles in journals such as *American Antiquity*, *American Anthropologist*, and *Native South.*

Gina Caison is the Kenneth M. England Professor of Southern Literature at Georgia State University, where she teaches courses in American literature, southern literature, Native American literatures, and documentary practices. Her first book, *Red States: Indigeneity, Settler Colonialism, and Southern Studies* (2018), won the 2019 C. Hugh Holman Award for the best book in southern literary studies. From 2020 to 2022, she served as president of the Society for the Study of Southern Literature. During the 2020–2021 academic year, she was a research fellow at the Institute for Advanced Study at Central European University in Budapest, where she completed her second book, *Erosion: American Environments and the Anxiety of Disappearance,* published in 2024 by Duke University Press.

Keith Cartwright is chair of the Department of English at the University of North Florida. He has coauthored *Gulf Gothic: Mexico, the U.S. South and La Llorona's Undead Voices* (2023), with Dolores Flores-Silva, and published two prior books: *Sacral Grooves, Limbo Gateways* (2013) and *Reading Africa into American Literature* (2002). His work has appeared in journals such as *American Literature*, *PMLA*, *Callaloo*, and *Yearbook of Comparative and General Literature.*

Dolores Flores-Silva is a professor of Latin American literature and cultures at Roanoke College and the coauthor of *Gulf Gothic: Mexico,* *the U.S. South and La Llorona's Undead Voices* (2023) and *Rosario Ferré y Mayra Montero: Entre la espada y la cruz* (2009). She has published on Mexican, US southern, and Indigenous writing in journals such as *Native South*, *World Literature Today*, *New Literary History*, and *La Palabra y el Hombre*. She has been collaborating with Keith Cartwright on a set of literary-historical studies of the region of the Gulf of Mexico, including a documentary film series and work archived on the site: https://gulfsbetweenus.domains.unf.edu.

Elizabeth Coonrod Martínez, Sonoma State University (1995–2010), where she received the Teaching Excellence award in 2006; and DePaul University, where she was also editor of the journal *Diálogo* (2010–2021). Martínez earned an MA from New York University and a PhD from the University of New Mexico, Albuquerque, in Latin American literature. Her books include *The Women of Mexico's Cultural Renaissance: Intrepid Post-Revolution Artists and Writers* (2023); *Teaching Late Twentieth-Century Mexicana and Chicana Writers* (2021); *Josefina Niggli, Mexican American Writer: A Critical Biography* (2007); *Lilus Kikus and Other Stories by Elena Poniatowska*, translation and "Introduction" (2005); and *Before the Boom: Latin American Revolutionary Novels of the 1920s* (2001).

Miriam Melton-Villanueva would like to thank the National Endowment for the Humanities for a yearlong research fellowship that generously supported this study (NEH HB-267886-20). She received her PhD from UCLA in 2012 and is a Founding Senior Ford Foundation Fellow. As associate professor in the Department of History at the University of Nevada, Las Vegas, her research program explores the cultural strategies and status of women and men in Mexico's Indigenous communities. Her first monograph, based on previously unknown, unstudied, and untranslated texts, *The Aztecs at Independence: Nahua Culture Makers in Central Mexico 1799–1832*, represents the first ethnohistory of Mexica/Nahua *altepetl* to extend beyond the colonial period, a time when written traditions were supposed to have ended. Readers will also find her 2018 *Ethnohistory* article of special interest: "Cacicas, Escribanos, and Landholders: Indigenous Women's Late Colonial Mexican Texts 1703–1832." Using Indigenous archival records, Melton-Villanueva underpins her analysis with ethnohistorical methods as a way to bring marginalized voices into history.

David G. Moore is professor emeritus of anthropology at Warren Wilson College, in Asheville, North Carolina. He is the author of numerous book chapters and articles for peer-reviewed journals as well as the books *Catawba Valley Mississippians: Ceramics, Chronology, and Catawba Indians* (2002); and *Fort San Juan and the Limits of Empire: Colonialism and Household Practice at the Berry Site* (2016) along with Christopher Rodning and Robin Beck.

Josh Platt is an adjunct instructor and the GIS lab supervisor for the Department of Geography and Planning at Appalachian State University, where he has taught courses in cartography and geospatial technologies. He has maps published in books across a variety of disciplines, including *The Violent World of Broadus Miller: A Story of Murder, Lynch Mobs, and Judicial Punishment in the Carolinas* by Kevin Young and *Heartsick and Astonished: Divorce in Civil War-Era West Virginia* by Allison Fredette. He is currently working on a guidebook of cycling routes and tours of Western North Carolina.

Christopher B. Rodning is professor of anthropology at Tulane University, New Orleans, Louisiana. He is coeditor with Robin A. Beck and David G. Moore of *Fort San Juan and the Limits of Empire: Household Archaeology at the Berry Site* (2016), coeditor with Jane M. Eastman of *Archaeological Studies of Gender in the Southeastern United States* (2001), and author of *Center Places and Cherokee Towns: Archaeological Perspectives on Native American Architecture and Landscape in the Southern Appalachians* (2015).

Paul M. Worley is a settler scholar from Charleston, South Carolina, and professor of Spanish at Appalachian State University, where he serves as chair of the Department of Languages, Literatures, and Cultures. Cowritten with Rita M. Palacios, his most recent book, *Unwriting Maya Literature: Ts'íib as Recorded Knowledge* (2019), was given an honorable mention for Best Book in the Humanities by the Latin American Studies Association's Mexico Section. Together with Melissa D. Birkhofer, he is cotranslator of Miguel Rocha Vivas's *Word Mingas* (2021), whose Spanish edition won Cuba's Casa de las Américas Prize in 2016. He has also translated selected works by Indigenous authors such as Hubert Matiúwàa (Mè'phàà), Celerina Sánchez (Mixteco), Manuel Tzoc (K'iche'), and Ruperta Bautista (Tsotsil).

Appalachian Futures

Black, Native, and Queer Voices

Series editors: Annette Saunooke Clapsaddle, Davis Shoulders, and Crystal Wilkinson

This book series gives voice to Black, Native, Latinx, Asian, Queer, and other nonwhite or ignored identities within the Appalachian region.

Black Freedom Struggle in Urban Appalachia
Edited by J. Z. Bennett, Christy L. McGuire, Lori Delale-O'Connor, T. Elon Dancy II, and Sabina Vaught

Affrilachia: Testimonies
Chris Aluka Berry with Kelly Elaine Navies and Maia A. Surdam

Teresa Martín & Luisa Menéndez: Indigenous Women from Appalachia in the Spanish Colonial Record
Edited by Melissa D. Birkhofer and Paul M. Worley

No Son of Mine: A Memoir
Jonathan Corcoran

To Belong Here: A New Generation of Queer, Trans, and Two-Spirit Appalachian Writers
Edited by Rae Garringer

Tar Hollow Trans: Essays
Stacy Jane Grover

Nobody's Psychic: Finding & Losing Yourself
Dani Lamorte

Deviant Hollers: Queering Appalachian Ecologies for a Sustainable Future
Edited by Zane McNeill and Rebecca Scott

Reading, Writing, and Queer Survival: Affects, Matterings, and Literacies across Appalachia
Caleb Pendygraft

Queer Communion: Religion in Appalachia
Edited by Davis Shoulders

Appalachian Ghost: A Photographic Reimagining of the Hawk's Nest Tunnel Disaster
Raymond Thompson Jr.